I0166611

# Aquinas and Bioethics

## Contemporary Issues
## in the Light of Medieval Thought

CRAIG PAYNE

Payne, Craig.
  Aquinas and bioethics: contemporary issues in the light of medieval thought.
  Includes bibliographical references.
**ISBN-13:**
**978-0692304488**
**ISBN-10:**
**0692304487**

Vision Publishing
311 East Alta Vista
Ottumwa, Iowa 52501

*Aquinas and Bioethics*

*Aquinas and Bioethics*

# Aquinas and Bioethics
## Contemporary Issues in the Light of Medieval Thought

## Table of Contents

# Part Two: Aquinas and Contemporary Bioethical Issues

# ACKNOWLEDGMENTS

Over the past few years, the author's personal life and attempts at scholarship have been enriched and benefited, in one way or another, by many people. Thanks are due to my extraordinary family, Desirae, Nathan, and Erin; to Pastors Larry Ulrich and Dr. Nancy Ulrich; to Dr. Neil Messer of the University of Winchester; to Dr. Francis Beckwith of Baylor University; to Fr. Joseph Koterski of Fordham University; and to all the members of UFFL (University Faculty for Life), especially Dr. Anne Barbeau Gardiner, Professor Emerita of English at John Jay College of the City University of New York, for their kindness, support, and ongoing labors. Thanks to Edwin Mellen Press for permission to use excerpts from a previous book, *Why a Fetus Is a Human Person from the Moment of Conception: A Revisionist Interpretation of Thomas Aquinas's* Treatise on Human Nature (2010). To me, all these people are no longer merely colleagues.

*Aquinas and Bioethics*

# Abbreviations Used

Several works by Thomas Aquinas will be used throughout this book. The following will be abbreviated in footnotes due to their frequency of citation:

CT        *Compendium Theologica.* Cyril Vollert, S.J., trans. [1947]. New York: Sophia Institute Press, 1998.

*De Ver.*   *De Veritate.* Robert W. Mulligan, S.J.; James V. McGlynn, S.J.; and Robert W. Schmidt, S.J., transs. Chicago: Henry Regnery, 1952-54.

SCG       *Summa Contra Gentiles.* Anton C. Pegis, James F. Anderson, Vernon J. Bourke, and Charles J. O'Neil, transs. Notre Dame: University of Notre Dame Press. Reprinted edition, 1975.

ST         *Summa Theologica.* Fathers of the English Dominican Province, transs. [1920]. New York: Benziger Bros., 1947.

*Aquinas and Bioethics*

# Introduction: Two Questions

The essence of something is made known through the definition; only through the (essential) definition is the thing intelligible. Each thing is not comprehended until one knows its definition—therefore the "quest" for the definition. This is the terminus of the desire to know....The definition is not an assumption that one stipulates at the outset but something that one seeks. It is the terminus of speculative reason.[1]

## 1.  Ethics and the Natural Law

In many debates over ethical issues today, the argument swirls around a central question: "What exactly is a human?" The corollary questions to this include "When does human life actually begin?" and "How does one know when human life actually begins?" Other questions frequently heard in contemporary ethical conversations follow from these: Is there a difference in kind between "human-ness" and "personhood"? Between a human "being" and a human "person"? And yet more questions seem to follow: If there is in fact a difference in kind between "human-ness" and "personhood," between a human "being" and a human "person," does that difference entail a difference in ethical or legal considerations and treatment of the two? Is a "person" a moral being with certain rights, but a "human" not? If one must treat a "person" as a rights-bearing, fully fledged human, may one legitimately *not* so treat what some might see as "pre-persons" (i.e., in the cases of abortion or embryonic stem cell research) or as "post-persons" (i.e., in the case of involuntary euthanasia)?

In the spirit of full disclosure, let me say at once that my sympathies lie with those who give the same answer to these last several questions: "No." Many argue that the commonly presented distinction between human-ness and personhood is based on mistakes both factual (scientific and theological) and logical (philosophical), and that therefore the favorable difference in treatment of the human "person" as

---

[1] Jan Aertsen. *Nature and Creature: Thomas Aquinas's Way of Thought*. Leiden: Brill, 1988, pp. 65 and 67.

opposed to the mere "human" is arbitrary and artificial.[2] James Trefil, Professor of Physics at George Mason University and well-known science writer, asserts, "There is no right answer to the question, What is a human being?"[3] However, as philosopher Baruch Brody has pointed out, such terminological and conceptual vagueness often arises when a term "has, as the criterion for its application, a set of conditions to be satisfied, but it is not specified how many of them must be satisfied. When some, but not all, of these conditions are satisfied, it is then unclear whether the term is applicable."[4] This book seeks to address this conceptual vagueness and some of the bioethical implications resulting from it, by defending a specific definition of the human person. This definition will be based upon Thomistic anthropology as considered in the light of modern genetics and embryology. (In philosophical discussions, "anthropology" is not the analysis of human societies, but human nature itself, the human person.)

Occasionally the objection is raised that these issues revolve around "religious" claims and are therefore unsuited for the framing of public policy, the constructing of technical philosophical arguments, or the defining of personhood under the law. For example, according to Leonard Glantz, "Although the law rarely lends itself to blanket statements, it can be clearly stated that a fetus is not a person under the law. However, this does not mean that we may not offer it certain protections or rights. This conclusion means, instead, that fetuses are not required to be protected."[5] However, even though this confident assertion may be accepted (everyone, after all, knows that abortion-on-demand is legal in the U.S., the U.K., and elsewhere, and that fetuses are not required to be protected under the law as persons), it is somewhat beside the point. The question is not "What does the law require?" but rather "What does the moral nature of the fetus require?" Should the

---

[2] In particular, I wish to acknowledge my indebtedness in this regard to Robert P. George, Ralph McInerny, Peter Kreeft, Francis Beckwith, Neil Messer, and J. Budziszewski, whose works will be quoted frequently throughout the following. Although they may disagree on some aspects of Thomistic interpretation, these writers are in basic unanimity regarding the bioethical issues raised in this book.

[3] Trefil, "What Is a Human Being?" World Economic Forum Annual Meeting, 29 January 1999. Weforum.org, n.p. Accessed 19 February 2006.

[4] Brody, *Abortion and the Sanctity of Human Life: A Philosophical View*. Cambridge, Massachusetts: MIT Press, 1975, p. 67.

[5] "Is the Fetus a Person? A Lawyer's View." *Abortion and the Status of the Fetus*. William B. Bondeson et al., eds. Dordrecht, Holland: D. Reidel Publishing, 1983: 107-17, p. 116.

fetus be considered as a human being, or perhaps as a "person"? If it should be so considered, how must the law be changed? In the U.S. at one time in its history, a black slave also was "not a person under the law," as seen in the 1857 Dred Scott decision. One presumes that the change in the law did not thereby change the moral nature of black slaves, but only recognized the moral status the slaves possessed all along. Similarly, appealing to the current laws regarding the rights of the unborn does little to aid discussion regarding those rights or regarding the morality of those very laws.

In another objection to the questions surrounding the topic of human-ness, one theologian points out, "The empirical and reduction-istic cast of modern thought worries over the abstract character of [descriptions of] human nature. Considering all the dynamics and structures implied in what and who we are, no simple description seems possible today."[6] However, a close relationship between philosophical and theological anthropology does exist, as well as a close relationship between applied public ethics and both. As professor Robert Sokolowski puts it, "Ethics in general, and medical ethics in particular, are obviously related to human self-understanding, to what we could call philosophical and theological anthropology." He goes on later to say:

> Our understanding of ourselves as human beings is related to our understanding of the good and virtuous human life. This end or *telos* of human beings is disclosed by virtuous action, by human beings existing and acting well as human beings.[7]

A comprehensive understanding of this human *telos* is foundational to the idea of a "natural law" for humans, a set of principles by which humans fulfill themselves and flourish as humans *qua* humans. Further, this set of natural principles serves as a natural moral boundary, especially in the area of *bioethics*—what humans *are* as humans (anthropology) immediately circumscribes what humans *should and should not do* to themselves and to fellow humans (ethics):

> The idea of a natural law has long served as a framework within which to draw out the moral implications of centrally important theological doctrines, including the goodness of creation and the

---

[6] Anthony J. Kelly. *An Expanding Theology: Faith in a World of Connections*. Sydney: E.J. Dwyer, 1993, revised 2003: Section 7.1. For a more extended critique, see also Pauline C. Westerman, *The Disintegration of Natural Law Theory* (Leiden: Brill, 1997).

[7] Robert Sokolowski. "What Is Natural Law? Human Purposes and Natural Ends." *The Thomist* 68 (2004): 507-29, pp. 507 and 527.

status of the human person as a free participant in God's universal providence.[8]

Although a view more characteristic of modernity would place these value-laden "moral implications" within the realm of "culture" rather than within the fact-laden realm of "nature," such a dualistic division between culture and nature does not seem representative of the unclassifiable complexity of humanity's lived experience. Most Christians would dispute this artificial division, arguing that factual statements can have clear cultural, moral, and religious implications. More specifically, it may be possible that moral implications for human behaviour (natural law) be derived from the facts of human nature discernible by deduction and by induction based on humanity's lived experience; in the words of Mircea Eliade, "For religious man, nature is never only 'natural'…. Nature always expresses something that transcends it."[9]

Therefore, to define one's ontological status as a human must at least implicitly, and perhaps explicitly, also define what it is one must be and do in order to be an example of a "good" human. These reflections must also define what sort of attitude and behavior we should adopt when it comes to other human beings who possess the same ontological status as we have and consequently deserve the same treatment as we do, both in the moral domain and under public law: "A nature limits what a being can do and have done to it."[10]

This is not to say that a correct understanding of human nature will necessarily lead directly to a correct cataloguing of ethical prescriptions. Again in Sokolowski's words, "It is not the case that we could work out a comprehensive description or definition of human nature as a purely theoretic enterprise and then apply this knowledge to practical issues."[11] Although the present work may seem like just such an attempt, such is not its intent. Rather, from beginning to end, I hope with this book to bring out the idea that the *telos* of humanity, the mature, normal condition of the species *Homo sapiens*, not only defines but simultaneously prescribes, so that the moral applications will arise naturally

---

[8] Jean Porter, *Nature as Reason: A Thomistic Theory of the Natural Law*. Grand Rapids, Michigan: Eerdmans, 2005, p. 45.

[9] Mircea Eliade. *The Sacred and the Profane: The Nature of Religion*. Willard R. Trask, trans. New York: Harcourt, Brace & World, 1959, pp. 116 and 118.

[10] Derek S. Jeffreys. "The Soul Is Alive and Well: Non-Reductive Physicalism and Emergent Mental Properties." *Theology and Science* 2.2 (October 2004): 205-25, p. 214.

[11] Sokolowski, "What Is Natural Law?" p. 507.

out of the definition of human being and even be contained *within* the definition. These applications will be "a set of ethical imperatives drawn from human nature and known through reason."[12]

Another way of saying the same thing is to say that, in natural law theory, the laws themselves are "natural" to humans because they are inherent to human "nature." The prescriptions surrounding human behavior exist as they do because of their rootedness in the human constitution, a constitution discovered through both observation and introspection. Human moral obligations are "based upon being," as Josef Pieper writes, and therefore, "Reality is the foundation of ethics. The good is that which is in accord with reality."[13] An anthropological description of human nature will thus also be at least partially a moral description as well, for once one knows what humans are, one may begin to see what are the right sorts of things for humans to do, both in order to flourish as humans themselves and in order to treat other humans as they should be treated.

## 2. Central Questions

In this book, therefore, the primary project will be to present an anthropological discussion which results in a comprehensive definition of the human person. Secondly, this book will address the questions contained in the first paragraph of this Introduction—and not only address the questions surrounding the concepts of human-ness and personhood, but also draw out a few of the bioethical implications these concepts of human-ness or personhood might entail. This book, therefore, addresses two questions: What is the definition of human-ness and/or personhood? Secondly, What are the bioethical implications following from this definition? For the first objective of this project, the definitions of human-ness and personhood, I will turn to the Scholastic theologian and philosopher Thomas Aquinas, whose analysis of human nature is articulated primarily in his *Summa Theologica* in the "Treatise on Human Nature."[14] The second objective, on bioethical implications, will follow naturally from the first: Once the nature of humans is discussed, the nature of what may and may not rightfully be done to humans will become more apparent. This clearly

---

[12] Stephen J. Grabill. "Foreword" to David VanDrunen's *A Biblical Case for Natural Law*. Grand Rapids, Michigan: Acton Institute, 2000: i-iii, p. i.

[13] Josef Pieper. *Reality and the Good*. Chicago: Regnery Publishing, 1967, p. 5.

[14] All quotes from the *Summa Theologica* throughout this work are taken from the translation of the Fathers of the English Dominican Province [1920] (New York: Benziger Brothers, 1947). The Treatise on Human Nature is found in ST I.75-102.

will be a "natural law" theory of ethics in that the ethical principles put forward will be laws drawn from the "nature" of humans. As ethicist Neil Messer puts it,

> According to Thomas Aquinas' account of natural law, we can draw conclusions about how we ought to behave from observations of ourselves and the world [ST I-II.94]. In a sense, natural law arguments move from an "is" to an "ought". . . . [for] in Thomas' natural law theory the facts themselves are not neutral but value-laden. The theory claims that human beings have been created by God with particular ends or purposes. This is a factual claim about the kind of thing a human being is: when we say "human being," part of what we mean is "a being that exists for these ends." But this factual claim has an evaluative claim built in: a human being is the kind of being whose good consists in fulfilling these ends. Given Thomas' first principle of practical reason—"that good is to be sought and done, evil to be avoided" [ST I-II.94.2]—it follows that right actions are those that help us to fulfill our ends.[15]

So from the start the central questions of this work, as previously stated, are two in number: (1) First and foremost, what is a Thomistic definition of a human being? In order to explore this definition, Thomistic views of "hominization" and of "personhood" must also be explored. Although Aquinas himself does use the terms *homo* and *persona* for "human being" and "person," he does not use either of the terms "hominization" or "personhood"; therefore, the Thomist discussing the coming into existence of the human person must base such a discussion upon Thomas's general metaphysical principles, not upon explicit statements. We should also note that the philosophical definition of "hominization" does not correspond to the scientific use of the term as meaning the process of development of the human race; rather it refers to the process by which "unformed" matter receives the human "form" and actually becomes a human being. Secondly: (2) How might this definition aid in addressing contemporary bioethical issues? The subsequent discussion of these questions must also therefore be two-fold in nature: (1) Justification must be provided for the claim that Aquinas provides the definition of "human-ness" that best describes our complete humanity, even though a Thomistic anthropological framework and account of hominization may need to be buttressed by advances in contemporary genetics, embryology, and other relevant sciences. (2) Secondly, it must be shown how this Thomistic anthro-

---

[15] Neil Messer. *Selfish Genes and Christian Ethics: Theological and Ethical Reflections on Evolutionary Biology.* London: SCM Press, 2007, p. 105.

pology adequately enables one to unravel perplexing contemporary human-life ethical issues.

Obviously, this type of anthropological examination might very well produce widely varying descriptions, a spectrum of definitions of humanity brought about primarily by the investigator's attitude toward the relationship between the corporeal and non-corporeal, between the "matter" and the "form" of the human being. These descriptions might vary so widely, in fact, as to be apparently incommensurable. "Theological" anthropology, for example, often reflects on humanity in its relationship to God's salvific purposes, purposes revealed through the categories of Creation, Sin, Redemption, Eschatology, and so on, while a more "philosophical" anthropology reflects on humanity as it can be known apart from the revealed knowledge of a faith tradition. Other anthropologies emphasize one or another of the characteristics of humans, such as their material attributes, for instance. Max Scheler, one of the founders of modern German philosophical anthropology, mentions some of these "apparently incommensurable" philo-sophical/theological anthropological conceptions of humanity which have arisen from antiquity to the present day. Here are three of his examples:

There is (1) the Judeo-Christian conception of humanity in terms of Creation in God's Image, the Fall, original sin, and Redemption.

There is (2) the conception of humanity as a creature qualitatively distinguished from all other creatures by the divine spark of reason (the classical, and especially Aristotelian, view).

Thirdly, there is (3) the modern scientific conception of man as a developed animal.[16]

However, these "apparently incommensurable" conceptions do not in fact appear to be incommensurable, unless the third conception, the "modern scientific" one, is taken in a wholly materialistic sense. This presentation of a "Thomistic anthropology" will comprise elements of all three—the first two because Aquinas himself attempted to synthesize the Judeo-Christian biblical view of humanity's *Imago Dei* and its fallenness with the classical Aristotelian conception of humanity as set apart from other creatures by its rational nature, and the third "scientific" view because Aquinas attempted to use the science known to him in his description of humanity and the human soul/body composite:

---

[16] M.J. Inwood. "Philosophical Anthropology." *The Oxford Companion to Philosophy.* Ted Honderich, ed. Oxford and New York: Oxford University Press, 1995: 38-39, p. 39.

[Aquinas] did not blindly follow any human authority, even Augustine or Aristotle. What he did was take the soundest philosophical system available—a controversial, highly suspect one—and the most enlightened scientific ideas of his time and use them to explain the contents and implications of faith.[17]

Therefore it seems plausible that a Thomist today, based on Aquinas's own principles of inquiry, would use modern DNA analysis and genetic descriptions of human-ness, without necessarily abandoning the necessity of the soul as impelling the development of the human substance. "Aristotle and St. Thomas could learn much from modern research," as one author writes, "and the novel facts would stimulate and require them to extend and modify their theories in detail, even though fundamental principles remained unaltered."[18]

It may seem suspiciously convenient to speak of what Aquinas "would" and "would not" say were he "alive today," instead of merely reporting what he did (in fact) say when he was (in fact) alive. However, especially in the area of scientific advances in understanding, Aquinas himself makes the following point: "Our intellect's proper and proportionate object is the nature of a sensible thing. Now a perfect judgment concerning anything cannot be formed, unless all that pertains to that thing's nature be known."[19] Given Aquinas's description of the human constitution, therefore, a Thomist today should certainly take advantage of advances in genetic and embryological information: "Thomism is bound to no particular scientific theory. St. Thomas. . . uses the theories current in his day by way of illustration, but with the proviso that these theories may well be discarded by a later generation and that such a discarding would have no effect upon his thesis."[20] One should not, however, regard a change in *attitudes* toward something's nature as an actual advance in knowledge; for example, whether or not a society's attitudes change toward the acceptance or non-acceptance of infanticide would not represent any sort of advance in knowledge

---

[17] William A. Herr. *Catholic Thinkers in the Clear: Giants of Catholic Thought from Augustine to Rahner. Basics of Christian Thought, Vol. 2.* Todd Brennan, ed. Chicago: The Thomas More Press, 1985, p. 112.

[18] Mortimer Adler. "Introduction." Robert Edward Brennan, O.P. *Thomistic Psychology: A Philosophic Analysis of the Nature of Man.* New York: Macmillan, 1941: vii-xiv, p. xi.

[19] ST I.84.8.

[20] Gerald Vann, O.P. *The Aquinas Prescription: St. Thomas's Path to a Discerning Heart, a Sane Society, and a Holy Church.* Published London: Hague and Gill, 1940. Reprinted Manchester, New Hampshire: Sophia Institute Press, 1999, pp. 94-95.

regarding the actual nature of the action itself. A societal change in attitudes may, in fact, arise from a willful rejection of knowledge, not an advance. At any rate, it remains true that, as Jean-Pierre Torrell has written, the greatness of the *Summa Theologica* lies in its ability "to inspire solutions to problems for future generations because of the breadth of the great intuitions that govern it. Therein lies, no doubt, the major reason for the *Summa*'s lastingness and its enduring fruitfulness.'[21]

It should be made plain, therefore, that this present work is not an effort in historical theology regarding Aquinas himself, but rather an effort of philosophical theology using Thomistic principles as understood by the author and applied to contemporary debates. The assumption maintained by me throughout the following book is clearly expressed by Baruch Brody: "When . . . I use the phrase 'human being,' I mean 'a member of the species *Homo sapiens* who has a right to life similar to the right to life had by you, me, and so on.' My initial assumption that the fetus is a human being is an assumption about its rights, and not merely about the species to which it belongs."[22]

Finally, this work will then seek to apply this Thomistic anthropology to some problems raised within contemporary bioethical discussions, in the hopes of clarifying these problems and possibly even attaining a degree of resolution.

---

[21] Jean-Pierre Torrell. *Aquinas's* Summa: *Background, Structure, and Reception.* Benedict M. Guevin, O.S.B., trans. Washington, D.C.: Catholic University of America Press, 2005, p. x.
[22] Brody, *Abortion and the Sanctity of Human Life*, p. 3.

# Part One: Aquinas and the Human Person

# Chapter 1:  Aquinas and the Natural Law

How can laws bind the conscience of an individual? Wherein lies, properly speaking, the ethical foundations of the coercive power of the state's legal and moral order?[23]

## 1.  A Thomistic Account of Natural Law

The pages of this book form a small piece of an immense tradition. More studies have been written on Aquinas than on any other philosopher or theologian in history.[24] Furthermore, natural law theory itself seems cyclically to decline in popularity, only to return in full force with different statements and re-statements. In Francis Oakley's formulation, whenever "the demise of natural law theory" is confidently proclaimed, "the obituary turns out, once more, to have been altogether too premature"[25]; the natural law is "perhaps the most ancient and historically persistent concept in Western ethics."[26] Over and over like the return of spring, this perennial philosophy rises in theological and philosophical discussions, is attacked and fairly summarily dismissed, and yet eternally reappears, continuing to flourish by engaging its critics, responding to their arguments, and advancing its own ideas with new vigor.  As Gerald Vann writes:

> If we have a warning . . . in the unhappy history of those Scholastics who, during the Renaissance, continued to speak, and to think, in terms that had lost their vitality for the contemporary world, and

[23] Heinrich A. Rommen. *The Natural Law: A Study in Legal and Social History and Philosophy* [1947]. Thomas R. Hanley, O.S.B., trans. Indianapolis: Liberty Fund, reprinted 1998, p. 4.
[24] Peter Kreeft. *A Summa of the Summa.* San Francisco: Ignatius Press, 1990, p. 19.
[25] Francis Oakley. *Natural Law, Laws of Nature, Natural Rights: Continuity and Discontinuity in the History of Ideas.* London: Continuum, 2005, pp. 16-17.
[26] Russell Hittinger. "Natural Law." *Encyclopedia of Bioethics.* Volume 4. Warren Thomas Reich, ed. New York: Simon & Schuster Macmillan, 1995: 1805-12, p. 1805.

who refused to face the problems that were of primary importance to the contemporary world, we have also a positive example in the person of St. Thomas himself. If we do in our day, so far as we may, what he did in his, we shall be contributing as we ought to the growth of Thomism....But we have to enlarge and enrich the [Thomistic] synthesis with the findings of later and contemporary thought and to recast it in terms of contemporary thought.[27]

(1)   *God and the Natural Law*

As it is typically used today, the term "natural law" refers to the idea that objective moral knowledge is available to humans by the use of the light of natural reason (*lumen naturale*); the natural law is "the foundational principles of right and wrong which are both right for all and at some level known to all."[28] These principles are "known" by reflecting both on human nature and on the ways that human nature has governed itself throughout history. Hence natural law principles are available to humanity both deductively and inductively, both by analysis of the human's known natural constitution and by comparison of the similarities developed through the centuries among the moral codes of nations and cultures. An early example of the latter "inductive" approach is found in the Roman effort to formulate a *jus gentium*, a sort of "law of nations" based on the commonalities of law throughout neighboring lands, resulting eventually in compendiums such as the sixth-century *Corpus Juris Civilis*. A good twentieth-century example of the same sort of approach is found in the "Illustrations of the Tao" section of C.S. Lewis's *The Abolition of Man*.[29] This approach may be viewed as the overall "consensus of everyone everywhere," or slightly more narrowly as the consensus of those "whose exceptional wisdom everyone everywhere concedes."[30] Consequently, the "fundamental principles" of natural law ethics are not distinctive to Christianity, "for these are shared with all serious-minded people in whatever tradition they stand."[31]

Proponents of this view usually believe that this natural law has been implanted into humans and graciously made accessible to natural reason by God, but that salvific knowledge of God, or even belief in God's existence, is not strictly necessary for knowledge of natural law moral

[27] Vann, *The Aquinas Prescription*, pp. 171-72.

[28] J. Budziszewski. *Natural Law for Lawyers*. Jeffery J. Ventrella, ed. Nashville, Tenn.: ACW Press, 2006, p. 21.

[29] Lewis, *The Abolition of Man*. Oxford: Oxford University Press, 1943.

[30] Budziszewski,. *Natural Law for Lawyers*, p. 31.

[31] John Macquarrie. *Three Issues in Ethics*. London: SCM Press, 1970, p. 89.

guidelines, since an effect can be known without knowledge of its cause. An early and cautious statement of this latter view can be found in the argument of Hugo Grotius that human nature is "the mother of natural law." Grotius goes on to the most famous passage in all his writings: "What we have been saying would have a degree of validity even if we should concede that which cannot be conceded without the utmost wickedness, that there is no God" [*etiamsi daremus Deum non esse*, "even if we were to concede that there is no God"].[32] Of course, Grotius himself was a devout Christian, and he is not to be read as attempting a case for a "non-theological" natural law; he is simply saying that the natural law can be known by the light of *natural* reason, and thus applies to all, whether "religious" or not.

However, most natural law theorists, following Aquinas, argue that in order to possess the character of law, natural law must have behind it a rightfully authoritative Lawgiver "to whom it belongs to inflict penalties." Of course, there is more to God as Lawgiver than "that One inflicting penalties"; however, Aquinas points out that any lawgiver, including God, does more in the making of a law than the "private person" who "can only advise." The law must have "coercive power… in order to prove an efficacious inducement to virtue."[33] Without God's providential ordering of the universe, humans in themselves "cannot establish the obligatoriness of natural law,"[34] although humans in themselves may still be able to recognize its prescriptions:

> Natural law is "law" because it has the properties of all law. Its precepts are not arbitrary whims, but rules that the mind can grasp as right; they serve not special interests, but the common good; their legislator is not a private person, but the public authority of the universe; and they are not secret rules, for God has so designed creation that every rational being knows them.[35]

Of course, the Thomistic account of our knowledge of natural law does not necessarily depend on God's existence. However, what *does* depend on God's existence is the Thomistic account of natural law precisely in its character *as law*, in its character as obligatory and binding upon

---

[32] *Hugonis Grotii, De jure belli et pacis libri tres* [1646 edition]. J.B. Scott, ed. Oxford: Oxford University Press, 1913, p. 6.

[33] ST I-II.90.3.

[34] Michael Zuckert. *Natural Rights and the New Republicanism*. Princeton, New Jersey: Princeton University Press, 1994, p. 191.

[35] J. Budziszewski. "Natural Law." *New Dictionary of Christian Apologetics*. W.C. Campbell-Jack, Gavin McGrath, and C. Stephen Evans, eds. Leicester, England: InterVarsity Press, 2006: 473-76, p. 473.

human behavior, since for Aquinas any legitimate law requires an authoritative source behind it. Therefore, natural law guidelines ought not to be thought of as "a vain attempt at an autonomous human ethic"; in fact, "Natural law cannot be understood properly apart from the reality of God's creating this world in the way He did and in particular his creating man in his own image."[36]

A question might logically arise at this point: When referring to "human nature" and "natural law," what is meant by the terms "nature" and "natural"? In common parlance, nature is viewed scientifically, as "that uniform or regular behavior that things are observed to exhibit when isolated from the interventions of chance or deliberate human design."[37] However, in philosophic and theological usage, nature does not necessarily refer to the scientific view, to "the great outdoors," or even to anything specifically physical, for in Christian philosophy a nature can exist as a substance without being physically embodied.[38] (A "substance" is anything which exists in and as itself, not as a characteristic or "accident" of something else. For example, consider a brown squirrel; the "brown" is the characteristic or accident, while the "squirrel" is the substance.) For the purposes of this study, the term "nature" will be defined as "things belonging to a genus" or "things having an inherently constituted reason for being categorized together." Nature, in other words, really refers to "natural kinds." Although he does not commit himself to an endorsement of this perspective, Fergus Kerr thinks it certainly plausible to argue that "If there is a single notion that runs all the way through [Aquinas's *Summa Theologica*], underpinning one consideration after another, it is surely the notion of 'nature.'"[39]

Aquinas mentions two senses of "nature," one of which is here under examination: "Since it is through the form that the essence of everything is made complete, this essence, which is what a definition signifies, is generally called 'nature.'"[40] He also points out that "both matter and form [together] are called 'nature'"—so that nature can be

---

[36] VanDrunen, *A Biblical Case for Natural Law*, p. 14.

[37] Benedict M. Ashley, O.P. "The Anthropological Foundations of the Natural Law: A Thomistic Engagement with Modern Science." *St. Thomas Aquinas and the Natural Law Tradition: Contemporary Perspectives.* John Goyette, Mark S. Latkovic, and Richard S. Myers, eds. Washington, D.C.: Catholic University of America Press, 2004: 3-16, p. 4.

[38] For one explanation of how this is possible, see Augustine's *Confessions*, Book 7.

[39] Kerr, *After Aquinas: Versions of Thomism.* Oxford: Blackwell Publishing, 2002, p. 120.

[40] ST I.29.1.

thought of both as the essence of something, what causes it to be placed in a genus, and also as its specific embodiment in matter. Thus one's own "nature" is the human essence as such, one's spiritual nature or form, but also one's "nature" can be thought of as what one is as a complete human being, an embodied rational creature comprising both form and matter. This is what is called "human nature," a nature common to all humans in their normally developing condition; as nature "in the sense of the cause and principle of (some) beings," such a view may be distinguished from "the nature of nature as of a subsisting thing."[41] This, what John F. Wippel calls "the genus argument" for human nature, does not confuse *quod quid est* (the essence of something) with *esse* (that thing's "act of being"). Only in God are the essence and the act of being identical; therefore, only God cannot be located in a genus. Or, to put it a different way, if God is in a genus, God is the only possible member of that genus, and thus God's "genus" is not really a genus as such at all. On the other hand, even though every human's act of being is different from every other human's, the human essence or genus is the same.[42]

Similarly, in his work *The Resurrection of Nature*, J. Budziszewski discusses various Aristotelian concepts of human nature: "The term 'human nature' can be taken in three senses: that which is innate (sense one), that which is characteristic (sense two), and that which is the mark of our full and appropriate development as human beings."[43] Later he fleshes out this third sense as "what is in the highest sense natural for human beings, the thing wherein we come into our own, the thing wherein we flourish, the measure of our full and appropriate development, and the rule of our conduct. . . . [Human reason is therefore not merely] deductive, technical, or narrowly instrumental reasoning," but rather "the activity by which we understand ourselves, bring our lives into purposeful order, and keep them in this order."[44] The terms human nature, human rationality or reason, and the natural law, as used throughout the present work, will refer primarily to this third sense in Budziszewski's description of "nature." Nature is thus a

---

[41] Jan Aertsen, *Nature and Creature*, p. 32.

[42] See Part I of Wippel's *The Metaphysical Thought of Thomas Aquinas* (Washington, D.C.: Catholic University of America Press, 2000), for the fuller explanation of this point.

[43] J. Budziszewski. *The Resurrection of Nature: Political Theory and the Human Character*. Ithaca and London: Cornell University Press, 1986, p. 12.

[44] Ibid., p. 38.

generic term referring to the "full and appropriate" human essence, as discoverable by the natural rational activity of humanity.

(2) *Aquinas's Aristotelianism*

In its ethical sense, as it is derived from this "human nature" or essence or genus, natural law is "the rule of conduct which is prescribed to us by the Creator in the constitution of the nature with which He has endowed us."[45] Thus the basic Aristotelian recognition behind the teachings of Thomistic natural law is two-fold: that things come in different kinds, and that these different kinds have different and specific functions or ends—that is, they possess an inherent *teleology* or "directedness." Because of this teleology, certain moral characteristics such as sympathy and fairness are natural to humans, since "they are to some degree innate, and they appear spontaneously" within the typical human life.[46] This remains an Aristotelian recognition even though, as Alasdair MacIntyre argues in his discussion of the Aristotelian *megalopsychos*, the "great-souled" human, Aquinas not only adapts but corrects Aristotle's pre-Christian ethical sensibility: "Aquinas's account of the virtues not only supplements, but also corrects Aristotle's to a significantly greater extent than I had realized."[47] In other words, Aquinas not only "baptizes" Aristotle, but engages him critically as a philosopher, even expanding and at least partially "creating" the very Aristotelian terms (such as substance, form, and nature) upon which he relies for his own accounts.

Despite this caveat, however, Aquinas's thoroughgoing use of Aristotle leaves little doubt that Aquinas's anthropological and ethical orientations definitely remain fundamentally Aristotelian[48]; as Ralph McInerny puts it in a defense of Aquinas's Aristotelian categories of

---

[45] James J. Fox. "Natural Law." *The Catholic Encyclopedia, Volume IX*. Robert Appleton Company: 1910. *Online Edition* K. Knight: 2005. Newadvent.org/cathen, n.p. Accessed 2 July 2006.

[46] James Q. Wilson. *The Moral Sense*. New York: Free Press, 1993, p. 229.

[47] Alasdair MacIntyre. *Dependent Rational Animals: Why Human Beings Need the Virtues*. Chicago and LaSalle, Illinois: Open Court, 1999, p. xi.

[48] See María L. Lukac de Stier's "Aristotle's *De Anima* as Source of Aquinas's Anthropological Doctrine" (Jacques Maritain Center: Thomistic Institute, www2.nd.edu. Accessed 12 Sept. 2007). Fergus Kerr's dissenting view ("On the standard interpretation, Thomas is an 'Aristotelian.' This requires nuancing, in the light of recent scholarship, even if it is plausible at all") seems overstated (*After Aquinas*, p. 9). However, the points for which Kerr ultimately argues— that Aquinas is first and foremost a Trinitarian Christian, and that this commitment guides not only his theological writings but also his philosophy— should be readily accepted and incorporated into Thomistic exegesis.

thought, "The native habitat of the *praeambula fidei* [of Thomistic thought] is the *Metaphysics* of Aristotle."[49] In Aquinas's adaptation of this Aristotelian perspective, humans are seen as endowed by their Creator[50] with a constituted nature; to recognize and live by the constitution of this specifically human nature is to recognize and live by the precepts of "natural law," a natural law innately recognized to be true by all normally functioning adult humans. Hence, in the Thomistic synthesis, anthropology and ethics meet and merge.

Of course, these straightforward claims are easy enough to assert, but rather more difficult to demonstrate logically. In fact, the arguments against the existence of objective moral knowledge sometimes take on moral overtones of their own, especially in their assertion of moral relativism as the surest safeguard of tolerance and civility. In the next section, this assertion will be examined.[51]

## 2. The Objective Nature of Natural Law

Touching upon the relationship of moral relativism and tolerance, Peter Kreeft outlines a typical argument connecting the two,[52] with such arguments usually running as follows:

Premise 1: If there are no objectively true moral statements, people should be tolerant of others' moral beliefs, particularly in dealing with cross-cultural issues, and not think stubbornly of their own moral beliefs as universal in nature.

Premise 2: There are no objectively true moral statements; all moral statements are relative to time, place, and circumstances.

---

[49] Ralph McInerny. Praeambula Fidei: *Thomism and the God of the Philosophers*. Washington, D.C.: Catholic University of America Press, 2007, pp. 167-68. For a view that does not contradict McInerny's but rather supplements it, see *Aquinas the Augustinian* (Michael Dauphinais, Barry David, and Matthew Levering, eds. Washington, D.C.: Catholic University of America Press, 2007).

[50] In the present work, the existence of God will be assumed, God being the proper object of the science of theology (ST I.1.7), without thereby arguing either for or against the apologetic value of Aquinas's "Five Ways" of demonstrating God's existence (ST I.2.3). "The Deity is confessed by almost all, even against their will, when they come to treat of the first principles of the universe" (Athenagoras, *A Plea for the Christians*, p. 132, Ch. 7).

[51] The argument for the "objectivity" of natural law moral principles is meant only in the sense of contrast with "subjectivity" in morality. Any congruence with John Finnis's use of the term "objectivity" as a replacement for the term "nature" is not intended; see Finnis's *Fundamentals of Ethics* (Oxford: Oxford University Press, 1983, p. 10).

[52] Peter Kreeft. *A Refutation of Moral Relativism*. San Francisco: Ignatius Press, 1999, Chapter 6.

Conclusion (by *modus ponens*): People should be tolerant of others' moral beliefs and not think of their own moral beliefs as universal in nature.

Kreeft's outlined argument provides a good illustration of the fact that people tend naturally to use the language of objective morality, even when they are seeking to deny the *existence* of objective morality, and thus provide unintentional support for the concept of objectively existing, universal moral claims. One premise of this argument maintains that there are no objectively true moral statements. On the other hand, the argument concludes with a blanket, objective, one-size-fits-all moral claim—that "people should be tolerant of others' moral beliefs." It seems that the very same objective morality that persuades of the rightness of tolerance and public civility is also the objective morality that should persuade of right and wrong in other areas as well. In order to make a case for moral relativism, the writer must appeal to certain absolute or objectively existing virtues, namely (in this case) the traits of tolerance and civility in typical situations. This leads to a sort of "boomerang" effect—i.e., arguments against the existence of objective moral rules typically contain appeals to moral rules the relativists themselves treat as objectively existing, and which they think should be universally accepted. Relativists tend to "assume that tolerance is good—really good, good for everybody," and thereby assume "the very moral absolutism [they are] trying to refute."[53]

As Kreeft points out, the very idea of tolerance "always pre-supposes some objective morality, some objectively real good and evil. . . . We do not tolerate *goods*, only *evils*, in order to prevent worse evils."[54] (In the succinct words of another writer, "Toleration, by definition, implies disapproval."[55]) Often, as in the case of the preceding illustration, no explanation is given as to why others should exempt as objective and absolute the moral rules the relativists themselves desire to retain. However, "if no moral values are absolute, neither is tolerance." Therefore, neither is the claim that humans should be tolerant of the customs and beliefs of others. Obviously, this relativistic stance is self-contradictory. However, virtuous practices such as tolerating differences in others and refraining from unnecessary harm do, in fact, have a secure foundation—this foundation just does not lie

---

[53] Ibid., p. 96.
[54] Ibid., p. 95. Emphasis in original.
[55] Colin E. Gunton. *A Brief Theology of Revelation: The 1993 Warfield Lectures.* Edinburgh: T & T Clark, 1995, p. 96n19.

within the realm of relativism, and so "the absolutist can take tolerance much more seriously than the relativist."[56]

In his *A Theory of Justice*, John Rawls argues that natural law theory, and specifically Thomistic natural law theory, is actually intolerant and cannot allow for "even a limited tolerance."[57] However, Aquinas does take into account and allows for differences of customs; he writes, quoting Isidore, "Law should be possible both according to nature, and according to the customs of the country"; in fact, "Custom has the force of law."[58] He reasons that "those who are in authority" should "rightly tolerate certain evils, lest certain goods be lost, or certain greater evils be incurred"; therefore, "Human law rightly allows some vices, by not repressing them."[59] Moreover, human law is changeable according to the movement of reason's progression within human customs, since only the primary precepts of natural law are "one and the same for everyone at all times"; the secondary precepts, on the other hand, vary in their application of primary precepts to the exigencies of diverse social situations. They will "vary from society to society and sometimes within societies."[60] However, when it comes to opposing a society's custom to the primary precepts of natural law, Aquinas steadfastly maintains the objectivity of natural law, which *"cannot be changed by a custom* proceeding from the will of man."[61] One may therefore think of Rawls' statement as a profound mistake while still recognizing that such a mistake is plausibly made: "Since a Thomistic understanding of natural law commits those who possess it to asserting that human nature is such that rational practical principles are antecedent to and govern choice in rational well-functioning human beings, and that therefore those principles have to be discovered, not chosen, any defense of a Thomistic understanding of natural law is very easily construed as a threat to liberty," as Alasdair MacIntyre writes.[62] In fact, another writer goes so far as to point out that Aquinas "was an advocate of diversity in public debate, of introducing a wide variety of views for

---

[56] Kreeft, *A Refutation*, p. 98.

[57] Rawls, *A Theory of Justice*. Cambridge, Mass.: Harvard University Press, 1971, p. 216.

[58] ST I-II.96.2 and 97.3.

[59] ST II-II.10.11 and I-II.96.2.

[60] Alasdair MacIntyre. *God, Philosophy, Universities: A Selective History of the Catholic Philosophical Tradition*. Lanham, Maryland: Rowman & Littlefield, 2009, p. 89.

[61] ST I-II.97.3. Emphasis added.

[62] MacIntyre, "Theories of Natural Law in the Culture of Advanced Modernity." *Common Truths: New Perspectives on Natural Law*. Edward B. McLean, ed. Wilmington, Delaware: ISI Books, 2000: 91-115, p. 112.

rational inquiry and lively debate. It is in this respect, I suggest, we find an affinity between Aquinas and modern liberals who want to allow for diversity in the public realm."[63] Indeed, Aquinas himself sounds almost relativistic while examining the question "Whether the Natural Law Is the Same in All Men?"[64] (although he answers the question with a clear "Yes").

Moreover, anyone who desires "diversity in public debate" must allow as well for those who argue for the objective universality of certain moral rules. If any moral rule at all is in fact seen as universally binding, the character of that moral rule must also have some sort of "universal" quality to give it its universal applicability. One logical conceptual basis for the universal acceptance of certain moral rules, perhaps the *most* logical, lies in the objective and absolute nature of those rules, rooted in objectively existing human nature. Given this conceptual basis, these rules may be discussed as just as much features of the universe as carbon and hydrogen:

> Morality is built into the universe as deeply and inescapably as atoms and protons and neutrons. We are moral beings to the core—the very universe is moral. Right and wrong are embedded in the creation.[65]

As can be readily seen, this statement is somewhat hyperbolic, and it is not quoted to suggest that the physical universe itself is either moral or immoral. However, it does point out that moral knowledge is an inherent feature of the human constituted nature[66] just as surely as elementary particles are inherent features of the physical universe. Noted ethicist Gilbert Meilaender puts this idea and its implications nicely:

> We should not think of moral education as indoctrination, but as initiation. It is initiation into the human moral inheritance. . . . We initiate rather than indoctrinate precisely because . . . we have not decided what morality requires; we have discovered it. We transmit not our own views or desires but moral truth—by which we consider ourselves also to be bound. Hence, moral education is not an exercise of power over future generations.[67]

---

[63] John Jenkins, C.S.C. "Aquinas, Natural Law, and the Challenges of Diversity." *Common Truths: New Perspectives on Natural Law*. Edward B. McLean, ed. Wilmington, Delaware: ISI Books, 2000: 57-71, p. 68.
[64] ST I-II.94.4.
[65] Eugene H. Peterson. *Christ Plays in Ten Thousand Places*. Grand Rapids, Michigan: Eerdmans, 2005, p. 145.
[66] ST I.79.11-13.

This is what is meant by the "objective" character of the natural law rooted in human nature. It is not a system necessarily promulgated by those in power, but rather a system overarching those in power, a system to which those out of power can legitimately appeal. It is true that "the law of society comes before that law of nature in a psychological and pedagogical sense," in that the law of society restrains and educates us before our individual rational analysis of our own nature is fully formed; however, ontologically the natural law is foundationally prior to the law of society.[68] The educated conscience may owe its existence as such to society, but the fundamental laws of conscience in which it is educated do not. This "loosely knit body of rules of action," as one writer has labeled the natural law, must be "prescribed by an authority *superior to the state*," whether that authority be "derived from divine commandment; from the nature of humankind; from abstract Reason; or from long experience of mankind in community."[69] Often, as Meilaender writes elsewhere, "Moral education . . . does not look much like teaching. . . . [The transmission of right moral responses comes from] men and women for whom such responses have become natural—persons whose vision of human nature is shaped in accordance with the *Tao* [the principles of natural law]. . . . To educate the youth in the primeval moral platitudes is to lead him into his human inheritance."[70]

Contrary to this assertion, it may be argued that the concepts of "nature" and "natural" have in fact been used by the state itself in ideologically driven ways, to promote and safeguard the interests of those in power (e.g., Aristotle's justification of "natural" slavery). However, as J. Budziszewski argues, "In the name of every good evil has been done, and in the name of every truth lies have been propounded."[71] It seems fundamental to the idea of natural law, at the very "root of this tradition," that law in its essence is "something more than a convention or a command of the sovereign power."[72] If the only

[67] See Richard John Neuhaus, "While We're At It" (*First Things* 159 [Jan. 2006]: 66-76, p. 66).

[68] Yves Simon. *The Tradition of Natural Law: A Philosopher's Reflections*. Vukan Kuic, ed. New York: Fordham University Press. 2nd printing, 1967, p. 69.

[69] Russell Kirk. "The Case For and Against Natural Law." Lecture 469, Heritage Lecture Series. Washington, D.C.: The Heritage Foundation. 15 July 1993: 1-9, p. 1. Emphasis added.

[70] Gilbert Meilaender. *The Taste for the Other: The Social and Ethical Thought of C.S. Lewis*. Grand Rapids, Michigan: Eerdmans, 1978, pp. 212 and 228.

[71] J. Budziszewski. *Written on the Heart: The Case for Natural Law*. Downers Grove, Illinois: InterVarsity Press, 1997, p. 209.

law recognized is the positive criminal law instituted by the state, those out of power within the state have no lawful appeal to make *at all*: "In this state, man will not only lack protection, he will lack even the language to articulate his need for protection."[73] On the other hand, at least Aquinas's recognition of different kinds of law shows how these appeals on the part of those out of power may be lawfully founded. Overarching the positive laws of nations are the "laws of Nature and of Nature's God," as the Declaration of Independence of the United States of America has it. Even if these natural laws have no actual legislative force as such, they provide a foundation for assessing the rightness and wrongness of positive legislation, and can therefore be used to judge the actions of those in power, the legislators, in at least a moral sense even if practically in no other: "Natural law is not only an ideal for the positive law, for legislation to realize; it is also a critical norm for the existing positive law."[74] The moral judgment thus undergirds any practical action taken. As Fergus Kerr states, "The appeal to the natural law tradition in some form is motivated, obviously, by horror at the abuse of law by so many states. If justice is determined by what the state decrees, as the abandonment of traditional belief in something normative beyond positive law seems to involve, it is not surprising that we should want to return to the principle that the law is always finally subject to what 'natural justice' requires."[75] This position quite logically leads to what one writer calls "jurisprudences in conflict," a "battle royal" between "the natural legal tradition" and "legal positivism or legal realism."[76] Thus, while the idea of a natural law may be misused by the state at times, it may also be used quite properly as the moral foundation for positive law; further, the natural law may be used as the moral foundation for those standing in opposition to a government when it acts wrongfully: "Without the natural law, the

---

[72] Budziszewski, *Natural Law for Lawyers*, p. 9.

[73] Ian A.T. McLean. "Criminal Law and Natural Law." *Common Truths: New Perspectives on Natural Law.* Edward B. McLean, ed. Wilmington, Delaware: ISI Books, 2000: 259-89, p. 282.

[74] Heinrich Rommen, *The Natural Law*, p. 234.

[75] Fergus Kerr. "Natural Law: Incommensurable Readings." *Aquinas's* Summa Theologiae: *Critical Essays.* Brian Davies, ed. Lanham, Maryland: Rowman & Littlefield, 2006: 245-63, p. 250.

[76] Nathan A. Adams IV. "An Unnatural Assault on Natural Law: Regulating Biotechnology Using a Just Research Theory." *Human Dignity in the Biotech Century: A Christian Vision for Public Policy.* Charles W. Colson and Nigel M. de S. Cameron, eds. Downers Grove, Illinois: InterVarsity Press, 2004: 160-80, p. 165.

people have no basis other than the pragmatic and utilitarian on which to respond to unjust laws. The ability, provided only by natural law, to challenge the very validity of an unjust law is an important safeguard against the enactment and enforcement of such laws."[77]

As one consequently turns to this tradition, one discovers that what the natural law affirms is that "all human beings share a set of ethical norms and imperatives that they commonly perceive without dependence on supernatural disclosure and illumination. Humanity, in short, universally knows a body of morally binding laws that shape a common pattern of social behavior."[78] It is this natural law, not one's own circumstances or moral preferences, that "judges" the human regarding right and wrong. Proponents of natural law therefore typically argue for the conclusion that "There exist acts which *per se* and in themselves, independently of circumstances, are always seriously wrong by reason of their object."[79] Restrictions on these acts are morally binding upon all humans because the natural moral law undergirding the restrictions objectively applies to all humans.

### 3. The Non-Sectarian Nature of Natural Law

Another frequent misunderstanding of the natural law on the part of the general public involves the identification of natural law prescriptions with some sort of sectarian religious code. For example, just after Christmas of 2003, the American Associated Press released a story headlined "Why Keep Some Old Testament Laws and Discard Others?" for newspaper publication nationwide. The opening two sentences of the article read:

> Among the issues raised during the bitter dispute over homo-sexuality in the Episcopal Church this year is why Christianity has upheld some Old Testament laws and discarded others. Why eat pork, for instance, but oppose same-sex behavior?[80]

However, the question itself reveals a misunderstanding of the natural law source of the latter moral position. Despite the frequent assertion that "no one has the right to impose his or her religious beliefs on

---

[77] Charles E. Rice. *Fifty Questions on the Natural Law: What It Is and Why We Need It.* San Francisco: Ignatius Press, 1995, p. 55.

[78] Carl F.H. Henry. "Natural Law and a Nihilistic Culture." *First Things* 49 (January 1995): 55-60, p. 56.

[79] John Finnis. *Moral Absolutes: Tradition, Revision, and Truth.* Washington, D.C.: Catholic University of America Press, 1991, p. 2. See also Oliver O'Donovan, "John Finnis on Moral Absolutes" (*The Revival of the Natural Law: Philosophical, Theological, and Ethical Responses to the Finnis-Grisez School.* Nigel Biggar and Rufus Black, eds. Aldershot, Hants: Ashgate, 2000: 111-28, p. 112).

[80] Anon. Associated Press release, 26 December 2003.

anyone else," many contemporary moral issues do not revolve around explicitly religious doctrines. In fact, it is probably best not to argue on the basis of such doctrines in most public discourse; as Richard John Neuhaus writes, "For most purposes in the ordering of our common life, it is neither necessary nor wise to invoke an account of moral reality beyond what is required for the resolution of the issue at hand." Neuhaus goes on:

....On most issues, a sustainable measure of political equilibrium can be achieved by appeal to a widely shared and "thin" account of moral reality that is far less than comprehensive....People who are themselves devoutly religious may in the public square advance arguments that are not distinctly religious in character. This is notably the case with proponents of natural law theory. They proceed on the basis that human beings are naturally endowed with a rational capacity to discern the truth, including the moral truth, of things. In public argument, they generally prescind from religious or theological claims, contending that agreement on the ultimate sources and ends of human reason is not necessary to the exercise of human reason. Contrary to the critics of natural law theory, the theory and its practice is not discredited by the observation that many, if not most, of its practitioners do in fact have definite ideas on sources and ends.[81]

Even in pre-Christian times, the Roman writer Cicero argued that "right reason" or "the light of reason from the nature of things" enjoins "conformity to Nature's standard" in moral matters.[82] Further, according to the Stoic philosophers, the great rationality (the *Logos*) undergirding the natural universe also, in smaller measure, persuades humans of what is morally "according to nature" and therefore right (or wrong); for example, Marcus Aurelius in his *Meditations*, Book V, writes, "Reverence that which is best in the universe; and this is that which

---

[81] Richard John Neuhaus. "Human Dignity and Public Discourse." *Human Dignity and Bioethics: Essays Commissioned by the President's Council on Bioethics.* Edmund D. Pellegrino, M.D., chair. Adam Schulman and Thomas W. Merrill, eds. Washington, D.C.: Government Printing Office, March 2008: 215-28, p. 224.
[82] Cicero. *De Legibus*, Book II.10. A good discussion of Cicero's natural law ethics may be found in Hadley Arkes, "That 'Nature Herself Has Placed in Our Ears a Power of Judging': Some Reflections on the 'Naturalism' of Cicero" (*Natural Law Theory: Contemporary Essays*. Robert P. George, ed. Oxford: Clarendon Press, 1992: 245-77). See also J. Rufus Fears, "Natural Law: The Legacy of Greece and Rome" (*Common Truths: New Perspectives on Natural Law*. Edward B. McLean, ed. Wilmington, Delaware: ISI Books, 2000: 19-56).

makes use of all things and directs all things. And in like manner also reverence that which is best in thyself; and this is of the same kind as that." In Book II, he makes the highly Thomistic assertion, "Nothing is evil which is according to nature."[83] Many Christians accept the Stoic *Logos* as a pre-Christian awareness of the light of Christ Himself, revealed through the writers of the New Testament: "And the Word [Logos] became flesh and lived among us" (John 1:14). Aquinas himself distinguishes between "divine" laws which are directed specifically toward the human "supernatural end,"[84] and those "natural" laws which apply to all humans because of their common human nature, regardless of their religious beliefs or lack of beliefs. To use the Associated Press example, the command "Do not eat pork" is a "divine" law applying to observant Jews under the Mosaic Covenant, and is therefore not rationally derivable by an introspective analysis of the generic human nature. The command "Do not murder," on the other hand, is an example of a natural law applying to all people regardless of their views of the Bible, Christianity, Judaism, or religion in general. These "laws of Nature and of Nature's God" are not based on any specific religion, but are a general guide for all humanity. This does not mean that natural law has no revelatory component; it does mean, however, that natural law is a general and non-sectarian revelation as opposed to a specific and "divine" (to use Aquinas's term) revelation.[85]

Earlier the endowment of humans with a constituted nature by their Creator was mentioned. Any such endowment of a created or designed nature, of course, implies specific human ends, and thus human rights and wrongs as well. "If man is an artifact of God's," as one philosopher argues, "man has a nature that provides a measure of his actions. Acts that thwart his nature are bad; those that fulfill its potential are good. That is, there are criteria of good and bad action antecedent to this person's doing anything at all. He will be good if he fulfills the purpose his Maker has embedded in him, and bad if he does not."[86] As Aquinas writes, it is not only "religious" knowledge which helps humans

---

[83] *Meditations.* George Long, trans. New York: P.F. Collier & Son, 1909. Compare ST I-II.18.5, in which Aquinas writes, "Even in natural things, good and evil [may be recognized] inasmuch as something is according to nature, and something against nature."
[84] ST I-II.91.4.
[85] On the necessity of the divine law beyond the natural law, see ST I-II.91.4.
[86] Ralph McInerny. *Ethica Thomistica: The Moral Philosophy of Thomas Aquinas.* Washington, D.C.: Catholic University of America Press, 1982. Revised edition, 1997, pp. 53-54.

"discern what is good and what is evil," but also and initially "the light of natural reason" by which humans come to understand the human nature measuring their actions:

> The light of natural reason, whereby we discern what is good and what is evil, which is the function of the natural law, is nothing else than an imprint on us of the Divine light. It is therefore evident that the natural law is nothing else than the rational creature's participation of the eternal law.[87]

This *lumen naturale* enables humans to perceive wrongdoing against the laws of their nature, the moral laws governing human behavior; not only do humans see what is prohibited, but also what is permitted and what is positively commanded. Even apart from the revelation of Christ, humanity is thus able to avoid "an absurd battle against the nature of things."[88] To defend this view, one need merely ask a question: Did humans know murder was wrong before the transmission of the Ten Commandments to Moses? Obviously, the answer is yes; however, equally obviously, not all natural laws will be as readily recognized by natural reason.

The point being made here is that by this natural light humans perceive also the objective, factual basis for natural law moral guidelines. The natural law is "a dictate of reason," as Aquinas has it, and the function of natural reason is to lead from facts known to the inference of other facts. "Wherefore just as, in demonstrative sciences, the reason leads us from certain principles to assent to the conclusion, so it induces us by some means to assent to the precept of the law."[89] Although humans do not always seem to see the underlying dictate of reason in the case of human-made criminal laws, they do tend to do so in the case of natural moral laws, even if these laws are not superficially apparent and must first be pointed out to humanity in divine revelation. The objection might be raised at this point that many do *not*, in fact, see the "underlying dictate of reason," and that "appeal to natural law is disqualified if there is not a consensus among all reasonable men, and above all among all Christians, about its conclusions." However, as Cahal Daly points out, "There are, alas, many matters about which there is no longer a consensus, even among Christians, but which, nevertheless, do clearly belong to the sphere of natural, rational morality." Daly mentions a few of these matters, such as divorce, abortion, and

---

[87] ST I-II.91.2.
[88] David VanDrunen, *A Biblical Case for Natural Law*, p. 60.
[89] ST I-II.92.2.

euthanasia, and defends the role of supernatural revelation in bringing some matters before the attention of natural reason:

> Chesterton was right: without the Christian supernatural, no one has ever succeeded in being fully natural. There is a sense in which, without the supernatural, it is not possible either completely and certainly to know, or perfectly to do, the natural. It is both historically false and theologically foolish to say that if some moral proposition were taught only by the Church it would *thereby* be proved not to be rational or natural.[90]

Thus these natural moral laws are not subjective, sectarian religious commands or divine laws, but objective features of the human practical intellect, although the divine laws are certainly necessary to reinforce and clarify any given natural law.[91] The natural law therefore is not an imposition of private conscience, but is available to all through public reasoning.

Some may see these statements and the discussion preceding them as a reversion to "morality by fiat"—in other words, "If one does not see the truth of these natural *praecepta*, it is simply due to a lack of rational understanding." However, such is not precisely the case; other factors may also come into play in the apprehension of moral truths. For example, as Russell Hittinger points out (paraphrasing Aquinas):

> A habitual grasp of first principles [in the practical intellect, *synderesis*] hardly constitutes a morality. The agent needs the facts drawn from experience and inquiry; conclusions need to be framed in the manner of adequate propositions; and conclusions need to be applied to facts. Moreover, all of these need the institutions of moral training.[92]

It may be possible that in modern moral discourse, natural law guidelines have lost much of their persuasive power (which at first glance would not seem possible if the claims of natural law ethicists are true) because of a lack of adequate understanding of and support for the habitual dispositions naturally innate within the general populace. Therefore, there may in fact be a "lack of rational understanding" of the natural *praecepta*, especially at the level of the axiomatic features of the practical intellect and the first-order logical inferences from those axiomatic features. Despite this possibility, the perhaps uneasy and

---

[90] Cahal B. Daly. *Natural Law Morality Today*. Dublin/London: Clonmore and Reynolds/Burns & Oates, 1965, pp. 13-14. Emphasis in original.

[91] ST I-II.91.4.

[92] Russell Hittinger. "Examination of Conscience." *First Things* 189 (Jan. 2009): 59-61, p. 60.

unstable position here defended is that Thomistic natural law theory is theological in nature, but is also rationally compelling without the necessary appeal to theological presuppositions.

Again, this does not mean that all will attain to the understanding of natural laws; in fact, some may reject the natural law even while its prescriptions remain "rationally compelling."[93] According to Aquinas, the "general principles" of natural law are known to all, but not necessarily the secondary principles attained by reasoning from the general principles: "There belong to the natural law, first, certain most general precepts, that are known to all; and secondly, certain secondary and more detailed precepts, which are, as it were, conclusions following closely from first principles. As to those general principles, the natural law, in the abstract, can nowise be blotted out from men's hearts. But it is blotted out in the case of a particular action, in so far as reason is hindered from applying the general principle to a particular point of practice."[94] Therefore, even valid natural law guidelines will not always be understood or accepted by all people, although the general principles will be understood. "Good is to be done and pursued, and evil is to be avoided" is Aquinas's first principle of practical reason; anyone who does not accept such a law simply misunderstands the terms involved or else has a defective mind, according to Aquinas.[95] However, *in practical application* the conclusions to some natural law guidelines may not be readily known, even as some true conclusions of the speculative reason may not be known: "As regards the general principles whether of speculative or of practical reason, truth or rectitude is the same for all, and is equally known by all. As to the proper conclusions of the speculative reason, the truth is the same for all, but is not equally known to all; thus it is true for all that the three angles of a triangle are together equal to two right angles, although it is not known to all. But as to the proper conclusions of the practical reason, neither is the truth or

---

[93] On this point one should especially see Alasdair MacIntyre's essay "Intractable Moral Disagreements," in *Intractable Disputes About the Natural Law: Alasdair MacIntyre and Critics* (Lawrence S. Cunningham, ed. Notre Dame, Indiana: Univ. of Notre Dame Press, 2009: 1-52). In this essay MacIntyre argues for the position that "it is possible for some theses to be rationally vindicated without thereby being able to secure the assent of all rational agents" (p. 2) and even that "it is possible to establish that one moral standpoint may be rationally superior to others without securing the assent of highly intelligent, perceptive, and thoughtful adherents of those other points of view" (p. 4).

[94] ST I-II.94.6.

[95] ST I-II.94.2.

rectitude the same for all, nor, where it is the same, is it equally known by all."[96] The example given in this passage by Aquinas is "that goods entrusted to another should be restored to their owner." This is a "proper conclusion" of the practical reason; however, in application the conclusion may be complicated by further considerations. For instance, if one were entrusted with a box which was then discovered to be filled with weapons to be used in a revolt against one's country, the "proper conclusion" to the natural law principle would vary, and the goods would not be restored to the rightful owner. Aquinas has in mind a similar example when he states that the truth of the conclusions of the practical reason are not "the same for all"—he is certainly not legitimizing any sort of ethical relativism or subjectivism.[97]

If this natural law is indeed composed of objectively knowable and applicable precepts based on human nature, following the natural law would seem the obvious path to a "naturally" flourishing and fulfilled human life. As one writer says, "It is by the choices a person makes that he or she develops a moral personality open to integral human fulfillment."[98] In the next section, we will take up the topic of the full development and flourishing of the human nature by means of which the natural law is perceived.

### 4.   Human Flourishing and the Human *Telos*

Throughout this work the central inductively-based premises of natural law theory should be kept in mind: that things come in different kinds, and that these different kinds have different and specific functions, ends, or "directedness." These premises are also true in the case of philosophical and theological anthropology. First, humans are of a different kind of thing than other things; second, the kind of thing that humans are has a different and specific function or end, a *telos*. Finding and fulfilling this different and specific function or end would mean fulfilling a human's "nature"; it would be the logical path to a flourishing and fulfilled life for a human. In fact, for Aquinas, one of the special traits setting humans apart from the rest of the animal world is that human agents consciously direct themselves to the goods they recognize as fulfilling of their own natures.

---

[96] ST I-II.94.4.

[97] On this point, see also Robert P. George, "Natural Law and Human Nature" (*Natural Law Theory: Contemporary Essays*. Robert P. George, ed. Oxford: Clarendon Press, 1992: 31-41, pp. 38-39).

[98] Joseph M. Boyle. "Reverence for Life and Bioethics." *Linking the Human Life Issues*. Russell Hittinger, ed. Lake Bluff, Illinois: Regnery Gateway, 1986: 101-40, pp. 126-27.

What exactly are these goods toward which humans direct themselves? As MacIntyre asks, "The philosophical theorist has to enquire: What is the good specific to human beings?"[99] In the previous section, it was argued that there exists an objective, factual basis for natural law moral guidelines. What is this basis?—that is to say, can humans identify what it is which serves to fulfill their natures and which provides the *telos* toward which they naturally gravitate? In Aquinas's analysis, according to his treatise "Of the Natural Law,"[100] these goods which fulfill the human nature are divided into three basic levels of the natural law as it pertains to human beings:

First, the natural law describes what humans share with all other substances. Every substance has the inclination to preserve itself in existence as the kind of thing it is. In Thomas's words, this means that "every substance seeks the preservation of its own being, according to its nature."[101] Several inferences may follow from analysis of this inclination; for instance, the preservation of one's self leads to a possible justification for violent self-defense, but also leads to the condemnation of murder and suicide. One should also avoid activities, insofar as this is possible and reasonable, that endanger one's health.

Second, what humans share with other animals leads to more specialized inclinations, such as the dual-sexed unions typified by humans' natural bodies, the inclination toward the rearing of children, and so on; these are the inclinations toward "things which pertain to man more specially, according to that nature which he has in common with other animals."[102] Having and raising children is therefore a positive good, but includes the obligation to educate one's children in the best way possible and to sacrifice one's own interests, if necessary, in the interests of the next generation.

Third, a human has an inclination to the good of reason that is peculiar to him, or "an inclination to good, according to the nature of his reason, which nature is proper to him." This rational good teaches humanity "to shun ignorance, to avoid offending those among whom one has to live, and other such things."[103] Their rational nature leads

---

[99] Alasdair MacIntyre. *Three Rival Versions of Moral Enquiry: Encyclopaedia, Genealogy, and Tradition.* Notre Dame, Indiana: University of Notre Dame Press, 1990, p. 128.
[100] ST I-II.94.
[101] ST I-II.94.2.
[102] ST I-II.94.2.
[103] ST I-II.94.2.

humans to desire knowledge of God, to desire to live together peaceably in society, and so on.

What else might arise from examining this third, specifically human, inclination? "To shun ignorance," for instance, is an inclination opening many doors, e.g., the study of theology, philosophy, psychology, and the natural sciences; this particular good of reason also implies that a *lack* of intellectual curiosity is not only regrettable, but an actual moral flaw for humans. (By "intellectual curiosity" is meant the Thomistic virtue of studiousness, the "keen application of the mind to something," and not its opposing vice, *curiositas*, the "vanity of understanding."[104]) The analysis of the inclination to the good of reason leads even further afield—for example, the directive "to avoid offending those among whom one has to live" has implications for friendship, sociability, the moral duties necessary to maintain friendships and society, the good of government, the duties of government, and the rights and duties of citizens. "It is especially this third category, the ends of human nature," as one writer has it, "that gives rise to moral problems."

> In this category it is most difficult for us to discover what the ends truly are, because here our purposes and our ends become most entangled with one another. Our inclinations and desires give rise to purposes, and sooner or later a conflict arises between what we want and what we truly are.[105]

What all three of these inclinations have in common is that they all aim at some good.[106] None of them is identical with goodness itself, but they all share in goodness. All natural human actions therefore are bound together by "the over-arching goodness they seek in this, that, and the other thing. That overarching goodness, what Thomas calls the *ratio bonitatis*, is the ultimate end. It follows that anything a human agent does is done for the sake of the ultimate end."[107] So, according to Aquinas, all inclinations upon which humans act aim at the ultimate end of goodness, an ultimate end in which all of them participate: "Man

---

[104] Compare ST II-II.166.1 to 167.1 for this distinction.

[105] Robert Sokolowski, "What Is Natural Law?" p. 511.

[106] "The concept of good, then, has application only for beings insofar as they are members of some species or kind; Aquinas . . . speaks of our good *qua* being, shared with all other beings, our good *qua* animal being, shared with all other animals, and our good *qua* rational being, the common good of rational beings" (Alasdair MacIntyre, *Three Rival Versions of Moral Enquiry*, p. 134).

[107] Ralph McInerny and John O'Callaghan. "Saint Thomas Aquinas." *The Stanford Encyclopedia of Philosophy (Spring 2002 updated online edition)*. Edward N. Zalta, ed. Plato.stanford.edu/archives/spr2005, n.p. Accessed 14 Jan. 2006.

must, of necessity, desire all, whatsoever he desires, for the last end [or] as tending to the perfect good."[108]

At first reading, this last statement seems as if it could not possibly be true. It is obvious that humans act upon a multitudinous variety of motivations and inclinations, and probably the vast majority of these motivations take no conscious account of "the ultimate end." In fact, even if humans do take into account their ultimate end of *ratio bonitatis*, are they not often mistaken regarding what means will bring about this end, or even about the nature of the end itself? For example, what about a person needing money who decides to become a professional burglar in order to (1) come into possession of money, (2) meet his financial needs and the financial needs of his loved ones, and in consequence (3) achieve a life that is, if not good, at least better in some respects than his current life? In what way could his choice of a life of crime aim at the ultimate end of "goodness"? However, Aquinas does consider these arguments. Regarding the objection that a human's motivations often take no account of the ultimate end, he writes, "One need not always be thinking of the last end, whenever one desires or does something: but the virtue of the first intention, which was in respect of the last end, remains in every desire directed to any object whatever, even though one's thoughts be not actually directed to the last end. Thus while walking along the road one needs not to be thinking of the end at every step."[109] Regarding the first objection, that humans act upon a wide variety of motivations and inclinations, Aquinas flatly disagrees: "All men agree in desiring the last end, which is happiness."[110] Secondary objects of inclination eventually tend toward the primary object and are thus done for its sake.

Consequently, the simple fact of the variety of human motivations does not discount the idea of a single ultimate end; rational activity finds its way in a variety of situations, and the plurality of applications of rationality simply means there exists also a plurality of human virtues corresponding to those applications. Further, even in the example of the would-be professional burglar, Aquinas would maintain that the burglar, though mistaken in apprehension regarding the proper means to take to reach the desired end, still has the same end in common with all other humans:

> The fact that there are false or inadequate identifications of goodness does not mean that there is not a true and adequate

---

[108] ST I-II.1.6.
[109] ST I-II.1.6.
[110] ST I-II.1.7.

account of what is perfecting or fulfilling of human agents. Everyone acts on the supposition that what he does will contribute to his overall good; one's overall good is the ultimate reason for doing anything. But not everything one does under this aegis actually contributes to one's overall good. Thus in one sense there is one and the same ultimate end for every human agent—the integral human good—and there are correct and mistaken notions of what actually constitutes this integral good.[111]

This conception of human flourishing, or the end toward which humans reach in order to flourish as humans, provides humans with an ethical basis on which to proceed, as was already discussed in the previous section. However, this idea of the ultimate end in purely its formal sense, as can be seen in the example of the burglar, "is not some thing that could enable us to discriminate between good human agents and bad."[112] Human happiness, or flourishing, is only realized by attaining those various goals humans set for themselves which are actually perfecting or fulfilling of their human nature, not by attaining those faulty goals which do not tend toward their ultimate happiness:

> If someone's desires are not desires to do what reason discloses it is best for that person to do, or if that person's dispositions to act are not systematically organized and directed to serve such desires for the ends proposed by reason, then that person will be open to being moved by considerations which distract his attention from or otherwise make him ignore what he knows to be best, and so what he does will not be what it is best or even good for him to do.[113]

Extrapolating from this, we can see that one problem with sin is that the attainment of objects not truly suitable for one's ultimate happiness tends further to cloud the actual obligations one ought to be trying to fulfill: "To identify an end is not to identify a value-neutral fact but to identify a relation between an agent and some suitable object that establishes a practical obligation to act for that object."[114] As Aquinas writes, "Those who sin turn away from that in which the notion of ultimate end is truly found but not from the intention itself of the ultimate end, which they falsely seek in other things."[115] A natural end is

---

[111] McInerny and O'Callaghan, "Saint Thomas Aquinas," n.p.

[112] Ralph McInerny. *Ethica Thomistica*, p. 27.

[113] Alasdair MacIntyre, *Whose Justice? Which Rationality?* Notre Dame, Indiana: University of Notre Dame Press, 1988, p. 126.

[114] Mary Hayden. "Recovering Eudaimonistic Teleology." *The Monist* 75.1 (January 1992): 71-83, p. 72.

[115] ST I-II.1.6.

only attained by the natural conduct conducive toward that end; such conduct should also be considered obligatory upon the acting agent.

Understanding the constitution of human nature and the ultimate good toward which this nature reaches enables the human being to recognize a naturally constituted rule of conduct as well; to recognize and live by that naturally constituted rule of conduct is to recognize and live by the precepts of natural law; to live by the precepts of natural law is to flourish (naturally) as a human being. "Natural law precepts are the starting points of moral reasoning; the moral task is to pursue the goods they incorporate in the fluctuating and altering conditions of our lives."[116] These precepts of natural law arise out of this idea of an innate, structural teleology for humans, a teleology that does not vary throughout the "fluctuating and altering conditions" of human circumstances. They are not arrived at by a systematic logical inquiry; rather, they arise out of the observation of human nature and then *become* the foundation of systematic logical inquiry. The logical and experiential exploration of these precepts, these "starting points of moral reasoning," leads to a morally fulfilled and flourishing human life.

## 5.    Thomistic Anthropology and Human Standards

Despite the various criticisms of it, natural law, especially that of the Thomistic variety, has proven to be the most resilient and enduring of ethical theories; not only is it one of the most ancient of ethical theories, but it seems eternally to recur in ever more painstakingly argued forms.

Furthermore, the anthropology or view of human nature in which natural law is rooted and out of which it arises provides a robust and coherent framework to address contemporary ethical issues, especially those bioethical issues most intimately related to human life itself; natural law "provides a set of formal principles that have clear bioethical implications," as Jason Eberl puts it.[117] As mentioned earlier, the *telos* of humanity, the mature, normal condition of the species *Homo sapiens*, not only defines but simultaneously prescribes. Teleological descriptions are also moral descriptions in the sense that they not only help explain humanity logically but also entail recognition of human standards; thus an understanding of Aquinas's anthropological account would be fundamental to any bioethical applications of his natural law ethical theory. Rather than being an outmoded conceptual scheme,

---

[116] Ralph McInerny. *Being and Predication: Thomistic Interpretations.* Washington, D.C.: Catholic University of America Press, 1986, p. 23.
[117] Eberl, *Thomistic Principles and Bioethics.* London and New York: Routledge, 2006, p. 9.

therefore, Thomistic anthropology seems both viable and helpful, even when compared to more current views.

To a consideration of Thomistic anthropology and its application to some contemporary bioethical issues, therefore, we will now turn.

# Chapter 2: What Is a Human Being?

What then? Do I say man is not made for an active life? Far from it!
But there is a great difference between other men's occupations and
ours. A glance at theirs will make it clear to you. All day long they
do nothing but calculate, contrive, consult how to wring their profit
out of food-stuffs, farm-plots, and the like. Whereas, I entreat you
to learn what the administration of the World is, and what place a
Being endowed with reason holds therein: to consider what you are
yourself, and wherein your Good and Evil consists.[118]

## 1. Definitions of Terms

The phrase "Thomistic anthropology" has already been used several
times throughout the preceding chapters, along with the companion
phrase "Thomistic natural law," and while the latter has been defined,
the former has not. Since in this chapter an account of Thomistic
anthropology will be presented, perhaps it would be well to begin with
defining terms.

### (1) *What Is Meant by "Thomistic"?*

Of course, the term "Thomistic" means simply "derived from the
teachings of Thomas Aquinas"; however, one quickly discovers that "as
the historical Aquinas comes increasingly into sharper focus, the
essential meaning of his teaching remains a matter of debate."[119] A basic
tension exists between those who prefer to emphasize Aquinas's
Aristotelian philosophical commitments[120] and those who prefer to

---

[118] Epictetus. *The Golden Sayings of Epictetus.* Hastings Crossley, trans. New York:
P.F. Collier & Son, 1937, Ch. 24.

[119] Carl N. Still. "The Search for the Real Aquinas." *The Canadian Journal of
History* (April 2005): Online, n.p. Accessed 15 March 2006.

[120] For example, Robert Pasnau seeks to separate out the "theological stuff"
(his phrase) from what he considers to be Aquinas's *philosophical* work (*Thomas
Aquinas on Human Nature*, p. 11). Even though Aquinas himself maintains that
"sacred doctrine bears, as it were, the stamp of the divine science which is one

emphasize Aquinas's Christian theological commitments.[121] Out of which commitment does his natural law ethical teaching arise?

Aquinas himself certainly maintains the theological commitment as crucial; for example, he introduces the whole of the *Summa Theologica* immediately and primarily as *sacra doctrina*.[122] As David Albert Jones writes, "Thomas was a preaching friar who held a chair in theology, rather than in the arts faculty. His philosophical vision was constantly informed by theological concerns."[123] However, it may be possible (and is attempted in this work) to combine profitably both approaches, since many think Aquinas himself did so. For example, one writer claims that "Thomas has structured or set up sacred doctrine so that (1) *the more Aristotelian it is, the more scriptural it is* [and] (2) *the more Aristotelian it is, the more christoform it is*." This assertion is supported by the facts that "a discipline counts the more as an Aristotelian science the more it attends and returns to its first principles" and "sacred doctrine [as *scientia*], in the *Summa*, takes its axiomatic first principles from sacred scripture."[124] This of course does not entail that the doctrinal aspects of Aquinas's anthropological thought are not amenable to public reason, since the reasoning developing from the doctrinal aspects typically is presented as being in correspondence with objectively observable features of human nature: "A science is the more Aristotelian, therefore, the more it accounts for or discovers that integrity, that mutual fittingness, that quality of belonging to each other, of human beings and the world. It is

---

and simple, yet extends to everything" (ST I.1.3), Pasnau argues that Aquinas cannot be taken "at face value" in this expressed intention because in "actual practice" he does not adhere to it (p. 15). For a critical discussion of Pasnau's somewhat astonishing claim, see Denis Bradley, "'To Be or Not to Be?': Pasnau on Aquinas's Immortal Human Soul" (*The Thomist* 68.1 [2004]: 1-39, pp. 35-36). Another strongly argued "non-theological" reading of Aquinas may be found in Anthony J. Lisska's *Aquinas's Theory of Natural Law: An Analytic Reconstruction* (1996).

[121] Recent examples include Nicholas M. Healy's *Thomas Aquinas: Theologian of the Christian Life* (Aldershot, Hants, and Burlington, Vermont: Ashgate, 2003); and Volume 2 of Jean-Pierre Torrell's study of Aquinas, *Saint Thomas Aquinas: Spiritual Master* (Robert Royal, trans. Washington, D.C.: Catholic University of America Press, 2003).

[122] ST I.1.3.

[123] David Albert Jones. *Approaching the End: A Theological Exploration of Death and Dying.* Oxford: Oxford University Press, 2007, p. 92.

[124] Eugene F. Rogers, Jr. *Thomas Aquinas and Karl Barth: Sacred Doctrine and the Natural Knowledge of God.* Notre Dame and London: University of Notre Dame Press, 1995: pp. 17-19. Emphasis in original. See also ST I.1.8.

in unitary first principles that the integrity resides."[125] As Alasdair MacIntyre argues, Aristotle's thought "was developed by Aquinas in a way which enabled him to accommodate Augustinian claims and insights alongside Aristotelian theorizing"; hence one finds in Aquinas "an Aristotelian tradition with resources for its own enlargement, correction, and defense."[126] Likewise, while theologian Fergus Kerr points out, "The important point is that, while the concept of natural law has a long history, there is no single theory," Kerr does not end there, but immediately continues: "The common core is that in some sense or other the basic principles of morals and legislation are objective, accessible to reason, and based on human nature."[127]

Again, the reason for these features of the natural law (i.e., its objectivity, its accessibility to reason, and its being based on human nature) is theological in nature, according to Aquinas: Natural law prescriptions are objective and "accessible to reason" because they are first of all contained within the objective and rational Eternal Law established by God.[128] However, Aquinas himself argues for the use of philosophy for theological purposes, in the *Summa Contra Gentiles*[129]:

> But any things concerning creatures that are considered in common by the philosopher and the believer are conveyed through different principles in each case. For the philosopher takes his argument from the proper causes of things; the believer, from the first cause. . . . Hence, also, [the doctrine of the faith] ought to be called the highest wisdom, since it treats of the highest cause. . . . And, therefore, human philosophy serves her as the first wisdom. Accordingly, divine wisdom sometimes argues from principles of human philosophy.[130]

Therefore, for most moral purposes, the fact that the natural law is objective, accessible to reason, and based on human nature is enough

---

[125] Ibid., p. 30.

[126] MacIntyre, *Whose Justice? Which Rationality?* p. 402. See also MacIntyre's *Three Rival Versions of Moral Enquiry*, in particular Chapter 3, "Too Many Thomisms?"

[127] Kerr, *After Aquinas*, p. 98. See also Bruce D. Marshall's "Thomas, Thomisms, and Truth" (*The Thomist* 56.3 [1992]: 499-524).

[128] ST I-II.91.2.

[129] All quotes from the *Summa Contra Gentiles* throughout this work are taken from the translation of Anton C. Pegis, James F. Anderson, Vernon J. Bourke, and Charles J. O'Neil (Notre Dame: Univ. of Notre Dame Press. Reprinted edition, 1975).

[130] SCG II.4.4. See on this point Denis J.M. Bradley, "*Ephemerides Thomisticae Analyticae*: Metaphysics and Ethics in Stump's *Aquinas*." *The Thomist* 69.4 (October 2005): 593-620, pp. 596-97n3.

for its profitable use even apart from the consideration of its supernatural origin, since an effect (the natural law written in human hearts) may be known without necessarily knowing its first cause, or Cause. Further, as has been argued by Russell Hittinger, even if "two Thomisms" have developed—the theological branch used as a doctrinal standard especially within Roman Catholicism, and the philosophical branch used especially within mid-twentieth-century culture to address issues of modernity—this development does not in itself entail conflict between the two approaches. Rather, according to Hittinger (following the thought of John Paul II), the key to the *rapprochement* of the two approaches is the similarity of their metaphysical view of human nature: "Anthropology is the nexus of the two Thomisms."[131]

In the phrase "Thomistic anthropology," the term "anthropology," from the Greek *anthropos*, "man," may also require further explanation, especially since the philosophical and theological use of the term "anthropology" is much different than the use of the word in other disciplines, including the social science discipline of anthropology itself. Furthermore, several other related terms will need to be defined, since they will be used extensively in presenting this chapter's account of Aquinas's view of human nature.

(2) *What Is Meant by "Thomistic Anthropology"?*

For the purposes of this study, the term "anthropology" does not refer to physiological anthropology, the study of humanity in its physical dimension only, nor does it refer to cultural or social anthropology, the study of humanity in its cultural institutions and social behavior. Philosophical and theological modes of anthropology do not examine some aspect of humanity, but rather "man as such, man as a whole biological, acting, thinking, etc. being."[132] Anthropology in this sense does not examine what human biology is like (solely), nor what human cultures and societies are like (solely). Rather, it examines what a human *is* in the totality of that human.

Another way of saying this is to say that this type of anthropology examines the *substance* of human-ness, "substance" being used in its Thomistic sense. In this rather specialized sense, a "substance" may be defined as anything which exists primarily in and as itself, rather than as a characteristic of something else, while incidental characteristics ("accidents," in Aquinas's terminology) have their existence *in* something else as their subject.[133] A substance, in other words, possesses existence *as*

---

[131] Russell Hittinger. "Two Thomisms, Two Modernities." *First Things* (184) June/July 2008: 33-38, p. 38.

[132] M.J. Inwood, "Philosophical Anthropology," p. 38.

*itself*, while an "accident" only possesses existence as a characteristic of a substance. As Aquinas puts it in his treatise *On Being and Essence*, accidents or incidental characteristics "cannot be defined unless a subject is placed in their definition. And this is so because they do not have existence in themselves free of a subject."[134]

A substance must therefore be thought of as *an essential nature*; for example, a dog must have the essential nature of dog-ness (and the dog is therefore a substance, possessing existence as itself), but the dog could be a wide variety of colors without changing in substance, the dog's color not being the substance of dog-ness in itself, but rather an incidental characteristic or "accident" of the dog. As Aquinas puts it, "We must observe that things which are accidental do not change the species. For since to be colored is accidental to an animal, its species is not changed by a difference of color, but by a difference in that which belongs to the nature of an animal."[135] The dog itself has existence by virtue of its very own dog-ness, not by virtue of the existence of anything else of which "the dog" is a descriptive characteristic. On the other hand, the dog's color *does* depend on the existence of the dog for its own existence. Therefore, the color of the dog is not part of the substance of the dog. Neither are the dog's size, age, health, level of abilities, and so on. All of these can be changed readily through the natural process of growth, for the dog's growth brings about these "incidental changes" in the dog. On the other hand, the dog cannot be changed from being a dog without what is known as a *substantial* change, a change in its very substance of dog-ness.

Thus Thomistic anthropology examines "man as such," the very substance of humanity. Aquinas speaks of this human substance as existing because of the human "form," another term which will arise in this work quite frequently. The "form" of a human—actually, the form of anything living—is its innermost shaping principle, that which makes anything what it is, guiding its development toward its mature and completed expression. In Aquinas, Aristotle, and the Bible alike, this "form" in humans is often referred to as an aspect of the "soul," the *anima*, or the *psyche* [Gk. *psuche*]. This is certainly not meant to imply that the Bible speaks of the human soul in Aristotelian terms, or even that the biblical "soul" corresponds directly to the Aristotelian "form."

---

[133] ST III.77.1.
[134] Aquinas, *On Being and Essence*. Joseph Bobik, trans. Notre Dame, Ind.: University of Notre Dame Press, 1965: § 100. All quotes from *On Being and Essence* throughout this work are taken from this translation.
[135] ST I.77.3.

Rather, what is meant is that in the biblical account, as in the Aristotelian account, although *psuche* sometimes refers simply to the natural life of the body, it also often refers to the non-corporeal element of a human being and that which *provides* the animating life to the material body: "The first man, Adam, was made a living being [*psuchen zosan*]" (1 Corinthians 15:45). Likewise, with regards to the soul's non-corporeal nature, Christ's hearers are instructed, "Do not fear those who kill the body but cannot kill the soul [*psuchen*]" (Matthew 10:28).

Some may question this use of the term "the biblical account," since Jewish and Christian thinking on this subject seems to evolve throughout the Bible; for example, some may think the concept of the non-corporeal soul conflates the idea of "resurrection . . . with the belief in an immaterial and imperishable soul, forcing both into the catch-all term *afterlife*."[136] However, as used here, the phrase "the biblical account" is intended to refer to the developed biblical doctrine inclusive of both Testaments. Although hints of the "immortality of the soul" view crop up here and there in the Old Testament, they are only hints, which are spelled out more explicitly in the New Testament, especially in the Pauline epistles. For example, Paul writes, "Even though our outer nature is wasting away, our inner nature is being renewed day by day. . . . For we know that if the earthly tent we live in is destroyed, we have a building from God, a house not made with hands, eternal in the heavens. . . . We would rather be away from the body and at home with the Lord" (2 Corinthians 4:16, 5:1, 8). Furthermore, *psuche* is employed for a variety of meanings both in the Septuagint, where it is used over 900 times, and in the New Testament. In the Septuagint, *psuche* usually stands in for the Hebrew *nephesh* and as such "denotes that which makes a body, whether of a human or an animal, into a living being. . . . The actual power of the soul is seen first of all in the movement that it imparts to the body in which it lives."[137] However, as the meaning of *psuche* expands throughout its biblical usage and into the New Testament era, it becomes "regarded as the permanent part of the person, an independent soul in contrast to the body. . . . In all this [the employment of its various powers], the soul remains incorporeal."[138]

---

[136] Benjamin Balint. "The Life of the World to Come: Review of *Resurrection and the Restoration of Israel: The Ultimate Victory of the God of Life*, by Jon D. Levenson." *First Things* 170 (February 2007): 31-34, p. 32. Emphasis in original.
[137] Verlyn D. Verbrugge, ed. *"Psuche." New International Dictionary of New Testament Theology*. Grand Rapids, Michigan: Zondervan, 2000: 620-23, pp. 620-21.
[138] Ibid., pp. 620-21.

The subtlety of the Septuagint's use of *psuchen zosan* may be seen also in the Hebrew *nephesh chayyah*, humanity as a "living soul" or "living being" (Genesis 2:7). Upon first consideration, according to biblical scholar Edmond Jacob, this text appears to affirm that *nephesh* "is not given to man as a soul which might be considered as deposited in a body, but as the final result of divine activity which is a reality at once physical and spiritual." On the other hand, just as in the case of the Greek *psuche*, so the biblical use of *nephesh* "proliferates into many realities."[139] The term denotes the energy of physical "life," along with its related notions of "breath" and "blood." However, Jacob notes that "life [*nephesh*] also reveals itself in certain non-organic functions such as aspiration and desire," as well as "eagerness." Further, "The Israelites realized that bodily organs and functions were incapable of expressing the full reality and dynamism of life; so *nephesh* often has the sense of living being and of person."[140]

Thus one could reasonably conclude that commonly accepted Aristotelian and biblical anthropological accounts are at least similar in that they both include a belief in the non-corporeal aspect of human beings, an aspect typically referred to as the "soul." This belief could be seen as a form of dualism, since in much theological and philosophical writing a "dualist" is one who thinks of humans as being composed of both corporeal and non-corporeal elements. This would make both Aquinas and Aristotle dualists; however, in the present work, the term "dualist" will be used in the more specialized sense of one who thinks of the two human elements as being two separate substances. In this latter sense, Descartes would be a dualist, since he thinks of humans as composed of two separate substances, but Aquinas and Aristotle would not, since they think of humans as a hylomorphic unity: "Body and soul are not two actually existing substances; rather the two of them together constitute one actually existing substance."[141] Here again one notes that the hylomorphic view of humans as both a corporeal and non-corporeal reality, even if not directly spelled out in the biblical account, tends at least to approximate the fullness of the Greek *psuche* and Hebrew *nephesh*, as argued above.

Aquinas defends Aristotle's general definition of the soul as "the first act of a physically organized body,"[142] or the first act of a corporeal

---

[139] Edmond Jacob. *Theology of the Old Testament* [1955]. Arthur W. Heathcote and Philip J. Allcock, transs. New York: Harper & Row, 1958, p. 159.

[140] Ibid., p. 160.

[141] SCG II.69.2.

[142] Aristotle, *De Anima*. Hugh Lawson-Tancred, trans. New York: Penguin,

organic body, moving the body from potential to actuality; the soul is thus "the formal cause of the animal [and] the efficient cause of its motions."[143] While the body provides the matter with which the soul bonds, the soul provides act or form for the body; it converts the body's potential into actual substance: "Without the form, or the formal cause, it would be impossible to account for the unity and specific identity of any substance. In the human composite the form is the spiritual soul, which makes the organism a single entity and gives it its human character."[144] A human substance is not a dog substance because the human substance possesses a human form; it has a human soul, and the dog substance does not (if it did, it would not be a dog, but a human). The human being's form or soul impels the substance toward becoming a mature example of a human being. In order for it to become (for example) a dog, it would have to change forms, undergoing a "substantial change," and would consequently no longer be a human. This idea of "substantial change" will become useful later on during this work's bioethical discussions, for, as one writer puts it, "Since humanity is a natural kind, the only properties essential for being a human being . . . are those had essentially by every human being, are those such that their loss would mean that the human being in question would go out of existence."[145] Therefore a human being becomes a human being when its matter is infused with a human form or soul; the intellectual form plus the matter is the human substance. The lack of the human form would mean the lack of a human being; conversely, the presence of the human form would mean the presence of a human being.[146]

---

1987: II.412b5. All quotes from *De Anima* throughout this work are taken from this translation.

[143] Joseph M. Magee. "Thomistic Psychology." *The Thomistic Philosophy Page.* Aquinasonline.com, n.p. Updated August 27, 1999. Accessed 15 Sept. 2013.

[144] Avery Cardinal Dulles. "God and Evolution." *First Things* 176 (October 2007): 19-24, p. 22.

[145] Brody, *Abortion and the Sanctity of Human Life*, p. 102.

[146] The Thomistic philosopher W. Norris Clarke offers another "substance"-oriented definition of "human being": "(1) It has the aptitude to exist *in itself* and not as a part of any other being [Aquinas, as may be seen in ST III.68.11, argues that the conceptus is not technically a "part" of its mother]; (2) it is the unifying center of all the various attributes and properties that belong to it at any one moment; (3) if the being persists as the same individual throughout a process of change, it is the substance which is the abiding, unifying center of the being across time; (4) it has an intrinsic, dynamic orientation toward self-expressive action, toward self-communication with others, as the crown of its perfection, as its very *raison d'etre*" (W. Norris Clarke, *Explorations in Metaphysics.*

Consequently, it seems certain that the Thomist today, although taking advantage of scientific advances, especially in embryology and genetics, in his view of human nature, need not thereby succumb to an unnecessary and overly reductive philosophical materialism: "If there are good philosophical reasons to recognize the reality of substantial form, nothing we learn in the natural sciences will lead us to gainsay that claim."[147] In fact, Aquinas refers to the materialist view itself as "a reversion to a very primitive philosophy"[148]: "The philosophers of old [i.e., the Pre-Socratics], not being able to rise above their imagination, supposed that the principle of [living animation] was something corporeal: for they asserted that only bodies were real things, and that what is not corporeal is nothing."[149] However, in Aquinas's view, the body apart from the non-corporeal soul could not even live; after all, a dead body still possesses its corporeal nature, lacking only what animated it and made it live. Its mere corporeality, in other words, could not be its animating principle:

> Now the substantial form gives being simply; therefore by its coming a thing is said to be generated simply; and by its removal to be corrupted simply....Aristotle does not say that the soul is the act of a body only, but *the act of a physical organic body which has life potentially*; and that this potentiality *does not reject* [exclude] *the soul*....In like manner, the soul is said to be the *act of a body*, etc., because by the soul it is a body, and is organic, and has life potentially....so that the soul by its motive power is the part which moves; and the animate body is the part moved.[150]

This is what Peter Kreeft humorously calls the "Dead Cow Argument": "There appears to be no material difference (e.g., in size or weight or color) between the two cows [a living cow and a cow that has just died]. Yet something is clearly missing. What is it?"[151] The obvious answer is that the cow is "clearly missing" its *life*—its "soul" or *anima*, in other words, its animating principle or form, that which causes the cow to live and develop as a cow. Modernity might label this idea of the animating

South Bend, Indiana: University of Notre Dame Press, 1994, p. 105). Clarke's definition has provided much material for reflection toward my own definition of "human being," to be provided later in this chapter.
[147] Steven Baldner. "An Argument for Substantial Form." *The Saint Anselm Journal* 5.1 (Fall 2007): 1-12, p. 2.
[148] Peter Kreeft, *A Summa*, p. 244n2.
[149] ST I.75.1.
[150] ST I.76.4.
[151] Peter Kreeft and Ronald K. Tacelli. *Handbook of Christian Apologetics*. Downers Grove, Illinois: InterVarsity Press, 1994, p. 239.

principle "simplistic" or non-scientific; Celia Deane-Drummond is surely correct to note that looking to the soul as a "life principle" was "rejected early on in the history of biology."[152] However, as stated previously, a change in attitudes is not equivalent to an advance in knowledge. The modern Thomist might well reply that to label this argument as simplistic or outdated by modern scientific views simply means that modern science has abandoned the search for formal and final causality in favor of efficient and material causality; however, the formal causation is still required to convert the merely corporeal into the corporeal and animate. Although the Thomist today, as has been argued, should use the findings of contemporary science even as Thomas used the Aristotelian analysis of human ends, he should do so critically and cautiously, especially with regards to some of the metaphysical assumptions implicit in modern science; in other words, one accepting Aquinas's principles would never accept that mere physical electrical discharges could convert Frankenstein's monster into a living being apart from the creature's animating form, a form which cannot be physically infused, no matter how powerful the electrical jolt. To live and develop as a cow is exactly what the dead cow can no longer do: Although it still appears to have all the necessary corporeal equipment and retains its shape for a time, it no longer has a form.[153] As Avery Cardinal Dulles has put it (paraphrasing Etienne Gilson), "Francis Bacon and others perpetrated a philosophical error when they eliminated two of Aristotle's four causes from the purview of science. They sought to explain everything in mechanistic terms, referring only to material and efficient causes and discarding formal and final causality."[154] However, the life of the cow ends precisely when the cow loses its formal causality. In the concluding pages of his book *The Soul of the Embryo*, bioethicist David Albert Jones summarizes this idea rather bluntly: "Christians have talked about the soul in various ways, but the soul has been understood first and foremost as the principle of *life*.

---

[152] Celia Deane-Drummond. *The Ethics of Nature*. Oxford: Blackwell, 2004, p. 82n95.

[153] This discussion raises the related and interesting question, "Can animals have souls?" Obviously, the Thomistic/Aristotelian answer is yes (non-rational souls); moreover, this answer also seems to be the biblical answer as well, as is testified in the original Hebrew and Greek languages of the Bible. For example, *psuche*, for soulish or psychic life, is often used in connection with the life of animals; however, *pneuma*, the spiritual core, the spirit, is never used in connection with animals, but only in connection with supernatural beings (God, angels, etc.) and humans.

[154] Dulles, "God and Evolution," p. 22.

What has life has soul."[155] One might point out, with Derek Jeffreys, that scientific opposition to this view entails that one must argue "that the potentiality for conscious life and experience really does exist in the nature of matter itself. . . .We will continue to have the contradictory assertion that by themselves, qualitatively inferior natures produce qualitatively superior ones."[156]

Some other reasons may be adduced for accepting the idea of the substantial form within the living physical entity.[157] For example, a chair is a chair because of its spatial ordering and aggregation of parts, which is not the case with that which is alive: "Obviously, living organisms have a spatial ordering of parts, but that spatial ordering of parts is not what makes them alive. The corpse and the living man have the same spatial ordering of parts, but there is a rather dramatic difference between the two." (This may be seen as a variant expression of Kreeft's already-presented "Dead Cow" argument.) Secondly, the ordering of parts within a living organism arises from within the organism itself; it is not imposed from without by construction or accretion. Finally, the living organism manifests from within itself "new powers or energies" as a result of its living status: "Living organisms manifest a whole range of powers that cannot in any way be found in the organic elements out of which they are composed: growth, self-repair, reproduction, respiration, self-motion, sensation, and so forth."[158] To this list may be added the specific intellective powers of the natural human substance, such as the faculty of understanding perceptions over and above the bare perceptions themselves. However, if only efficient and material causality are admitted in its description, the living substance must be thought of as being made up *entirely* of the aggregate of non-living elements, with "life" being thought of as the result of the interactions of the aggregate. Further, if the life of the living substance grants that substance a range of powers nowhere to be found in its non-living elements, this range of powers must also be thought of as arising out of the interaction of the aggregate of non-living elements.

On the other hand, if the animating principle or form is required for the life of an animate organism, why is it no longer considered as an interrogative principle of contemporary science? In fact, occasionally

---

[155] Jones, *The Soul of the Embryo*, p. 248. Emphasis in original.
[156] Derek S. Jeffreys, "The Soul Is Alive and Well," p. 215.
[157] The following paragraph is drawn from Baldner's "An Argument for Substantial Form," pp. 2-3. Baldner presents five arguments; three of these are used in the present work.
[158] Ibid., p. 3.

the very idea of form or formal causation is rather contemptuously dismissed in scientific discussion, as in the following:

> One of the basic tenets of modern biology is that all of the phenomena of life are governed by, and can be explained in terms of, chemical and physical principles. Until early in the [20th century] most people, biologists and laymen alike, held that life processes differed in some fundamental way from those of nonliving systems. With the vast increase since then in our understanding of chemical and physical principles it has become clear that the myriad phenomena of life, although much more complex than nonliving systems, can be explained in chemical and physical terms without postulating some mysterious vital force. The properties of living cells and organisms that at one time seemed so mysterious, now appear to be quite straightforward.[159]

In like manner, ethicist and philosopher of science Michael Ruse notes, "Looking at organisms as though they were designed does not mean that they have vital forces. Anything but. They were made . . . in a good old-fashioned mechanical way."[160] But is it in fact the case that living beings can be explained more or less completely "in chemical and physical terms without postulating" an ordering and animating principle such as the substantial form or soul? As one considers the central presupposition of the contemporary scientific method, the idea of methodological naturalism, one sees that given this presupposition, the final and even formal causation of something cannot enter into a description of that thing, since those causal features are non-physical in nature and naturalism treats only of the physical. Philosophical problems arise only when naturalism as a scientific method elides into naturalism as a metaphysical claim, i.e., the claim that material and efficient causality fully describe all that there is to describe in a living being. Although the naturalistic presupposition enables the scientist to trace material and efficient causality more effectively, it also excludes the scientist from philosophical knowledge of the object under consideration. This is so "because final causality is not a physical thing. It is mental and spiritual. Purposes and ends and goals and goods and designs have no color or shape."[161] The same is true of formal causality;

---

[159] Claude Villee and Vincent Dethier. *Biological Principles and Processes*. Philadelphia: Saunders, 1976, p. 12. Quoted in Steven Baldner, "The Soul in the Explanation of Life: Aristotle Against Reductionism" (*Lyceum* 3.2 [Fall 1991]: 1-14), p. 1.
[160] Michael Ruse. *Darwin and Design: Does Evolution Have a Purpose?* Cambridge, Massachusetts: Harvard University Press, 2003, p. 282.

the "form" of an animate being is non-corporeal, and thus the animating principle of an animate being is itself also non-corporeal.

In Aquinas's view, final causality does not replace the efficient causation of actions, but does work through it; for example, even a materialist speaks of sea turtles coming ashore *in order to* lay their eggs, or blood clotting *in order to* prevent bleeding.[162] Ruse speaks of such questions as illustrations of "metaphor," and possibly even of misleading metaphor, but approves of them nonetheless because without them science "at the practical, real-life level" would cease questioning.[163] However, it seems to make just as much if not more sense to refer to such questions not as illustrations of metaphor but rather as illustrations of the practical recognition of formal causality in the natural world. As John W. Keck of the Institute for the Study of Nature writes:

> A comprehensive knowledge of nature will require not only resolving the modern notion of matter into Aristotelian terms, but even more the recovery of undiluted formal and final causality. Recovery of substantial form and intrinsic final causality has the additional benefit of allowing modern science to assimilate into the whole of human knowledge.... At the heart of the modern scientific conception of the world is the assumption that nature is a knowable order.... That things happen "always or for the most part" indicates finality or purpose.... Although chance events often obtain, the natural world is inherently teleological.... Far from being opposed to modern science, teleology is its *conditio sine qua non.*[164]

"Moreover," as a different writer adds, "the matter, i.e., the constituents that make up the body, are constantly changing while the animal [the embodied creature] persists—[but] the animal's form or functional organization, i.e., organization of material parts by which an animal accomplishes its vital functions, remains the same."[165] Consequently a theory of exceptionless materialism not only lacks sufficient explanatory power in the case of human nature, but also in the case of the existence of *any living organism.* Of course, a materialist might respond, "Science, especially evolutionary biology, can explain functional organization in terms of material cause and effect without remainder—so what more

---

[161] Peter Kreeft, *A Refutation of Moral Relativism*, p. 127.

[162] The sea turtle example comes from Ric Machuga, *In Defense of the Soul*, p. 84.

[163] Ruse, *Darwin and Design*, pp. 284-85.

[164] John W. Keck. "The Natural Motion of Matter in Newtonian and Post-Newtonian Physics." *The Thomist* 71.4 (October 2007): 529-54, pp. 531-33.

[165] Joseph Magee, "Thomistic Psychology," n.p.

explanatory work is left to do?"[166] However, the "remainder" is precisely what is under discussion; to describe organization in itself in terms of material causation alone is not to describe the animating principle of that organization, nor all of that organization's consequent effects (e.g., consciousness and intellectual understanding, in the case of humans).

## 2. What Is a Human Being?

Therefore, having considered Scheler's three anthropological conceptions listed earlier in the Introduction (the Aristotelian conception of humans as rational creatures, the Judeo-Christian conception of humans as *Imago Dei*, and the modern scientific conception of humans as developed animals), a Thomistic anthropology might well describe humanity in three ways simultaneously:

(1) As separated from the rest of the corporeal creation by its *rational*, non-corporeal nature (the classical, Aristotelian view); but also:

(2) As created in the image of God, yet spiritually and morally flawed and fallen (the biblical view); and:

(3) As specified *physically* by its genetic endowment as *Homo sapiens* (the scientific, but not necessarily metaphysically neutral, view).

These, taken together, constitute what is meant by the phrase "human being." Perhaps a fuller discussion of each in turn would be helpful:

---

[166] According to Neil Messer, "Whereas Aristotelian science was teleological in character [incorporating formal and final causality in its descriptions], there was a powerful move in early modernity to exclude teleological thinking from the natural sciences. This non-teleological programme was more easily implemented in the physical than the biological sciences, and even after Darwin, opinion has been divided as to whether the theory of natural selection supports or disposes of teleological thinking in biology" ("Humans, Animals, Evolution and Ends." *Creaturely Theology: God, Humans and Other Animals*. Celia Deane-Drummond and David Clough, eds. London: SCM Press, 2009: 211-27, p. 215). For example, as is under discussion, Michael Ruse argues that evolutionary theory and indeed all of biology "would be dreadfully impoverished without a perspective that asks 'what for'"—in other words, a perspective that is at least implicitly teleological (*Darwin and Design*, p. 283). However, as Messer responds, "Whereas Aquinas could define the *good* as 'what all things seek after,' all that modern biology can say is that 'what all [living] things seek after' is survival and reproductive success. Biology *qua* biology gives no grounds for equating these ends with the *good*, in any morally informative sense, or for concluding that they are *proper* ends. They may be, but biology cannot tell us that they are" ("Humans, Animals, Evolution and Ends," p. 215. Emphasis in original).

First, the human being is a *rational* creature. Not only does the human form have potentiality for rationality, but it continually develops toward the mature actualization of that potential throughout its embodied existence. Even though in the early stage of its embodiment the human zygote lacks a cerebral cortex, it is still a creature developing toward rationality and the actualization of its intellectual nature, in a way that other animate embodied creatures are not and cannot, regardless of whether or not they *ever* develop a cerebral cortex. This intellectual nature is "the *telos* that defines a human zygote's internally directed, individuated, and unitary development from its temporal beginning."[167] Thus, to use the Aristotelian and Thomistic phrase, humans are rational animals throughout their development, and therefore also persons throughout their development.

Secondly, the human being is a creature *created in God's image*, but *fallen*. The human race has lost its original innocence, the "gift of original justice,"[168] and now possesses an inclination to evil, an inclination that grows ever stronger as it is indulged in thoughts, words, and actions. This fallenness is a part of humanity's heritage even from conception: "Indeed, I was born guilty, a sinner when my mother conceived me" (Psalm 51:5). However, according to Aquinas, humanity retains its natural powers of the soul, such as free will and rationality, although these powers are readily misused precisely because of the human inclination toward evil.

Thirdly, the human being is an *embodied* creature, recognizable genetically by its DNA structure. It possesses (1) the DNA of the species *Homo sapiens*, which is (2) separately and uniquely expressed, and (3) capable under normal circumstances of further development into a mature example of the human species. (The argument for these genetic specifications will be given in the next chapter.) This human comes into being at conception, not by human Creation, but by human *pro*-creation.[169] Its Creation is divine and involves the infusion of the intellectual soul into the corporeal conception. Therefore, without the action of God, there is no substantial form of the human, but apart from the role of the parents, there is also no human being:

> It is possible to affirm that God is involved in some particular and intimate way in the creation of each human soul and that the soul is

---

[167] Denis Bradley, "To Be or Not to Be," p. 32.

[168] ST I-II.85.1.

[169] For a discussion of this concept, see Neil Messer, *The Ethics of Human Cloning* (Cambridge: Grove Books, 2001, pp. 18-20); see also O'Donovan's *Begotten or Made?* (1984).

not reducible to material causes, and yet also to hold that God gives to parents a true role in generation of the new human person. Only God can create (*ex nihilo*) but parents can cooperate in this action.[170] This is not intended to isolate the (human) biological from the (divine) spiritual, which would be "at odds with the insistence seen elsewhere throughout Thomas's work that the spiritual soul is at one and the same time the form of a living body."[171] It is rather intended simply to highlight once more the unity of the natural embodiment and the supernatural infusion in creating the living human being.

*Rationality, createdness, fallenness, and embodiment:* From human conception to human death an entity exists satisfying all of these descriptions, at one level of development or another. Even after the time of bodily death, the rational human form may survive, to be (in the Christian hope) re-united one day with a resurrected body and individuated as a completed human substance. Therefore, since from conception to death an entity exists satisfying all of these descriptions, one is now in a position to answer this chapter's titular question, "What is a human being?" Earlier it was mentioned that a Thomistic classical and biblical anthropology would need to take into account factual advances in modern science, specifically in the areas of genetics and embryology, in order to arrive at a definition for "human being." Drawing upon the discussions of these first chapters, one is here able more fully to articulate that completed, "buttressed" definition, as follows:

"A human being is a rational, embodied member of the species *Homo sapiens* (the species being determined by the genetic structure of its embodiment), created in God's image but fallen, at any level of development, from conception to death."

---

[170] David Albert Jones, *The Soul of the Embryo*, pp. 106-107.
[171] Ibid., p. 122.

# Chapter 3: Are a Human Being and a Human Person the Same Thing?

At its highest level, the lower attains to the higher by participating in the latter's dignity through an imperfect resemblance. This principle is decisive for an anthropology that excludes all dualism from its vision of man, for there is no rupture, but rather continuity, between the biological, the sensory, and the spiritual in the human creature. The same soul is in each of them.[172]

To our bodies turn we then, that so
Weak men on love reveal'd may look;
Love's mysteries in souls do grow,
But yet the body is his book.[173]

## 1.  Aquinas on Personhood

Having proceeded through several pages of argument to reach the definition of "human being" at the close of the previous chapter, one immediately calls to mind objections both small and large in scope. For example, well-known bioethicist Peter Singer has called into question the entire project of the use of genetic information to establish moral claims, thinking it both logically and morally indefensible. He writes:

> When opponents of abortion say that the embryo is a living human being from conception onwards, all they can possibly mean is that the embryo is a living member of the species *Homo sapiens*. This is all that can be established as a scientific fact. But is this also the sense in which every "human being" has a "right to life"?[174]

However, for the purposes of this discussion, the specifically Thomistic point is that for Aquinas, one cannot be a human being without being a human person; in his thought, there is no clear distinction between the

[172] Jean-Pierre Torrell, *Saint Thomas Aquinas, Volume 2: Spiritual Master*, p. 255.
[173] John Donne. "The Exstasie." *Poems of John Donne, Volume I*. E.K. Chambers, ed. London: Lawrence & Bullen, 1896: 53-56, p. 56.
[174] Peter Singer and W. Walters, eds. *Test-Tube Babies*. Oxford: Oxford Univ. Press, 1982, p. 60.

two. As Eleonore Stump puts it even more straightforwardly, "For Aquinas, there is no difference between a human person and a human being."[175] A "person" might not necessarily be a "human being" (as in the case of angelic intelligences), but a "human being" is always a person. A human *person* is "identical to a particular in the species *rational animal*"[176]; however, the exact same definition would for Aquinas suffice to define the human *being*. Since he accepts Boethius's definition of "person" as "an individual substance of rational nature,"[177] he would not accept the ethical distinction made by such writers as Dombrowski and Deltete when they differentiate between a "human being" as such, and "a human person in some morally relevant sense."[178] The definition "individual substance of rational nature" suffices both for personhood and human-ness, with the additional qualification in the case of human-ness that a human is also embodied (as opposed to, say, angels, which are persons but not humans). Further, Aquinas "contends that only the *potentiality* for rational thought must be present" to justify the claim of human-ness and hence personhood: "It is important to recall here that Aquinas, in his account of embryo-genesis, never asserts that a fetus must *actually* think rationally in order for it to be a human being."[179] As Stephen D. Schwarz has pointed out, being a person is not always exactly the same condition as being able to function as a person; the functional ability may fluctuate while the personal identity does not.[180]

As Aquinas advanced further and further away from acceptance of any sort of Platonic substance dualism, the idea of humanity as the soul/body hylomorphic union became more and more important to his anthropological thought. This hylomorphic union arises because the substantial form of the human expresses itself completely only in its embodied state. Further, because in the hylomorphic union one can distinguish between the "substantial" aspects of humanity and the "incidental" aspects, this view of humanity seems to lead to the rejection of the modern division of the "genetic" human *being* (characterized by certain "accidents" of functionality, or the lack of

---

[175] Stump, *Aquinas*. London and New York: Routledge, 2003, p. 486n73.

[176] Ibid., p. 53. Emphasis in original.

[177] ST III.2.2.

[178] Dombrowski and Deltete, *A Brief, Liberal, Catholic Defense of Abortion*. Champaign, Illinois: Univ. of Illinois Press, 2000, p. 7.

[179] Jason T. Eberl, "Aquinas's Account of Human Embryogenesis and Recent Interpretations." *Journal of Medicine and Philosophy* 30.4 (August 2005): 379-94, p. 384. Emphasis in original.

[180] Stephen D. Schwarz. *The Moral Question of Abortion*. Chicago: Loyola University Press, 1990, p. 94.

functionality) from the "rights-bearing" human *person* (characterized by the human substance); as Aquinas writes, "It belongs to every man to be a person, inasmuch as everything subsisting in human nature is a person."[181]

Other writers have commented upon this division using different terminology; for instance, Robert P. George differentiates between the view of human life as "instrumentally" good and the view of human life as "intrinsically" good. If life is viewed as merely instrumentally good, then the rights-bearing "person" who may derive some instrumental good out of his or her own death (suicide) or the death of another (abortion and euthanasia) may perfectly well choose these options. Usually those who hold this view believe that "apart from special revelation, we have no reason to affirm the intrinsic goodness and moral inviolability of human life."[182] This view has been summarized as typically holding that "The value and interests of science and the rest of society *may override* the value and interests of the individual human being; the human being is of instrumental value."[183] However, George points out that this view is inherently dualistic (in the strong Cartesian sense of the term) and that this "metaphysical dualism of the person and the body" is "rationally untenable"; it holds "a particular under-standing of the human person as an essentially non-bodily being who inhabits a non-personal body."[184] This instrumental view of the goodness of human life, "which contrasts with the Judeo-Christian view of the human person as a dynamic unity of body, mind, and spirit," sees the human person as "the conscious and desiring 'self' as distinct from the body which may exist (as in the case of pre- and post-conscious human beings) as a merely 'biological,' and thus sub-personal, reality."[185] In a similar vein, Joseph Atkinson writes, "In the modernist perspective the body is only an instrumental good and the person and the body are not intrinsically linked. This leads inevitably to a serious distortion of the understanding of the human person and the human act."[186]

[181] ST III.16.12.

[182] Robert P. George, *The Clash of Orthodoxies: Law, Religion, and Morality in Crisis.* Wilmington, Delaware: ISI Books, 2001, p. 9.

[183] Teresa Iglesias. "What Kind of Being Is the Human Embryo?" *Embryos and Ethics: The Warnock Report in Debate.* Nigel M. de S. Cameron, ed. Edinburgh: Rutherford House Books, 1987: 58-73, p. 63. Emphasis in original. (Iglesias herself disagrees with the quoted sentence.)

[184] On this point, see also Patrick Lee's provocatively titled "Human Beings Are Animals" (*Natural Law and Moral Inquiry.* Robert P. George, ed. Washington, D.C.: Georgetown University Press, 1998: 135-51).

[185] George, *The Clash of Orthodoxies*, p. 9.

On the other hand, the view of human life as "intrinsically" good sees no such division between (*a*) a human's life and (*b*) the instrumental uses a human "person" may have for that human's life, whether his own or another's. In fact, this division was explicitly denied by Aquinas, who saw "that it is by no means logically (or, for that matter, theologically) necessary to identify the human person with the soul as distinct from the body, and thus to deny that bodily life is intrinsic to the human person. . . . As the doctrine of the resurrection of the body makes clear, human beings are saved and exist in eternity as bodily persons, not as disembodied souls."[187] The body, in other words, should be seen as part of the identity and reality of the human person. "It is properly understood, therefore, as fully sharing in the dignity—the intrinsic worth—of the person and deserving the respect due to persons precisely as such."[188]

Some implications of this perspective are stated succinctly by George:

> Even the life of an early embryo or a severely retarded child or a comatose person has value and dignity. Their value and dignity are not to be judged by what they can do, how they feel, how they make us feel, or what we judge their "quality" of life to be. Their value and dignity transcend the instrumental purposes to which their lives can be put. They enjoy a moral inviolability that will be respected and protected in any fully just regime of law.[189]

A human being does not *become* a "person"; rather, a human being is a human person by virtue of his or her very human-ness. On the other hand, human persons may or may not still exist as such after having lost part of their complete humanity, through physical death. The only distinction recognized by Aquinas between the human being and person occurs in this post-mortem state, when the soul is separated from the body and thus receives knowledge via the "influx" of the "light of grace" rather than via the more normal sensory apparatus of the "light of nature."[190] In this condition, this post-mortem, bodiless soul may be a subsistent "human being" without possessing the human bodily

---

[186] Joseph C. Atkinson, "*Familiaris Consortio*: The Biblical and Theological Foundation of an Adequate Anthropology." *Life and Learning XI: Proceedings of the Eleventh University Faculty for Life Conference.* Joseph Koterski, S.J., ed. Washington, D.C.: University Faculty for Life, 2001: 248-66, p. 253.

[187] George, *The Clash of Orthodoxies*, p. 326n6.

[188] Ibid., p. 10.

[189] Ibid., pp. 8-9.

[190] ST I.89.1.

completeness of the "human person."[191] As Robert P. George and Patrick Lee put it, "Such souls are rational entities, even though . . . they are not, strictly speaking, persons, since having a complete nature is part of what is meant by 'person,' and a separated soul is in its nature incomplete."[192]

However, the crucial premise being brought out here is that for Aquinas, just as for George, the *human person* is the hylomorphic union; the person is not some future entity a human *being* may one day become, given enough functionality. In the words of Catholic writer Dave Armstrong, "Conception as the point of beginning for any human being is an undisputable scientific fact, and playing around with the additional 'right' of becoming a 'person' at some logically absurd later stage does nothing to change that fact."[193] This Thomistic view stands in stark contrast to the common philosophical practice today of separating physical human-ness away from metaphysical personhood in order to deny rights to the former and grant rights to the latter: "Strange to say, the persons of bioethical theory seem to be almost immaterial. At the very least they always possess big dualistic wardrobes."[194]

Of course, these assertions do not yet form an argument; Aquinas's own thoughts regarding personhood remain to be examined.[195] One

---

[191] For a more extensive discussion, see Anton C. Pegis's article "The Separated Soul and Its Nature in St. Thomas" (*St. Thomas Aquinas 1274-1974: Commemorative Studies.* Toronto: Pontifical Institute of Mediaeval Studies, 1974, pp. 1:131-58).

[192] Robert P. George and Patrick Lee. "Bodies: The Exhibition." "On the Square: Observations and Contentions." Firstthings.com (14 August 2006), n.p. Accessed 14 August 2006. See also Jason Eberl, *Thomistic Principles and Bioethics*, p. 9: "Although a rational soul is capable of existing on its own, because it is the substantial form of a material body, it does not subsist with a complete specific nature; a soul alone is not completely 'human.'"

[193] David Armstrong. *Family Matters: Catholic Theology of the Family.* Melvindale, Michigan: Lulu Publishing, 2007, p. 8.

[194] Jenny Teichman. "The False Philosophy of Peter Singer." *The New Criterion* 11.8 (April 1993): 25-30, p. 29.

[195] Maureen Junker-Kenny writes that the "definition of the beginning . . . of human personhood is caught in a practical hermeneutical circle. We define its starting point because we want to act in a certain way, and we act according to how we have defined it" ("Embryos *in vitro*, Personhood, and Rights." *Designing Life? Genetics, Procreation and Ethics.* Maureen Junker-Kenny, ed. Aldershot: Ashgate, 1999: 130-58, p. 133). However, it is hoped that the arguments in the remainder of this chapter will steer the reader toward recognition of the logical preferability of the identification of "human-ness" and "personhood," as in the Boethian and Thomistic definition.

way a Thomist might arrive at the identity of "human-ness" with "personhood" is to reflect, as does Aquinas, on the meaning of the biblical text, "Let us make humankind in our image, according to our likeness," found in the account of human creation (Genesis 1:26). "Image" and "likeness" are not identical, according to Aquinas; X can have likeness to Y without being the image of Y. However, X cannot be the *image* of Y without having likeness to Y as well; in the latter case, the likeness of something signifies "the expression and perfection of [its] image."[196] In that restricted sense, only humans are created in both the image and likeness of God: "While in all creatures there is some kind of likeness to God, in the rational creature alone we find a likeness of 'image.'"[197]

Aquinas divides this idea of creation in God's image into two different senses: "First, so that this preposition 'to' points to the term of the making, and then the sense is, 'Let Us make man in such a way that Our image may be in him [Aquinas quotes the first chapter of Genesis as reading that God made humans "like 'to' His image"]." The second way of understanding is also relevant to this discussion: "Secondly, this preposition 'to' may point to the exemplar cause, as when we say, 'This book is made (like) to that one.' Thus the image of God is the very Essence of God, Which is incorrectly called an image forasmuch as image is put for the exemplar. Or, as some say, the Divine Essence is called an image because thereby one Person imitates another."[198] In other words, God's essence is the exemplar of the image of God found in humans, and so God's creation in humanity in some respects "imitates" the nature of God Himself. Therefore, if God is a Person, or three Persons in one substance, as Christians maintain, and if humans are created in God's image, then to be created as a human is also to be created as a person: "Aquinas did not think it was possible to be a human being without being a human person."[199] Aquinas did not think of the early embryo as a human "person" simply because he did not think of the embryo as a human being; however, this is not a metaphysical judgment, but a judgment based on a less-advanced observation of the embryo's development. "In the light of modern biology, Aquinas's principles favor the view that the human embryo is a human being, and hence a human person, from conception."[200]

---

[196] ST I.93.9.
[197] ST I.93.6.
[198] ST I.93.5.
[199] David Albert Jones, *The Soul of the Embryo*, p. 220.
[200] Ibid., pp. 220-21.

Thus far in this book the argument has been presented that the intellectual soul is infused into the human conceptus at the time of conception. The argument now under consideration follows directly from that one. For example, Aquinas brings out the similarity to God of all created things in their various ranks of being: "Now it is manifest that specific likeness follows the ultimate difference. But some things are like to God first and most commonly because they exist; secondly, because they live; and thirdly because they know or understand; and these last, as Augustine says, 'approach so near to God in likeness, that among all creatures nothing comes nearer to Him.' It is clear, therefore, that intellectual creatures alone, properly speaking, are made to God's image."[201]

Some writers argue that the intellectual soul is not infused until several weeks into the embryo's development, and therefore the zygote cannot be said to be "made to God's image," in Aquinas's phrase. However, Aquinas follows Boethius in defining a "person" as "an individual substance of rational nature."[202] Therefore, to be created by God (and pro-created by human parents) as a human is also to be created as a person; other definitions of personhood seem unduly narrow. In other words, if any rational substance is a person, and the conceptus is an embodied rational substance, then the conceptus is an embodied human person ("human" due to the genetic nature of its embodiment as possessing *Homo sapiens* DNA, and "person" due to the nature of its substantial form). Only the zygote, alone among human cells, qualifies as such a hypostasis:

> By *hypostasis*, the word "person" can mean not the individual who exercises the rational function or capacity but a being of that natural *kind* whose mature representatives *normally do* exercise it, and of which the individual is an instance. In this sense all human beings are persons. . . . [for] all belong to the natural kind whose members do exercise such capacities in the due course of development, and when no impediment such as sleep or injury intervenes.[203]

Another response is rather simpler and also less theological: One could argue that the human conceptus is a person because its progenitors are persons. Human persons conceive human persons, as zebras conceive zebras. Common objections to this stance, as has been seen, usually involve a division of personhood off from the essential characteristics

---

[201] ST I.93.2.

[202] ST III.2.2.

[203] J. Budziszewski. *The Line Through the Heart: Natural Law as Fact, Theory, and Sign of Contradiction.* Wilmington, Delaware: ISI Books, 2009, p. 99.

of humanity; as the pro-choice slogan has it, "An acorn is not an oak tree!"[204] However, an acorn, once germinated, actually *is* an oak tree, at its earliest stage of development. It is an oak tree because its ancestors are oak trees and not apple trees; it is living and developing as an oak tree, and its DNA is that of an oak tree. Another objection is more refined, but similar in thought; a critic might argue, "Just because the progenitors are human persons does not make the conceptus a human person. The progenitors might be red-haired, or airline pilots, or automobile mechanics, or good at tennis, or six feet tall. None of those attributes make the conceptus red-haired or a pilot or good at tennis or six feet tall; all of those are attributes which might or might not manifest themselves at a later date in the development of the conceptus. Likewise with personhood: Even if the progenitors are persons, that in itself does not make their conceptus a person."

However, to return to a familiar Thomistic theme, "We must observe that things which are accidental do not change the species."[205] Furthermore, characteristics of the species of anything must be defined by examining the mature, fully flourishing example of that species. One could easily be a mature, fully flourishing human without being a pilot or having red hair or possessing superior tennis ability. These are "accidental" characteristics which do not change the substance of human-ness. On the other hand, one could not be a mature, fully flourishing human without *being a person*, an "individual substance of rational nature." The conclusion following is straightforward enough: Personhood must be seen as a defining characteristic of the human species, and the conceptus is a member of the human species. To the objection, "No, personhood is a defining characteristic of the *mature* example of the species, not the undeveloped," one must again differentiate between those substantial characteristics which are in the species because of what sort of thing it is and those incidental characteristics which are not. For example, young children are not sexually developed in the sense that adult humans are, but the characteristic of mature sexual expression is "in" every human undergoing its maturation as the human develops; in other words, every human possesses sexuality at some stage of development. Skill at tennis, on the other hand, is not

---

[204] The most famous use of this slogan is that of Judith Jarvis Thomson in her well-known essay "A Defense of Abortion" (*Philosophy and Public Affairs* 1.1 [Fall 1971]: 47-66, p. 47). This essay will be discussed in Chapter 6, "Opposing Arguments."
[205] ST I.77.3.

resident "in" every human and will not naturally undergo maturation unless the human is encouraged and trained in that skill.

The question therefore arises: Is human personhood, like human sexuality, an innately held characteristic which is activated by the mere plain facts of being conceived by human parents and divinely infused with the human form, or is it an acquired characteristic like skill at tennis? Although this is perhaps too optimistic a stance, one would hope that to pose the question is to see the answer: It is the former, an innately held characteristic which exists at some stage of development in all human beings. Of course, personhood, like sexuality, can be stunted or thwarted or given immature or unnatural expression. However, the conceptus is a human being, which means it is also a human person.[206] The vastly lesser question of whether or not it is also a good tennis player would remain to be answered, much later in its development.

A salient objection might arise at this point, since a critic could object that personhood is "in" the zygote, but latently, not yet actively. Just as it is impermissible to involve children in sexual activity precisely because their sexuality has not reached mature expression, so also, this critic might argue, it *is* permissible to kill the zygote precisely because the latent personhood of the zygote has not yet reached mature expression. However, as stated previously, every human being possesses sexuality and merely develops into its mature expression; that is, every human being possesses a sexual nature despite that nature's level or lack of development or expression. Moreover, the fact of both the possession of sexuality on the part of children and its immaturity logically imposes restrictions on the behavior of those around the children. The immaturity of the sexuality of a child should not be a license for its misuse, but rather a boundary marker. Likewise every human being possesses personhood and merely develops into its mature expression, and the conceptus, as has been argued, is a human being; that is, it is an individual substance of a rational nature despite that

---

[206] To inject a personal misgiving: It seems not only a rhetorical blunder but a factual mistake to refer to the conceptus as an "unborn baby" until a certain stage in its development is reached. It is a "rhetorical blunder" because even those sympathetic to the pro-life viewpoint do not usually see a zygote as a "baby" (nor should they, since it factually is not). The relevant point for which to argue is that the conceptus is a human being, no matter its stage of development. The zygote is involved in the process which will *make* it a human baby, a human child, a human teen-ager, a human adult—because of what it already is, a human.

nature's level or lack of development or expression. In John Finnis's expression, it remains a person although it may not yet be "paradigmatic":

> Any entity which, remaining the same individual, will develop into a paradigmatic instance of a substantial kind already is an instance of that kind. The one-cell human organism originating with the substantial change which occurs upon the penetration of a human ovum by a human sperm typically develops, as one and the same individual, into a paradigmatic instance of the rational bodily person, the human person; in every such case, therefore, it is already an actual instance of the human person.[207]

The fact that the personhood of the conceptus is not fully expressed, and perhaps cannot be expressed at all in its current state, should not be construed in itself as licensing the aborting of the conceptus, but should rather be construed as imposing a "boundary marker" around its development. A human person does not lose personhood simply due to not being "a paradigmatic instance" of a person.

## 2. Three Criteria for Human-ness

This general principle of the human substance as constituted by the union of the animating form with the embodied presence of DNA from the species *Homo sapiens* might be able to stand as stated. However, to ward off some potential objections, the genetic criteria for human existence need to be more explicitly outlined; a discussion of these criteria will therefore now follow.

### (1) *Human "Plus" Something Else*

As I walk along the footpath in the field outside my window, I might kick a rock from time to time, for no special reason except that I feel like doing so. However, if I encounter another human on this footpath and decide to kick him or her, I need to have prepared a rational explanation for the attack. This explanation is required because there are things humans can do to inanimate objects that they cannot do to animate creatures without good reason, and especially "there are things which we [can] do to non-persons which we ought never to do to persons."[208] What gives rise to the vast majority of bioethical disagreements is the simple question, "Is there a difference in kind between a 'human' and a 'person'?" The answer to this question will determine what it is humans can do to another "human," if in fact the

---

[207] John Finnis. "Abortion and Health Care Ethics II." *Principles of Health Care Ethics.* R. Gillon, ed. New York: Wiley, 1994: 547-57, p. 550.
[208] Neil Messer. *Theological Issues in Bioethics: An Introduction with Readings.* London: Darton, Longman & Todd, 2002, p. 65.

human is a non-person. On the other hand, if the human *is* a person, that will also entail limitations on the permissible actions that can be done to him or her. What kind of action is it that is being chosen? Even those who are "pro-choice" are not "pro" all "choices."

The term "person," when used in opposition to "human being," usually highlights "a set of capacities—usually including consciousness and self-awareness, ability to feel pain, at least some minimal capacity for relationship with others, and perhaps some capacity for self-motivated activity."[209] A human being, in this view, might not possess personhood, and consequently could easily be excluded from the list of "protected" persons: "Personhood arguments, exclusive rather than inclusive in their understanding of human community, seem in many ways to have turned against the long and arduous history in which we have slowly learned to value and protect—for Christians, to see Christ in—those who are least among us."[210] Some have even suggested that the concept of "personhood" must include the "capacity to live without the mercy of others" or even that the concept must include the state of being "lovable."[211] Of course, the immediate logical extension of these capacities would exclude many conscious, rational, and self-aware adults from the category of personhood, as well as the unborn. As Gilbert Meilaender notes:

> In the last several decades it has become common to define personhood in terms of certain capacities. To be a person one must be conscious, self-aware, productive. The class of persons will widen or narrow depending on how many such criteria we include in our definition of personhood. But, in any case, the class of human beings will be wider than that of persons. Not all living human beings will qualify as persons on such a view—and, we must note, it is persons who are now regarded as bearers of rights, persons who can have interests that ought to be protected.[212]

If the criterion for recognizing personhood and defining those members of humanity possessing human rights revolves around (for instance) rational ability, the comatose are of course also immediately deprived of innate human rights, and perhaps not even just the

---

[209] Gilbert Meilaender, *Bioethics: A Primer for Christians*. Grand Rapids, Michigan: Eerdmans, 1996, p. 32.
[210] Ibid., p. 33.
[211] This attitude, extreme though it may sound, has been brought up by some and is discussed in Paul Ramsey's *Ethics at the Edges of Life: Medical and Legal Intersections* (New Haven and London: Yale University Press, 1978), p. 206.
[212] Meilaender, *Bioethics*, p. 6.

technically comatose. More and more frequently simple disability is substituted for lack of consciousness in determining personhood. As one writer points out, "If we do not accept the substitution of disability for lack of consciousness, then the evidence is indisputable that Permanent Vegetative State [PVS] is not necessarily permanent and not unquestionably insentient."[213] Some do appear ready to accept the logical conclusion of denying human rights to the comatose; as one ethics professor succinctly argued, "The unborn are not human and the brain-dead are no longer human; therefore, the prohibition against killing an innocent human does not apply in their cases."[214] Similarly, Peter Singer writes:

> The fact that a being is a human being, in the sense of a member of the species *Homo sapiens*, is not relevant to the wrongness of killing it; it is, rather, characteristics like rationality, autonomy, and self-consciousness that make a difference. . . . Killing [a human being lacking these characteristics], therefore, cannot be equated with killing normal human beings, or any other self-conscious beings. This conclusion is *not limited* to infants who, because of irreversible intellectual disabilities, will never be rational, self-conscious beings.[215]

Moreover, when one is designated by the label "brain-dead," it will be noticed (especially when this label is mis-applied to PVS patients), even the ability to breathe normally and maintain a steady heartbeat without mechanical assistance might not qualify one as retaining any specific human right to life—even if one is not technically unconscious or comatose. In fact, cycles of sleeping and waking, or "intermittent wakefulness manifested by the presence of sleep-wake cycles," are accepted as part of the condition of the Permanent Vegetative State, along with "variably preserved cranial-nerve reflexes (pupillary, oculophalic, corneal, vestibulo-ocular, and gag) and spinal reflexes."[216]

This attitude toward limiting the expansion of basic human rights seems symptomatic of the tendency to "define humanity up"—that is, to define a "human person" as "a human being *plus* something else," the

---

[213] Chris Borthwick. "The Permanent Vegetative State: Ethical Crux, Medical Fiction?" *Issues in Law and Medicine* 12.2 (1996): 167-85, p. 179.
[214] Gregory Landini. Lecture, "Introduction to Ethics." The University of Iowa, Iowa City, Iowa, Summer 1995.
[215] Peter Singer, *Practical Ethics*. 2nd edition. Cambridge: Cambridge University Press, 1993, p. 182. Emphasis added.
[216] Multi-Society Task Force on PVS. "Medical Aspects of the Persistent Vegetative State: Part 1." *The New England Journal of Medicine*. 330.21 (1994): 1499-1508, p. 1499.

"something else" being a specific function or functions located on a variable list of abilities. Bioethical dilemmas arise when disagreements spring up, as they inevitably must, over which functions are the "defining" functions.

(2) *Two Corporeal Criteria and One Non-Corporeal*

Could a "functionalist" definition of personhood involving active rationality, self-awareness, and self-expressive consciousness, such as is proposed by Singer and others, be a solution to many of the bioethical issues faced today? In one respect, the answer is yes—that is, if a functionalist definition of personhood is accepted, it certainly would allow for a simple solution to many issues, along with wide latitude regarding "morally acceptable" bioethical decisions. However, this definition, along with all types of "functionalist" definitions, para-doxically also seems far too restrictive or "exclusive rather than inclusive," in Meilaender's phrase, when it comes to common cases dealt with today. Perhaps a better definition of human being[217] would restrict *itself* rather than attempting to restrict the category of human-

---

[217] The objection has been raised by Mary Anne Warren (in her essay "On the Moral and Legal Status of Abortion"), along with others, that the type of argument being made here conflates the terms "human being" and "person" and thus commits the fallacy of equivocation. However, a central claim of the current argument is that the initial *separation* of these two terms itself can be disputed, no matter on what grounds the separation is made; in Aquinas's view, an embodied human being simply *is* a human person, and vice versa. As one writer puts it, "If [it] is right that the human soul is that which organizes the activities of a human being and that ensouled humans are persons, embryos are persons from conception" (Jan Deckers, "Why Eberl Is Wrong: Reflections on the Beginning of Personhood." *Bioethics* 21.5 [June 2007]: 270-82, p. 270). Interestingly, Deckers is responding to an earlier essay by Eberl; in his more recent work (published the year before Deckers' article appeared), Eberl argues, "In normal cases, a human zygote has an active potentiality to be an actually thinking rational human being, and this is sufficient to conclude that it is informed by a rational soul. By applying Aquinas's metaphysical principles to contemporary embryological data, I conclude that a human being begins to exist at conception" (*Thomistic Principles and Bioethics*, p. 42). In fact, in his response to Deckers' article, Eberl begins in the first paragraph by pointing out, "Further research since the publication of that article has led me to conclude that the account I previously defended is not sufficiently compelling to negate the conclusion that, from a Thomistic metaphysical perspective, a human embryo is rationally ensouled at conception" ("A Thomistic Perspective on the Beginning of Personhood: Redux." *Bioethics* 21.5 [June 2007]: 283-89, p. 283). Indeed, after his introductory remarks regarding Deckers' "Why Eberl Is Wrong," the first section of Eberl's article is entitled "Why Deckers Is Right"!

ness. For example, here are two criteria, both of which can be seen as corporeal in nature rather than functional, which seem irreducibly necessary in order for one to qualify as a human being:

(1) One must possess a DNA code from the species *Homo sapiens.*

(2) One must possess a separate and uniquely expressed DNA code. (The DNA codes of identical twins are likewise identical; however, these codes are still "uniquely expressed." Although the genotypes of identical twins may be the same, their phenotypes (the total expression of their genotypes) is different, including differences in physical characteristics such as fingerprints.)

To these two corporeal criteria a third criterion must immediately be added. However, this criterion is non-corporeal in nature and refers back to the earlier discussion on the necessity of the human "form":

(3) One must possess the potential, under normal circumstances, to develop into a mature example of *Homo sapiens.* (This criterion necessitates the presence of the human form because of the need for the animating principle of human development, not merely the presence of the human's genetic "blueprint.")

It might seem that by presenting a requirement for a "potential," this criterion falls back into the same type of argument presented by those arguing for a "functionalist" definition of humanity; for example, philosopher Robert Pasnau argues for a distinction between having "a capacity in hand" and having the "potential to develop such a capacity."[218] However, the developmental capacity described in the present definition is not a functional ability attained or learned by the human, which is what Pasnau means by "capacity"; nor for that matter can it be lost, except by death. This remains true even if the human is damaged or disabled in some way, and even if this damage is mortal in nature, as is the case when the pregnant woman's body spontaneously rejects the implantation or development of the fertilized ovum. The fertilized ovum up to that point still would possess the capacity, *under normal circumstances*, to develop into a mature example of *Homo sapiens.* It should also be noted that this potential is held by those extra-uterine ova fertilized under laboratory conditions, even apart from the mother's womb. Under normal conditions they also would develop into mature examples of *Homo sapiens*—in fact, they also would possess all three of the criteria listed in this section. Therefore, this third criterion should not be seen as implying a more liberal stance than I intend. It does not mean, for example, that a conceptus, embryo, or fetus with a severe genetic disease that will result in death within a few weeks of birth is not

---

[218] Pasnau, *Thomas Aquinas on Human Nature*, p. 115.

therefore a human being. The presence of the mortal disease is not a "normal" condition even if congenital, and if the conceptus were returned to normal conditions, free of disease, it would possess the capacity to continue to develop normally. Such a presence of mortal disease should therefore be seen as a characteristic or "accident" in such cases (using Thomistic terminology) and not as a feature of the substantial form of the conceptus. "Under normal circumstances" every embodied substantial form will develop, via the animation of the intellectual soul and the self-organization of the genetic blueprint, into a mature example of *Homo sapiens*. Consequently, every human conceptus, healthy or not, is included in this definition of "human being." Under normal circumstances, every human conceptus has this potential for development, even if no functional abilities are present.

On the other hand, in her article "The Morality of Killing Human Embryos," Bonnie Steinbock argues against this view by means of this very state of affairs, that of viable non-uterine embryos with no *de facto* future: "For unlike a fetus, an extra-corporeal embryo is not developing into someone with a valuable future. Left alone (that is, not aborted), the fetus will (most likely) develop into someone with a valuable future. But the same is just not true of an embryo, whether left-over from IVF or deliberately created for research. Left alone, an extra-corporeal embryo will just die."[219] However, the particular definition of "human being" under discussion seeks to avoid Steinbock's objection by highlighting the fact that such extra-corporeal embryos, no matter how they are produced, would develop into maturity *under normal circumstances*. The mere fact that extracorporeal embryos exist under such highly abnormal circumstances points to the troublesome aspects of the research itself, but the type of existence the extracorporeal embryo possesses does not add to or subtract from the definition of the embryo as such. Again, extracorporeality in these situations is an accidental characteristic and not part of the embryo's substantial form, any more than it would be part of a human's substantial form to be located in Mexico City rather than in London.

The Thomistic distinction to which Pasnau is alluding when he differentiates between having "a capacity in hand" and having the "potential to develop such a capacity" is the distinction between two types of "first act" or first actuality: "[Actuality] is twofold: first and second. The first act is the form and integrity of a thing; the second act is its operation." The first act "is said to be in potentiality to the second

---

[219] Steinbock, "The Morality of Killing Human Embryos." *The Journal of Law, Medicine & Ethics* 34.1 (Spring 2006): 26-34, p. 33.

act, which is operation."[220] So for example, if one were actually thinking rationally, one would be in second actuality, which is the actual operation of something hitherto in potential only. As a human, one can enter into this second actuality of rational thought more or less at will; however, even if one is not presently thinking rationally (while sleeping, for instance), the "capacity in hand," which is the first type of "first actuality," still distinguishes one as a rational human. The second type of first actuality, which is the "potential to develop such a capacity," according to Pasnau is not enough of an actuality to distinguish one as a rational human; therefore, since the conceptus only has the second type of first actuality (potential to develop) and not the first type of first actuality (capacity in hand, with no further actualization required), he concludes that the conceptus is not yet a human being.

However, one can use these very terms to rebut Pasnau's conclusion. Aquinas clearly asserts that the actual operation of a potentiality (the second actuality) is incidental to the existence of the soul containing these potentialities in first actuality.[221] Therefore, whether or not the capacity for rational thought is a "capacity in hand" or simply a potential to develop a capacity in hand, this distinction seems to lack the importance Pasnau finds in it. What is important is that the rational soul may inform a developing conceptus even apart from the "second actuality," that of actual operation of its potentiality for rational thought: "Since a rational soul is a human body's substantial form.... it is inconsequential whether such operations are actually exercised in a body for a rational soul to inform it."[222] The ongoing development toward fully fledged rational thought indicates the presence of the human rational soul, even if that soul is not currently rationally thinking (second actuality) or even cannot currently undertake rational thought at all (i.e., it has no "capacity in hand," the first type of first actuality).

To return to the discussion of the three criteria for human-ness: One benefit of this third non-corporeal criterion is that it rules out "growths" or "organs" as human beings, even though they may satisfy the first two corporeal criteria. A wart would possess human DNA, for example, and (should the human die from whom the wart was removed) could even possess a separate and uniquely expressed human

---

[220] ST I.48.5; 76.4.

[221] See, for example, ST I.79.2, in which Thomas discusses the "passive power" of the soul, manifested in its "potentiality" for rational understanding.

[222] Jason T. Eberl, *Thomistic Principles and Bioethics*, p. 28. Thanks are due to Eberl for his lucid discussion of this point (pp. 26-ff.), which first brought it to my attention.

DNA code. However, it would still lack the animating principle of development granted by the substantial form; consequently, under normal circumstances, the wart could never develop into a mature example of the species *Homo sapiens* and thus is not a rational human substance, or a *hypostasis*, to use Aquinas's term.[223] Aquinas himself uses the example of a severed hand, not a wart, but the lack of substantial form would be the relevant issue in both examples. This applies also to the more standard example often given of the anomalous placental-tissue growth of hydatidiform moles (HMs), which may even contain partial aspects of non-viable embryonic development. However, the HM is not simply a more extreme example of a non-viable embryo, or an embryo with a fatal chromosomal disease; it seems something else entirely, a result of a sperm-egg union that is not itself a conception, and which may in fact develop into a choriocarcinoma, a form of cancer. As Francis Beckwith points out, "One who holds that a human being begins to exist as a single organism at conception is not arguing that everything that results from the sperm-egg union is necessarily a conception. . . . Hence, the sperm-egg union is a *necessary* condition for conception, but not a *sufficient* condition. . . . [Hydatidiform moles] do not result from normal, biologically complete, conceptions but arise from entities that are in fact flawed or deficient 'fertilizations' and thus have no intrinsically directed capacity to develop into a normal human being."[224] Typically an HM arises when an empty ovum (lacking its DNA) is penetrated by one or more sperm cells; thus an HM may be seen as importantly differing from an embryo which is non-viable due to a mortal chromosomal disease, for the latter would under normal circumstances (i.e., without the accident of the disease) continue to develop into a mature example of a human being.[225] The HM would not; it is therefore not a hypostasis, and not a human being.

---

[223] E.g., in ST III.16.12*ad* 2-3.

[224] Francis J. Beckwith, *Defending Life: A Moral and Legal Case Against Abortion.* New York: Cambridge University Press, 2007, pp. 74-75 and 82-83. Emphasis in original.

[225] A related question might arise at this point: What about an embryo which develops as a human being, but which possesses a chromosomal differentiation which affects the future child to such an extent that it may even qualify the child's personal identity (e.g., a child with trisomy 21 or Down's syndrome)? What are the "normal circumstances" of such a child's development—in other words, if the chromosomal disorder were to disappear, would the Down's syndrome child still be the same child, in the way that, for example, a child with skin cancer would still be the same child if the skin cancer were to disappear?

Such a question requires further consideration; in the meantime, one might

Further, this third criterion (that "One must possess the potential, under normal circumstances, to develop into a mature example of *Homo sapiens*") addresses occasional objections such as those of Dombrowski and Deltete, who argue by a sort of *reductio* that a genetic determination of human-ness would lead to ridiculous situations: "If potentiality for X [human life] entitles one to X, then the silly line from a Monty Python film should be taken quite seriously: every sperm is sacred." They go on later:

> If an organism is a human person merely through possession of human genetic capital, then not only is a heart ready for transplant a human person, as is each living cell in a body that is brain dead and whose heart has stopped beating, but also every single cell of the zygote, the morula, or the blastula, since each one of these may, if separated early enough from the others, survive with its human genes intact.[226]

However, given the three criteria listed above, one readily sees that these human organs and cells, and even human sperm cells and ova, do not represent even *potential* humans, since they lack the animated self-organization of the human zygote. Earlier Aquinas's position on this point was paraphrased from ST III.16, but he presents a similar argument in Part I of the same work: "Not every particular substance is a hypostasis or a person, but that which has the complete nature of its species. Hence a hand, or a foot, is not called a hypostasis, or a person."[227] A severed foot, or a removed organ, would not satisfy the three specified requirements: (1) It does possess human DNA, but (2) its DNA is not separately and uniquely expressed, and (3) it has no potential to develop into a mature human being (it lacks this potential because it is not a substance in itself). Therefore, a severed foot, an ovum, or a sperm cell, considered in itself, could not be called a human being, or any other type of hypostasis.

---

simply say, with Robert P. George and Christopher Tollefsen, "To be a complete human organism (human being) an entity must possess a developmental program (including both its DNA and epigenetic factors) oriented toward developing a brain and nervous system; that is, it must, by virtue of its biological makeup, possess, at least in root form, capacities for characteristically human mental activities, even if disease or defect should at some point impede the further actualization of those capacities" (*Embryo: A Defense of Human Life* [New York: Doubleday, 2008], p. 137). The child with Down's syndrome is certainly such a complete organism, and is therefore according to this argument a human being and person from conception.

[226] Dombrowski and Deltete, *A Brief, Liberal, Catholic Defense*, pp. 47 and 51.
[227] ST I.75.4.

At this point, a summary of the discussion surrounding this third criterion might be of benefit: First, the human's required "potential" is neither a functional ability nor a "capacity in hand," but rather the "potential to develop such a capacity" (understanding "capacity in hand" and "capacity" as having essentially the same meaning as "functional ability"). Secondly, under this criterion, a diseased embryo would still qualify as fully human, since the disease would be one of the "accidental qualities" of the embryo and not a feature of its substantial form. Thirdly, this criterion applies only to the conceptus as hypostasis, not to its component cells or organs. The substantial form is the form of the human body, not of its organs: "A proof of which," as Aquinas writes, "is, that on the withdrawal of the soul, no part of the body retains its proper action … wherefore the soul must be in the whole body."[228] No isolated part of a human, consequently, can be considered a human being in itself, unless it has the innate potential to continue its development as a human being. Hypothetically, a totipotent stem cell (a single cell, such as a zygote, with the ability to divide and produce all of the cells and organs of an organism) brought into being from an adult cell might appear to contradict this conclusion. However, the conclusion still applies: Until such an event is brought about, the adult cell is not itself developing as a unitary human being. If such an event were to be brought about, the newly developing cell would be a separate human being, similar in nature to an identical twin.

Conception, however, produces an entity that does satisfy all the three requirements specified above, and therefore the conceptus may justly be called a human being.[229] So also would the comatose patient with a diagnosis of PVS: Since the patient satisfies the first two corporeal criteria, and since *under normal circumstances* the patient's human development would continue normally, the patient is a human being. Any call for the death of the patient on the grounds of the patient's lack of personhood must therefore be seen as a call for the killing of a human being merely because of that human being's medical condition. This call for the killing of the patient would not be based on the nature of the patient himself or herself, but on the special character of the

---

[228] ST I.76.8.

[229] "On any biologically precise and morally apt description, sperm and ova are not 'potential humans'; their only relevant innate potential is to fuse with the other so that each can provide one half of the DNA for a new, genetically distinct, one-cell organism. Only the one-cell zygote is an organism with properly human potential because, arguably, it already is human" (Denis Bradley, " 'To Be or Not To Be,'" p. 33).

patient's circumstances. Upon considering the human-ness of both the conceptus and the comatose patient, it does not seem that their circumstances could justify such killings.

# Chapter 4: The Soul and Body Composite

### 1.  Aquinas's View of Human Nature

Aquinas in general accepts Aristotle's analysis that souls are of three different kinds: the vegetative soul, the sensitive soul, and the rational soul.[230] Each different kind possesses consecutively higher powers without losing the powers possessed by the lower kinds, and without becoming multiple souls in one being, since each of the higher kinds supervenes upon the kind(s) beneath it: "Thus there is only one soul in any particular [being]; there is a hierarchy of souls and of vital functions, such that the higher souls subsume the lower."[231]

Plants possess the first kind of soul or animating principle, the vegetative, which allows them to reproduce themselves and take in nutrition. The sensitive (sensory) soul allows higher animals to take in sensory data from their environment and to direct their own motions, while the rational soul in humans allows rational, abstract reflection and communication. Language itself in its fullest sense, as incorporating abstract symbols as well as concrete signals, is an exercise of the power of the rational soul. Entities with souls thus progressively live, sense, move, and think as one rises up in the hierarchy of animating principles. However, "Given man's intermediate position between the world of bodies and the world of the spirit, we easily grasp that the problem put to anyone who reflects on human reality is precisely how to understand the nature of the link that holds the two disparate principles of being, spirit and matter, together."[232]

---

[230] ST I.78.1-ff.

[231] Joseph Magee, "Thomistic Psychology," n.p. See also ST I.76.3, where Aquinas argues that the human soul is "numerically one"; and Jason Eberl: "Aquinas claims that...the sensitive and vegetative souls that had previously informed a developing embryo are annihilated once a rational soul is created [in order to] counter the claim by some of his contemporaries that there are three souls—vegetative, sensitive, and rational—existing at the same time in a fully developed human being" (*Thomistic Principles and Bioethics*, p. 130n12).

[232] Jean-Pierre Torrell, *Saint Thomas Aquinas, Volume 2: Spiritual Master*, p. 255.

## (1)  *The Composite Human Being*

For Aquinas a human is an embodied (and hence mortal) rational animal: "The term *what* refers sometimes to the nature expressed by the definition, as when we ask: What is man? and we answer: A mortal rational animal."[233] The "animal" part of this definition refers partially to the sensitive faculties humans share with the other living members of nature, for humans' interactions with the external world around them come through their senses, just as is the case for other creatures. "As to sensible forms [i.e., our soul's powers in regard to the sensible world] there is no difference between man and other animals"[234]—indeed, if there is a difference at all, it would be in *favor* of the other animals of the world, or at least the higher animals, which possess far more finely tuned faculties for encountering the physical world than humans do.

However, as Aquinas immediately points out, humans do not perceive merely through the senses, but also through a "coalition of ideas," a coalition which is not an immediate feature of the sensory perception.[235] If humans are embodied rational animals, it seems the parts of the definition of "human" more important than the "animal" part are the "embodied" and "rational" parts. To take the description of "rational" first: Because of their powers of rationality, humans surpass "all other animals" in their "faculty of understanding"; in fact, "the proper operation of man as man is to understand."[236] Humanity is therefore of the same *genus* as other animals, but of a different *species*, not only in a biological sense, but in the sense of its differentiating or "speciating" capabilities.[237] For both Aquinas and Aristotle, the "rational" in "rational animal" is what makes humans specifically human, no matter what other features they may share with other animals. Therefore, human rational faculties set humans apart from the other corporeal creatures of the world. If humans were only "embodied" but not "rational," they would be mere mortal animals not essentially different from any other.

On the other hand, if humans had *only* rational faculties without corporeal embodiment, they would be in the same category as non-corporeal rational intelligences (angels, for example), which they obviously are not; unlike angels, humans possess non-completed potential. Humans are mortal, transient, changeable, and so on. So the

---

[233] ST I.29.4.
[234] ST I.78.4.
[235] ST I.78.4.
[236] ST I.76.1.
[237] ST I.75.3.

other part of a human's definition specifically as *a human* is the "embodied" (and hence mortal) aspect: "There is a twofold nature in man: rational nature and the sensitive nature."[238] The "sensitive nature" is the nature of the "embodied" human self; the "rational nature" is the nature of the "spiritual" human self. Lacking one or the other, humans become angels or beasts, neither of which designates accurately the specifying human nature:

> Very early in the history of mankind the attempt was made to get along without the material world. A no less energetic denial of the spiritual world dates from the Greek materialists and is almost universal in America today. Naturally, if either matter or spirit is denied in human nature, that quiet, peace-loving creature we call man is replaced by a monster.[239]

In some philosophies, the tendency to reduce humans to minds capable of non-corporeal existence ("angelism") is uppermost; one thinks of Descartes' *Cogito*, for example. In this view, simply because I am able to think, I know I exist at least as a mind, even if I cannot as of yet be sure of the existence of my body, given the untrustworthy nature of my physical senses. As one writer (who disagrees with this tendency) puts it, "Since it is rational nature which spells the difference in man, the tendency to reduce man to his specific difference would seem warranted and valid from a definitional standpoint. The intellect is the chief thing in man which tends to undermine and overshadow the bodily part of his nature."[240] In other philosophies, especially some prevalent today in scientific materialism, the opposite tendency is uppermost, namely the tendency to reduce humans to their physical component. The present work argues that the more difficult, but veridically and ultimately more fruitful and satisfying, view of humanity is that of the middle ground, the common-sense intuition of human nature as the union of spiritual and material: "It is the substantial unity between man's body and soul (which is intellectual) that holds the key in understanding man as a special kind of composite."[241] This is certainly Aquinas's view: "His overall metaphysical account stakes a middle ground between Platonic/

[238] ST I-II.71.2.
[239] Walter Farrell. *A Companion to the Summa. Volume I—The Architect of the Universe.* New York: Sheed and Ward, 1945, p. 279.
[240] Liza Ruth A. Ocampo. "The Question of the Definition of Man in Thomas Aquinas's *De Unitate Intellectus Contra Averroistas.*" *Talastasan Series 2005.* Diliman, Quezon City: Univ. of the Philippines, Sept. 2005: 1-7, p. 4.
[241] Ibid., p. 4.

Cartesian substance dualism, in which a person is identified as an immaterial soul, and reductive physicalism."[242]

This view of the human being as composite immediately creates a tension between the corporeal body and non-corporeal intellect. Aquinas believes that the soul exists as the form of the body and as the principle by which animate sensation takes place; on the other hand, he also believes that the soul possesses its own subsistent existence independently of the body and that abstract intellection takes place without involving the body or its senses either by way of mixture or any sort of physical contact.[243] As he puts it, "The intellectual principle which we call the mind or the intellect has an operation *per se* apart from the body."[244] Aquinas resolves this tension by arguing that the soul and body together make up the human substance, the substantial form of the human being, but that the soul also possesses "its own act of existence which it communicates to the body."[245] Therefore, the "act of being" belongs to the soul "as its principle, and in keeping with its very own nature," but the very same act of being is communicated to the body as its recipient.[246] Here one sees on display Aquinas's "Augustinian habit" of "holding two apparently contradictory (but not *really* contradictory) teachings together without compromising either."[247] Thus Aquinas argues for the soul's existence independent of the body while the soul simultaneously acts as the non-corporeal form of the body's corporeal matter; together the soul and body make up the human person, in what is often referred to as a "hylomorphic unity," a "version of Aristotelian hylomorphism."[248] A "person" is any individual substance possessing a rational intellectual nature; God and angels are persons because they have rational natures without material bodies. On the other hand, the human person is the soul and body combined, and thus *as a person* becomes "more like God" even in the composite state: "The soul that is united to the body is more like God than the soul that has been separated from its body because the former more perfectly possesses its own nature."[249]

---

[242] Jason T. Eberl. "Aquinas's Account of Human Embryogenesis," p. 380.
[243] SCG II.56.5-6.
[244] ST I.75.2.
[245] Joseph Magee, "Thomistic Psychology," n.p.
[246] SCG II.68.5.
[247] Peter Kreeft, *A Summa*, p. 257n19.
[248] Denis Bradley, " 'To Be or Not To Be?'" p. 6.
[249] *Quaestiones Disputatae de Potentia Dei*. English Dominican Fathers, transs. [1932]. Westminster, Maryland: Newman Press, reprinted 1952: V.10.ad5. All further quotes from this work will be taken from this translation.

So exactly how do human spiritual and material natures co-exist? In what manner does Aquinas describe the precise relationships between the rational and embodied sides of the human being, between the soul and the body? In order to present an answer to this question, we must turn again to the Treatise on Human Nature in Part One of the *Summa Theologica*.

### (2) *The Soul and Its Nature (ST I.75)*

After having discussed both the spiritual and corporeal creations separately in the preceding sections of the *Summa*, Aquinas turns to a consideration of humans, who are *qui ex spirituali et corporali substantia componitur*, "composed of [both] a spiritual and corporeal substance."[250] This is something of an ambiguous phrase, since it appears that it could mean humans have both a spiritual substance *and* a corporeal substance, leading to a Cartesian "substance dualism"; however, in context it appears to mean simply that the human is a single substance composed of both the spiritual and the corporeal, and is addressed directly in I.76.4: "Of one thing there is but one substantial being.... [T]here is no other substantial form in man besides the intellectual soul." This interpretation is also borne out in the Prologue to ST I.50, where Aquinas looks forward to Question 75 as a discussion *de creatura composita ex corporali et spirituali*. One notes the lack of any reference to *substantia* in relation to either *corporali* or *spirituali*; humans are merely seen as creatures composed of both "the corporeal and the spiritual."[251]

Even though the human DNA code provides the "blueprint" for the organization and development of the human, it in itself is merely another corporeal feature, almost an organ, of the body. This may seem a rather odd way of describing DNA; however, it is in accord with Aquinas's account of the human soul requiring organs through which to manifest its operations.[252] Although they contain the *information* necessary for organized development—that is, they contain the material organization "sufficient for the development of those organs that support all of the operations proper to the human species"[253]—the purely physical properties of the genetic code cannot account for its own *power* of organized development. Such organized development still requires the animating principle of the human substantial form/soul— as argued previously, it is by means of the formal causality herein

---

[250] ST I.75.1.
[251] On this point, see also Bradley, " 'To Be or Not To Be?'" pp. 3-4.
[252] SCG II.89.3; see also Haldane and Lee's "Rational Souls and the Beginning of Life (A Reply to Robert Pasnau)" (*Philosophy* 78.4 [October 2003]: 532-40).
[253] Haldane and Lee, "Rational Souls," p. 533.

referred to as its soul that the unformed matter takes on the form of whatever sort of being it is, while by means of the primary efficient causality of its internally self-directing DNA code, this being develops toward its terminal shape and structure as an embodied entity.[254] Moreover, since the corporeal exists in the fashion it does because of its relationship to the spiritual (the soul), the spiritual is primary and must be considered first.

A threefold approach to this consideration will include that of "essence [what a human soul is in itself], power [its capabilities], and operation [how it functions as it does]."[255] We will begin, as Aquinas does, with the soul's essence, its nature.

Aquinas first argues that the soul is not corporeal. An immediate objection to this view might be that, since Aquinas sees the soul as animating the body (its "first principle of life"), the soul must be also bodily in nature, since "contact is only between bodies."[256] It seems that the soul must somehow physically *touch* the body in order to effect the body's movement. However, Aquinas differentiates between contact of "quantity" between physical objects, and contact of "power." A writer's thoughts, for example, can compel him to put down words on his computer screen by an inward compulsion, even though there is nothing *physically* compelling him to do so; no physical contact is required. Although the materialistic or "bodily" view of the soul "can be proved to be false in many ways,"[257] the primary argument Aquinas uses in the *Summa Theologica* is a relatively simple one. The principle of life and animation cannot belong to bodies as such; if it did, that would mean that every physical body would possess this principle, and thus every physical body would be living and animated. A boulder, for example, would be just as living and animated as a human. There is nothing inherently implausible or illogical about a living, animated boulder; therefore, since boulders are not living and animated, animate life must arise from some principle not found in mere corporeality:

> Therefore a body is competent to be a living thing or even a principle of life, as *such* a body. Now that it is actually such a body,

---

[254] Genetic information is not the sole efficient cause of the human's development of physical characteristics, since other biological and environmental factors also play their part. However, for the most part the DNA code is the most obvious efficient cause of said development, and will be presented as such throughout this work.

[255] ST I.75, Prologue.

[256] ST I.75.1.

[257] ST I.75.1.

it owes to some principle which is called its act. Therefore the soul, which is the first principle of life, is not a body, but the act of a body.[258]

A devout theologian might at this point argue that Aquinas's description seems to ascribe too much authority to the soul, since as a "first principle of life" and first act of the body, the soul seems itself to be an unmoved mover of the body, "Unmoved Mover" being a description reserved only for God. However, Aquinas distinguishes between things that are "moved essentially," such as the body, and things that are "moved accidentally . . . and [do] not cause an invariable movement," such as the soul.[259] If God is the cause of beings *qua* beings, God is also, by that very fact, the cause of the proper differences of being as such. One of those proper differences would be the difference between what is contingent and what is necessary. Therefore, since caused to exist by God, even the contingent (or "accidental") actions of a free human agent are not the actions of an unmoved mover or a prime mover unmoved.[260]

Aquinas maintains the subsistence or independent existence of the soul, even though the soul is incorporeal. The soul exists both as an incorporeal intellect and as the form of the body. As form, it must be embodied in matter, but as intellect, it is incorporeal. The soul and the body are not the same—and so, although the soul requires the body's sensory apparatus for bodily perceptions of exterior objects, neither the sensory apparatus nor the perceptions themselves are to be identified with the "act of understanding" which takes place in the soul.[261] Since the act of understanding is not a *bodily* operation, and since this act of understanding does in fact take place in humans, the soul in which the act of understanding takes place must be capable of an existence separate from the body: "Since the intellectual soul has an operation independent of the body, it is subsistent."[262] A non-physical operation must take place in a non-physical arena of operation. As one theologian somewhat over-optimistically writes, "There cannot be any serious doubt regarding the existence of an intellectual soul in man"; he goes on

---

[258] ST I.75.1.

[259] ST I.75.1.

[260] Craig Payne. "Fatalist Attraction: Determinism, Freedom, and Moral Choice." *De Philosophia* 14.2 (Fall/Winter 1998): 253-71, p. 271n12.

[261] ST I.75.2. On this point, see also Joseph M. Magee's *Unmixing the Intellect: Aristotle on Cognitive Powers and Bodily Organs* (Westport, Connecticut: Greenwood Press, 2003).

[262] ST I.118.2.

to explain: "Man has vital actions and therefore must have a vital principle or soul. Because man has the vital activities of understanding and willing, which transcend the level of sense life and cannot be reduced to it, man must have a soul which differs from that of mere animals."[263]

Aquinas discusses this act of understanding in *De Veritate* as well:

Truth is in both the reason and the faculties of sense perception, but not in the same manner. It is in the reason as the result of the act of knowledge, and simultaneously as known by the reason. . . . In the faculties of sense perception [on the other hand] truth is known as the result of their act [but] not as known by the senses. Though the faculties of sense perception make true judgments regarding things [objects of knowledge], yet they do not know the truth by which they make true judgments.[264]

The senses serve to provide perceptions, but do not reflect upon their own acts of perception. Reason, however, not only provides the act of understanding, but also reflects upon its own act to provide a completed comprehension of the objects of knowledge. "The conceptual faculty—whether we call it intellect, mind, or soul—is capable of a certain reflexivity: It knows that it knows," according to one writer. "Such powers depend on the neurophysical system to some degree, but clearly their operations extend beyond the identifiable limits of neuroscientific classification."[265] Not only does this act of understanding separate the human soul from the human body and its sense perceptions (separate logically, not in the actual substance of the human), but it also separates the human form from the purely animal form. Those operations which seem to take place within the animating principle of animals do not necessarily have to exist separately from the animal's body; consequently, Aquinas concludes that animals do not require a spiritual existence after the death of the body, as humans do.[266] Whether or not one agrees with his assessment of the spiritual existence of animals after their death would, in this argument, depend on whether

---

[263] Henry J. Koren, S.T.D. *An Introduction to the Philosophy of Animate Nature.* London and St. Louis: Herder, 1955. Revised edition, 1960, p. 246.
[264] *De Veritate* 1.9. Robert W. Mulligan, S.J.; James V. McGlynn, S.J.; and Robert W. Schmidt, S.J., transs. Chicago: Henry Regnery Company, 1952-54. All quotes from *De Veritate* throughout this work are taken from this translation. Questions 1-9 translated by Mulligan (1952); Questions 10-20 translated by McGlynn (1953); Questions 21-29 translated by Schmidt (1954).
[265] Adam G. Cooper. "Redeeming Flesh." *First Things* 173 (May 2007): 27-31, p. 30.
[266] ST I.75.3.

or not one thought of higher animals as possessing any sort of faculty of *understanding* in addition to their highly developed faculties of *perception*. However, whether or not one agrees with Aquinas regarding animal existence does not take away from his previous argument regarding the human soul, since it is readily apparent that at least humans do possess this faculty of understanding and hence possess a non-corporeal nature in addition to the corporeal. Therefore, the corruption of the corporeal brain and other organs after human death does not entail likewise the corruption of the non-corporeal nature, which is thus incorruptible in that sense.[267]

To say this does not imply one must take the further step to say that the spiritual nature *is* the human, and that humans are therefore spiritual creatures bound by *maya*, the chains of material illusion (to use the Hindu term). Aquinas quotes Augustine's *City of God*, "Man is neither the soul alone nor the body alone, but each of these is a part, and the man is the whole of which they are the parts,"[268] and goes on to say:

> To the nature of the species belongs what the definition signifies; and in natural things the definition does not signify the form only, but the form and the matter.[269]

So the human soul is non-corporeal, a spiritual nature which when united with a physical nature makes up a human. The soul is the principle of life and animation, the first act of the corporeal organic body, and therefore humans are to be identified neither solely with the soul nor solely with the body. Humans are composite creatures, with soul and body somehow united.

## 2. The Union of the Soul and Body (ST I.76, 91, 118)

The soul as an intellectual principle, according to Aquinas, is in fact united to the body; this remains the case even though the soul can exist separately after the body's death. "As life appears through various operations in different degrees of living things, that whereby we primarily perform each of all these vital actions is the soul"; however, the specific nature of the human soul's operation is rational understanding. Thus "the proper operation of man as man is to understand."[270]

---

[267] ST I.75.6.
[268] From 19.3. All quotes from *The City of God* throughout this work are taken from the translation of Gerald G. Walsh, Demetrius B. Zema, Grace Monahan, and Daniel J. Honan. New York: Image Books/Doubleday, 1958.
[269] ST I.75.4.
[270] ST I.76.1.

How is it that the soul survives the temporary loss of the body in death? Aquinas points out that the power of the form's operation exceeds the elementary matter of which its body is composed. For example, the *life* of a plant exceeds a mere summary of all the minerals and chemicals of which the plant is composed.[271] Even if the identical minerals and chemicals were mixed together and shaped into a plant-like structure, they would not add up to an actually living organism, i.e., an organism with innately directed growth, development, reproduction, and so on: "Mechanism may give a true account of most biological phenomena, but it does not for all that necessarily give a true philosophical account of natural reality in its fullness."[272] Likewise the human soul has an operation and power (intellection) "in which corporeal matter has no share whatever"[273]; even if the various materials of a human corporeal body were somehow cobbled together, one would not thereby have a human. Therefore it seems plausible that the non-corporeal soul, existing as an intellective power, can survive even the death of the corporeal body.[274] It should be noted, however, that in

---

[271] Scientist Craig Venter, famous for his work on the Human Genome Project, has created an artificial chromosome for *Mycoplasma genitalium*, currently the tiniest bacterium known to biology. According to Venter, the bacterium managed to survive with 20% of its DNA replaced by the artificial chromosome, which was made up of 381 genes. However, even in this instance, the artificial chromosome was added to the previously existing life form, and depended on the metabolism and replication capabilities of the existing entity. Venter is seeking for a "minimal genome" for the production of a truly artificial living cell, an artificial genome inserted in the shell of a bacterium. If such a discovery is made, and such a cell is innately capable of actual life, the relationship between the Thomistic substantial form and life itself could require reformulation to accommodate these new possibilities.

[272] Steven Baldner, "An Argument for Substantial Form," p. 4. As Baldner further says, "If . . . philosophical knowledge is general whereas scientific knowledge is specific, then it might be reasonable to expect that a specific and detailed analysis could profitably leave out of account certain realities that must be included when one is giving a general account. Contemporary empirical sciences, which are very highly specialized, regularly leave out of consideration—and rightly—any consideration of general philosophical categories. Their methods require a prescinding from the general. In so doing, they tend to view nature in a reductionist and mechanist way. There is nothing wrong with such a focusing of attention. The only mistake, I would claim, would be that of supposing that reductionism or mechanism is a *complete* account of nature" (p. 4, emphasis in original).

[273] ST I.76.1.

[274] ST I.89.1.

order for this soul to be *a human person*, it must be re-united with its matter to become the human substantial form.

The objection might be raised that the soul/body relationship seems somehow improper, perhaps even indiscreet, like the marriage of an angel and a donkey—the idea is that the intellective powers of a human's soul are so far removed from the human's animal physicality that some other arrangement would surely have been more fitting. Aquinas even quotes from the Bible the seemingly insulting verse, "God made man of the slime of the earth."[275] Further, to bring to an end the animal physicality humans possess, a corporeal nature which seems almost unnecessary to the human spiritual self, comes the final degradation of physical death. How is it that the human intellectual nature looks up to heaven even as the human corporeal nature sinks back to earth?

However, Aquinas addresses these objections in a rather bracingly matter-of-fact tone. If it is said that God could have avoided the present form/matter arrangement, the reply is, "In the formation of natural things we do not consider what God might do, but [rather] what is suitable to the nature of things." Humans are not naturally gifted with knowledge, as are the angels (in the human case, this would have to be a "super-natural" gifting, although it is "natural" for a completely non-corporeal intellect); therefore, humans require bodily senses in order "to gather knowledge from individual things." As far as human death is concerned, God has "provided in this case by applying a remedy against death in the gift of grace."[276]

Human souls and bodies are simultaneously as closely joined to each other and as distinct from each other as a piece of wax and the shape of the wax.[277] On the one hand, the wax and its shape are in one respect inseparable and form a unified whole. On the other hand, the wax and its shape can certainly be separated logically, as they possess different orders of being. When we see a statue in marble, we do not say to ourselves, "Here is a chunk of marble no different from any other chunk of marble." In fact, usually we would not think of the statue as "a chunk of marble" at all; we would think of it as an image of a horse, or historical figure, or whatever else might be its shape. Likewise the human form is united to the human body without itself necessarily participating in the corporeal nature of that body. We do not look at a living thing, such as a human, and think to ourselves, "Here approaches

---

[275] ST I.91.1, where Aquinas is quoting Genesis 2:7.
[276] ST I.76.5.
[277] ST I.76.7, where Aquinas borrows this analogy from Aristotle.

an animated chunk of matter." We think of these things in terms of their form and matter making up unified wholes: "Here approaches a human."

Aquinas makes a clear demarcation between the "sensitive [sensation-receiving] soul," which humans share with all creatures with sensory apparatus, and the intellectual soul. The sensitive soul is generated by the act of procreation, as is the case with all animals,[278] while the intellectual soul "comes from without," being begotten "through creation by God."[279] As the intellect is non-corporeal, it cannot be generated in a corporeal fashion. Aquinas thinks of the intellectual soul as supervening upon the sensitive soul, without thereby losing the powers of the sensitive soul, and so in Aquinas's view the developing human embryo does not possess the human form until it is infused by God with the intellectual soul.

However, Aquinas in these instances errs in his view of the development of the corporeal embryo; he is passing along the faulty embryological information available to him, virtually unchanged from the time of Aristotle. As Robert Edward Brennan writes:

> In matters of empirical observation, both Aristotle and Aquinas were men of their age, which was definitely a pre-scientific age. This means that extreme caution must be used to dissociate the permanent philosophic analyses from the useless and outmoded scientific formulas with which these analyses are often overlaid. The record of Aristotle's and Aquinas's theories in the field of science is, for the most part, without value, except as a moment in the history of their mental development.[280]

Aquinas does not think of the developing embryo as possessing the human form until that form is recognizable visually. The form of a human, he thought, could not be thought of as present until there was enough of the *physical* human to express that human's (specifically human) differentiation from other creatures. With our knowledge of DNA, of course, we today would recognize that the differentiation is there from the beginning, and so we would see Aquinas as wrong on this particular biological point. However, simple mistakes in biology and other physical sciences can be corrected with additional empirical information. Philosophical mistakes, on the other hand, set the wrong course of one's investigations from the beginning; for example, the *a priori* exclusion of the soul's or form's relationship to the body or matter

---

[278] ST I.118.1.

[279] ST I.118.2.

[280] Brennan, *Thomistic Psychology*, p. 4.

of the human being leads inevitably to an account of humanity which will be greatly incomplete.

Since "the fundamental principles of his philosophy of man are independent of his obsolete biology,"[281] Aquinas's mistaken scientific views need not threaten one's adoption of a Thomistic anthropology. The embryological development of humans is not the point; the point is the nature of the human thus developing.

[281] "An Approach to a Key Theological Question." American Bioethics Advisory Commission Report, Part 10. all.org/abac/clontx10.htm, n.p. Accessed 13 Dec. 2013.

# Chapter 5: The Soul's Power to Make True Moral Judgments

The very essence of man as a moral, social being points to the nature of law. For all men are born natural-law jurists because in the human soul lies the ineradicable demand that the law must live in morality. All law must be just: only then can it obtain that power which primarily holds together and continually renews every community, and in particular every political community, the power to bind in conscience. But the proper function of the natural-law doctrine is precisely to show forth the connection between morality and law. Consequently it must, for the sake of the very existence of man and his concrete legally ordered communities, ever recur, and it does in fact always return wherever the genius of law seeks out its own foundations.[282]

## 1. The Soul's Powers

As his discussion of human nature develops, Aquinas makes what seems at first reading to be a rather startling claim regarding the powers and operations of the human soul: He asserts that humans have a wider variety of powers than non-corporeal intelligences such as angels. However, this means nothing regarding human superiority over angels; in fact, it means just the opposite. Because humans are composite, soul/body creatures, they occupy a position between material and intellectual powers, embracing both. They are like angels in some respects, capable of a perfected goodness, yet they require "many movements" toward that end, as compared to the angels' "few movements," and therefore require many powers:

Man can acquire universal and perfect goodness, because he can acquire beatitude. Yet he is in the last degree, according to his

---

[282] Heinrich Rommen, *The Natural Law*, p. 236.

nature, of those to whom beatitude is possible; therefore the human soul requires many and various operations and powers. But to angels a smaller variety of powers is sufficient. In God there is no power or action beyond His own Essence. There is yet another reason why the human soul abounds in a variety of powers: because it is [exists] on the confines of spiritual and corporeal creatures; and therefore the powers of both meet together in the soul.[283]

The essence of the human soul is not power itself. On the other hand, God's Essence is power, just as His Essence is love, and goodness, and wisdom, and any other perfection; God is not just loving and strong, but Love and Strength. (For example, see 1 John 4:8, "God is love," or Exodus 15:2, "The Lord is my strength.") In fact, whatever can be predicated of God truly can be predicated of God *absolutely*—this is the meaning behind Aquinas's discussion of God's "simplicity."[284]

Furthermore, in a simple being, being and that which is are the same. For, if one is not the other, the simplicity is then removed. But, as we have shown, God is absolutely simple. Therefore, for God to be good is identical with God. He is, therefore, His goodness.[285]

However, in all lesser beings, the essence of the soul is separate from its attributes—humans, for example, are composite rather than Simple in nature. A human might be loving, but not love; free, but not freedom; good, but not goodness.

This remains true even though the human soul considered in itself may be thought of as simple in nature. "All the powers of the soul, whether their subject be the soul alone, or the composite, flow from the essence of the soul, as from their principle. . . . From the one essence of the soul many and various powers proceed."[286] However, many of these powers are manifested only through means of the soul/body composite. Humans are thus not simple in nature, as is God. The human soul possesses many attributes, or powers, and therefore, "We proceed now to consider those things which belong to the powers of the soul."[287]

---

[283] ST I.77.2.

[284] See ST I.3.4, where this concept is presented as the divine identity of "essence" and "existence." On the difficulties of the doctrine of divine simplicity, and possible solutions to these difficulties, see Jeffrey E. Brower's "Making Sense of Divine Simplicity" (*Faith and Philosophy* 25.1 [January 2008]: 3-30).

[285] SCG I.38.6.

[286] ST I.77.6.

Since powers are directed toward actions, "we seek to know the nature of a power from the act to which it is directed." Occasionally the objection is raised, "But humans have such diverse powers, directed toward such diverse ends or objects—how on earth could we possibly derive any moral principles from human potentialities, as natural law theory attempts to do? The range of human potentialities is simply too broad." By way of response, one might again point out the distinction (which Aquinas also raises here again) between that which is substantial and that which is incidental: "We must observe that things which are accidental do not change the species. . . . In like manner, therefore, not any variety of objects diversifies the powers of the soul, but a difference in that to which the power of its very nature is directed."[288] The very nature of humanity, as has been previously discussed, is rational. The diverse uses and misuses of human rationality do not transform its nature; nor does the "broadness" of human potentiality. Therefore, there is a hierarchy or order to the soul's powers.[289] Not all of the soul's various powers are necessarily constitutive of the nature of the soul itself; some of them "are performed by means of corporeal organs," such as sight.[290] These powers are constitutive of the composite of soul *and body*; however, they are not permanently lost at death, the loss of the body and its sensory organs, since they await only the restoration of the body at the resurrection to be "re-ignited" within the soul/body composite. They remain "virtually" in the soul "as in their principle or root."[291]

As has been described, Aquinas divides souls into three different kinds: the vegetative soul, the sensitive soul, and the rational soul.[292] Moreover, each successive kind supervenes upon those coming before. For example, plants, possessing the vegetative soul, live but do not sense; some animals both live and sense, possessing both vegetative and sensitive souls, but do not move (Aquinas's rather dubious example of this "non-locomotive" type is shellfish); some animals live, sense, and move; lastly, humans live, sense, move, and think: "There are some living things which with these [i.e., along with possessing the vegetative and sensitive souls] have intellectual power—namely, men."[293] The

---

[287] From the Prologue to ST I.77.
[288] ST I.77.3.
[289] ST I.77.4.
[290] ST I.77.5.
[291] ST I.77.8.
[292] ST I.78.1.
[293] ST I.78.1.

vegetative soul contains within itself three powers: the power to pro-create, to "produce another like unto itself" ("generative" power); the power to ingest and digest sustenance, and thus to develop ("aug-mentative" power); and the power to grow as a unified living organism ("nutritive" power).[294] Likewise the sensitive soul contains five powers, namely the five senses.[295]

However, the intellectual powers are contained exclusively within the rational soul and are therefore powers speciating the human animal apart from other animal forms.[296] The intellectual power of human nature is both "passive" (perhaps "receptive" would be a clearer term) and "active." In the "passive" mode, the intellect is something like the Lockean *tabula rasa*; as Aristotle says, the intellect is "like a clean tablet on which nothing is written,"[297] and so the intellect exists in a state of "potentiality with regard to things intelligible."[298] On the other hand, Aquinas does not take this view to the Lockean extreme, for the intellect is also "active"—that is, the soul contains both passive and active powers within itself. This active power converts the impressions humans receive via their senses from being potentially intelligible to being actually intelligible; in other words, the intellect converts human sense impressions from potentiality to act, from potential knowledge to actual understanding:

> Now the human soul is called intellectual by reason of a participation in intellectual power. . . . Moreover it reaches to the understanding of truth by arguing, with a certain amount of reasoning and movement. . . . [So it is] necessary to assign to the human soul some power participating in that superior intellect, by which power the human soul makes things actually intelligible.[299]

There exists an ongoing philosophical controversy over whether the mind's operations gain knowledge via *a priori* or *a posteriori* means. Even though for the most part Aquinas may be placed solidly in the ranks of the empiricist, *a posteriori* epistemologists, here one can see that he

---

[294] ST I.78.2.

[295] ST I.78.3-4.

[296] In his *Devotions*, John Donne refers to this principle: "Man, before he hath his immortal soul, hath a soul of sense, and a soul of vegetation before that: this immortal soul did not forbid other souls to be in us before, but when this soul departs, it carries all with it; no more vegetation, no more sense" (Meditation XVIII, *Devotions upon Emergent Occasions and Several Steps in My Sickness* [1624]. Ann Arbor, Michigan: Univ. of Michigan Press, 1959, p. 116).

[297] *De Anima* III.4.

[298] ST I.79.2.

[299] ST I.79.4.

makes the major exception that in addition to the "passive" powers of the intellect, the soul also actively engages through the active intellect the impressions passively received. The human soul's ability to gain understanding thus seems to be *a priori* in nature, although the actual gaining of understanding first requires our *a posteriori* impressions: "Man's intellect, the lowest of all intellects, comes into being in a state of pure potentiality, actually knowing nothing, able to know all."[300] Consequently, in the debate over *a priori* and *a posteriori* categories of knowledge, as is the case in most philosophical controversies, we find Aquinas staking out a position somewhere in the middle.

Somewhat remarkably, the human intellect, in its limited fashion, participates in the mode of intellectual activity enjoyed fully only by God. Since God by definition has no potential for improvement or for additional knowledge to be imparted to Him, God exists eternally in the state of completely Active Intellect; God has no "potentiality" which could be converted to "act," possessing as He does the complete knowledge humans do not possess. However, by means of participation, "the active intellect is something in the [human] soul,"[301] incorporating within itself both memory and rationality.[302] Aquinas has already discussed understanding as the soul's operation, and now points out that rationality is a virtually identical operation: "For to understand is simply to apprehend intelligible truth, and to reason is to advance from one thing understood to another, so as to know an intelligible truth."[303]

Can this *description* of the rational human soul become a *prescription* for ethical human behavior? This question raises the specter of G.E. Moore's "naturalistic fallacy," the Humean principle that one cannot derive "ought" conclusions from "is" premises, or assertions of what we "should do" from statements of "what is in fact the case."[304]

---

[300] James H. Robb. *Man as Infinite Spirit: The Aquinas Lecture, 1974*. Milwaukee: Marquette University Press, 1974, p. 42.
[301] ST I.79.4.
[302] ST I.79.7-8.
[303] ST I.79.8.
[304] G.E. Moore. *Principia Ethica* [1903]. Amherst, New York: Prometheus Books, 1988, Chapter 1, § 10. The passage from Hume himself reads, "In every system of morality, which I have hitherto met with, I have always remark'd, that the author proceeds for some time in the ordinary way of reasoning, and establishes the being of a God, or makes observations concerning human affairs; when of a sudden I am surpriz'd to find, that instead of the usual copulations of propositions, is, and is not, I meet with no proposition that is not connected with an ought, or an ought not. This change is imperceptible; but is, however, of the last consequence. For as this ought, or ought not,

However, Aquinas here neatly avoids the naturalistic-fallacy trap by arguing that the theoretical ("speculative") and practical intellects "are not distinct powers,"[305] and so whether or not the intellect is directed to only the object of understanding (the theoretical intellect) or to the object of an operation (the practical intellect) does not involve the substance of the intellect:

> Now, to a thing apprehended by the intellect, it is accidental whether it be directed to operation or not, and according to this the speculative and practical intellects differ. For it is the speculative intellect which directs what it apprehends, not to operation, but to the consideration of truth; while the practical intellect is that which directs what it apprehends to operation. [However] the speculative and practical intellects are not distinct powers.[306]

Earlier, in the Introduction to this work, the goal was noted to bring out the idea that the *telos* of humanity, the mature, normal condition of the species *Homo sapiens*, not only defines but simultaneously prescribes, so that the moral applications will arise naturally out of the definition of human being and even be contained *within* the definition. Here is a wonderful illustration of this principle in action. For example, a Thomistic argument against murder might go like this (with regard to this point): The theoretical examination of human nature reveals within human souls, in the law "written on their hearts" (Romans 2:15), a rejection of the unlawful taking of an innocent human life. However, this is not merely a statement of a factual understanding of the human emotive self ("We don't like murder") which in itself cannot lead to the moral prescription "We should not murder"; rather, the moral prescription "We should not murder" is *itself* a factual understanding humans have of themselves, known by the *practical* intellect, and therefore just as much an object of knowledge as anything known by the speculative intellect.

---

expresses some new relation or affirmation, 'tis necessary that it shou'd be observ'd and explain'd; and at the same time that a reason should be given, for what seems altogether inconceivable, how this new relation can be a deduction from others, which are entirely different from it. But as authors do not commonly use this precaution, I shall presume to recommend it to the readers; and am persuaded, that this small attention wou'd subvert all the vulgar systems of morality, and let us see, that the distinction of vice and virtue is not founded merely on the relations of objects, nor is perceiv'd by reason" (David Hume, *A Treatise of Human Nature* [1739-40]. T.H. Green and T.H. Grose, eds. London: Longmans, Green, and Co., 1898: III.1.1).

[305] ST I.79.11.
[306] ST I.79.11.

As Alasdair MacIntyre puts it, the "peculiar task of human beings" is "to evaluate, to choose, and to act *qua* rational beings."[307] He notes later, paraphrasing Aristotle and through Aristotle Aquinas, that a human's "taking pleasure or pain in something is never by itself a reason, let alone a good reason, for action."[308] Thus the *telos* of humanity really has nothing to do with Bentham's "two sovereign masters" of pleasure and pain.[309] "The speculative intellect by extension becomes practical," as Aquinas puts it, "but one power is not changed into another."[310] For Aquinas, to describe a human just *is* to describe a being with a *telos*, a natural end, and thus humans possess practical knowledge of their natural rights and wrongs based upon recognition of their natural end, not based upon hedonistic utilitarian considerations:

> So "such and such is the good of all human beings by nature" is always a factual judgment, which when recognized as true by someone moves that person toward that good. Evaluative judgments are a species of factual judgment concerning the final and formal causes of activity of members of a particular species. . . . There is then no form of philosophical enquiry—at least as envisaged from an Aristotelian, Augustinian, or Thomistic point of view—which is not practical in its implications.[311]

The naturalistic fallacy has become a sort of "incantation" in today's philosophical *milieu*, according to Nancey Murphy, and simply results in "confusion," since modernity in general has forgotten "that the 'ought' statement—'You ought to do (or be) *x*'—is only half of a moral truth." The original and complete ethical claim would also provide the warrant for the "ought" statement: " 'If you are to achieve your *telos*, then you ought to do (or be) *x*.'" As Murphy argues, "This latter sort of ethical claim can be straightforwardly true or false; the 'ought' is no more mysterious than the 'ought' in 'A watch ought to keep good time.'"[312] If this *is* a watch, then this *ought* to do and not do certain things, given the nature and end of a watch. If this *is* a rational creature (such as a human

---

[307] MacIntyre, *Whose Justice? Which Rationality?* p. 133.

[308] Ibid., p. 305.

[309] "Nature has placed mankind under the governance of two sovereign masters, *pain* and *pleasure*. It is for them alone to point out what we should do." So run the opening two sentences of Bentham's *An Introduction to the Principles of Morals and Legislation* (1.1, 1780). J.H. Burns and H.L.A. Hart, eds. London: Athlone Press, 1970, p. 11.

[310] ST I.79.11.

[311] MacIntyre, *Three Rival Versions of Moral Enquiry*, pp. 128 and 134.

[312] Nancey Murphy. *Anglo-American Postmodernity: Philosophical Perspectives on Science, Religion, and Ethics*. Boulder, Colorado: Westview Press, 1997, p. 205.

being), then the same principle should hold true. Even though one cannot (as Hume argues) in the strictly logical sense derive an "ought" statement from simple "copulative" statements, to hold to this as an absolute principle "ignores the way in which states of affairs are ordered in ways that move us to acknowledge their goodness. . . . This obligation may or may not be moral, but it is obligation nevertheless"[313] Thus statements regarding what something is may lawfully elide into statements regarding what one ought to do or not do with that something.

So the voice of conscience within humanity speaks exactly as its root meaning says it should speak: *Con scientia*—"with knowledge." Basic natural law moral prescriptions are "what we can't not know," as J. Budziszewski writes; at some level of our being, "Everyone knows them; even the murderer knows the wrong of murder,"[314] unless perhaps the murderer has a defective *understanding*, i.e., is psychotic. In the cases of many murderers, this may very well be the fact, since a soul (*psyche*) which is actually incapable of recognizing the first principles of morality would be a severely damaged (psychotic) soul. However, even in these cases, Aquinas only allows for defective moral understanding in those whose actual organs connected with reasoning ability are actually damaged; apart from this particular type of brain damage, the knowledge of moral claims is as absolute as the knowledge of first principles of inferential reasoning.[315] As Stephen Pope puts it, murder "involves a voluntary and deliberate choice to do something that is *known* to be immoral."[316] Our theoretical knowledge of ourselves as humans is indissolubly linked with the practical knowledge of ourselves as humans who understand right and wrong, and who prescribe right actions: "We must have, bestowed on us by nature, not only speculative principles, but also practical principles."[317] Thus Aquinas here rejects "the emotive theory of value [which reduces] conscience to a subjective feeling"[318]— right and wrong are not merely what humans *want* them to be, but what humans *know* them to be: "Conscience is said to be the law of our

---

[313] Derek S. Jeffreys. *Defending Human Dignity: John Paul II and Political Realism.* Grand Rapids, Michigan: Baker Book House, 2004, p. 126.
[314] J. Budziszewski. *What We Can't Not Know: A Guide.* Dallas: Spence Publishing, 2003, p. 3.
[315] *De Ver.* 16.3.
[316] Stephen J. Pope. *The Evolution of Altruism and the Ordering of Love.* Washington, D.C.: Georgetown University Press, 1994, p. 101. Emphasis added.
[317] ST I.79.12.
[318] Peter Kreeft, *A Summa*, p. 282n32.

minds because it is the verdict of the reason, deduced from the law of nature."[319] In some respects, the assertion of the objectivity of natural conscience is a commonplace; in other respects, it is a "staggering assertion," as one writer puts it: "The claim that all people, of whatever culture, historical milieu, or religion, know the basics of what is right and wrong at the core of their being is a staggering assertion."[320]

The habitual disposition of the practical intellect and its activity of conscience, by which humanity has knowledge of the first principles of moral action, Aquinas calls *synderesis*. These first principles of moral action are equivalent to the foundational natural law prescriptions, as known naturally by normal humans:

> Much in the same way that we, without musical training, can judge certain tones to be off pitch, we have moral "perceptions" that some actions are good and some bad, without having any explicit training about such kinds of actions. I speak of these as moral "perceptions" not because they are equivalent to sense perceptions, but because of their immediacy and their unformulated quality; indeed, I believe them to be rational in several important respects, not least because they are cognitive acts and they are in accord with reality.[321]

Again, all humans possess this habitual disposition of the practical intellect: "The wicked, like all people, have knowledge of universal practical principles by means of synderesis, which is a 'natural habit' that parallels the natural knowledge of the first principles of reason."[322] Our wrongful habits of self-justification and avoidance arise in humanity's unnatural, fallen state precisely because humanity cannot avoid this moral knowledge: "In a particular activity [synderesis] may be said to be destroyed whenever one sins by choice. . . . But this does not destroy synderesis altogether, but only in some respect. Hence, absolutely speaking, we concede that synderesis is never destroyed."[323] Persisting "as a spark of illumination in every human being that enlightens, even if only dimly, the darkest of circumstances,"[324]

---

[319] *De Ver.* 17.1ad1.

[320] David VanDrunen, *A Biblical Case for Natural Law*, p. 1.

[321] Janet E. Smith. "Natural Law and Sexual Ethics." *Common Truths: New Perspectives on Natural Law*. Edward B. McLean, ed. Wilmington, Delaware: ISI Books, 2000: 193-215, pp. 196-97.

[322] Nicholas M. Healy, *Thomas Aquinas: Theologian of the Christian Life*, p. 159n11.

[323] *De Ver.* 16.3. For a more detailed exposition of this concept, see Luc-Thomas Somme's "The Infallibility, Impeccability and Indestructibility of Synderesis" (*Studies in Christian Ethics* 19.3 [2006]: 403-16).

[324] Somme, "The Infallibility, Impeccability and Indestructibility of Synderesis,"

synderesis includes both knowledge of the first principles of moral facts and the inner pressure to obey those facts; it is said "to incite to good, and to murmur at evil, inasmuch as through first principles we proceed to discover, and to judge of what we have discovered."[325] Synderesis is not therefore another of the powers of the speculative intellect, but rather the habitual disposition toward grasping the first principles of moral knowledge all humans know through the practical intellect, and also the habit of action, the *habitus*, based on that knowledge[326]; the action itself (of which synderesis forms the habit) is the action of obeying the voice of conscience: "Properly speaking conscience is not a power, but an act."[327] The "act" of conscience arises out of synderesis, the habitual disposition toward moral action which is founded on the moral truths "that are in the common domain, truths everybody knows."[328]

Aquinas explains this more clearly in another work:

> Thus, just as there is a natural habit of the human soul through which it knows principles of the speculative sciences, which we call understanding of principles, so also there is in the soul a natural habit of first principles of action, which are the universal principles of the natural law. This habit pertains to synderesis. . . . The act of the natural habit called synderesis is to warn against evil and to incline to good.[329]

This disposition toward the universal principles of the natural law, according to Aquinas, cannot be mistaken in its immediate actions, although humans may be mistaken in its *application*. He uses the example of those within Judaism who persecuted the disciples within the early

---

p. 404.

[325] ST I.79.12.

[326] "In Thomas's language, habitus (from the Greek *hexis*) is a key notion, which our English word 'habit' not only does not translate properly but suggests almost the contrary of the true meaning. Habit is a fixed mechanism, a routine; habitus is, instead, an inventive capacity, perfecting the human faculty in which it is rooted, to which it gives perfect liberty in its exercise. A worker's know-how is a habitus; so is the skill of a doctor or the knowledge of a scientist. Midway between a nature and its action, habitus is the sign and expression of its full flowering" (Jean-Pierre Torrell, O.P., *Saint Thomas Aquinas Volume 2: Spiritual Master*, p. 13).

[327] ST I.79.13.

[328] Ralph McInerny. "Are There Moral Truths that Everyone Knows?" *Common Truths: New Perspectives on Natural Law*. Edward B. McLean, ed. Wilmington, Delaware: ISI Books, 2000: 1-15, p. 5.

[329] *De Ver.* 16.1.

Church; since the persecutors "thought they were offering worship to God" by their actions, in one sense they were seeking to act rightly, for they were following "the universal judgment of synderesis, that worship should be offered to God." However, Aquinas argues that their actions were in fact wrongful because they were following a "false judgment... which considered the killing of the Apostles as pleasing to God." In an inferential syllogism in which one premise is true and the other false, the wrong conclusion is blamed on the wrong premise and not the right one. Just so, according to Aquinas, it is not synderesis itself which leads to wrongful applications of moral beliefs, for "there can be no error in it." In this the basic principles of practical moral knowledge are like the basic principles of theoretical knowledge:

> All speculative knowledge is derived from some most certain knowledge concerning which there can be no error. This is the knowledge of the first general principles, in reference to which everything else which is known is examined and by reason of which every truth is approved and every falsehood rejected. If any error could take place in these, there would be no certainty in the whole of the knowledge which follows. As a result, for probity to be possible in human actions, there must be some permanent principle which has unwavering integrity, in reference to which all human works are examined, so that that permanent principle will resist all evil and assent to all good. This is synderesis, whose task it is to warn against evil and incline to good. Therefore, we agree that there can be no error in it.[330]

Taken as stated, it almost sounds as if Aquinas were arguing for the inerrancy of synderesis based on utilitarian considerations—that is, since no certainty of moral knowledge could be possible unless humanity as a whole adopts the moral compass of synderesis as a basic, "unwavering" guide and agrees "that there can be no error in it," and since certainty of moral knowledge would be good even if only in a utilitarian sense for humanity to have, this stance toward the soul's moral knowledge should in fact be adopted. Would not one dedicated to moral relativism rightfully dismiss this argument with contempt?

However, as Aquinas points out, all inferential knowledge, especially in the speculative and theoretical realm, is derived from principles about which there can be no doubt. If some honestly doubt that A = A (which Aquinas does not think possible for normally functioning humans), one cannot *force* recognition of that truth upon them, just as one cannot force the recognition of green upon one who is color-blind.

---

[330] Ibid., 16.2.

As Aquinas writes, "Hence, the human soul, according to that which is highest in it, attains to that which is proper to angelic nature, so that it knows some things at once and without investigation." In the recognition of some things "at once and without investigation," the human soul is linked to angelic intelligence because "divine wisdom joins the ends of nobler things with the beginnings of lesser things"[331]; so it is that humanity is joined together with animal natures at one end of its existence due to its corporeal nature, and with created non-corporeal rational intelligences (i.e., angels) at the other end. Therefore, humans, upon consideration of their sensory experiences, can know by way of their intellective soul some truths immediately and without further argument or proof, such as the truth "The whole is greater than the part."

Furthermore (proceeding to the primary point, which is moral in nature), the same thing is also true regarding the practical intellect, since angels also possess a "double knowledge": the first is speculative and the second practical. By means of the practical intellect, angels serve God and are assigned their various duties, "according to which the orders of angels are distinguished." Aquinas, who in this passage is not really all that concerned with the nature of angelic intelligence, concludes: "Hence it is that *human* nature, in so far as it comes in contact with the angelic nature, must both in speculative and practical matters know truth without investigation. . . . Furthermore, this knowledge must be habitual so that it will be ready for use when needed. Thus, just as there is a natural habit of the human soul through which it knows principles of the speculative sciences, which we call understanding of principles, so, too, there is in the soul a natural habit of first principles of action, which are the universal principles of the natural law."[332] Although humans certainly may make moral errors, Aquinas "shifts the possibility of error to conscience, which he characterizes as an act that applies knowledge to action."[333] Thus the knowledge of basic principles will not be in error, even if the specific application is in error.

A passage from Alasdair MacIntyre makes this point clearly:

> On this Thomistic view, we all of us—except in certain exceptional, albeit very important, types of situations—know what the fundamental precepts of the natural law are and that they are true: that it is true that we ought not to take innocent life, that we ought to tell

---

[331] Ibid., 16.1.

[332] Ibid., 16.1.

[333] Somme, "The Infallibility, Impeccability and Indestructibility of Synderesis," pp. 405-406.

the truth and to keep promises, that we ought to respect the property of others, although not quite unconditionally, and so on. We also all know, on this Thomistic view, that all positive laws that conform to what reason requires by way of justice—and only laws that conform to reason and justice are genuine laws—either give expression to these precepts or provide for their application to a variety of concrete situations. We as plain persons know, on a Thomistic view, what must seem a surprising amount.[334]

Therefore (to summarize this discussion), the knowledge of moral truths is just that—*knowledge*, not emotive preference—and not a sort of societal indoctrination or cultural heritage, although both of these have their pedagogical part to play.[335] The primary moral natural law principles are known to the practical intellect by synderesis, which forms the natural habit of first principles of action; from this natural habit proceeds the specific act of the conscience, a moral act "with knowledge." Actions contrary to conscience are not therefore contrary to society or culture as such, but rather contrary to the soul's certain knowledge. As Aquinas writes, "Just as in the speculative part of the soul understanding of principles never errs, so in the operative part of the soul synderesis never errs."[336]

A wonderful example of this concept in action is found in Mark Twain's *Adventures of Huckleberry Finn*. Huck is debating within himself whether or not to give up to the law the runaway slave Jim, his friend. His "conscience," deformed by the society in which he has been raised, insists that he give up Jim to the authorities and return him to his life as a slave. However, Huck's *true* conscience, the act based on the knowledge of first principles of right action, eventually wins out; not only does Huck not give up Jim to the authorities, but he helps Jim escape, even while thinking that he will "go to Hell" for doing so.[337]

None of this knowledge of moral truths entails that humanity in itself is naturally capable of meritorious good actions before God, a viewpoint Aquinas dismisses as a form of Pelagianism. Since synderesis

---

[334] MacIntyre, "Theories of Natural Law in the Culture of Advanced Modernity," pp. 92-93.
[335] "A rule like the prohibition of murder reflects not a mere illusion or projection, but genuine knowledge. It expresses the actual moral character of a certain kind of act" (Budziszewski, "Natural Law," p. 473).
[336] *De Ver.* 16.1.
[337] *Adventures of Huckleberry Finn* (1876). Norton Critical Edition, 2nd ed. Sculley Bradley, Richmond Croom Beatty, E. Hudson Long, and Thomas Cooley, eds. New York: Norton, 1977, p. 169.

is not a power of action in itself, but rather a habitual disposition or a habit of action based on the soul's moral knowledge, God's gracious empowerment is still necessary for a human to perform a meritorious good action; as Aquinas writes, "A habit together with a power is enough for the act of that habit. But the act of the natural habit called synderesis is to warn against evil and to incline to good. Therefore, men are naturally capable of this act. However, it does not follow from this that a man with purely natural gifts can perform a meritorious act. To impute this to natural capability alone is the Pelagian impiety"[338]—that is, to think that humans can perform meritorious actions before God with purely natural gifts is to deny the necessity of God's grace to counter the effects of original sin. Synderesis in itself, as a natural gift, cannot enable humans to perform meritorious acts before God, although it can and does point out to humans what actions would be, in fact, truly meritorious and what actions evil: "The inner voice that approves good and opposes evil is the inner eye that the first murderer cannot flee."[339]

## 2. A Summary of Aquinas's Anthropology

At this point, a summary of five of the features of Thomistic anthropology outlined in the previous chapters will be of benefit. These comprise the features which will be most immediately useful to any subsequent argument:

First: *The soul of a human is not the human.* A human is not only a soul, but a complete entity composed of both soul and body. "The soul on its own can no more be called a person than a hand or a foot on its own. The person is the possessor of the complete nature of the species."[340] The human substance comprises both form and matter and is thus both non-corporeal and corporeal.

Second: *The human soul and body naturally belong together.* This helps explain the necessity for the Christian doctrine of bodily resurrection as opposed to the idea of a "spiritual" existence in eternity with God (or apart from Him). The "dualistic instincts" of Platonic philosophy, which "had elevated the 'soul' at the expense of the body," had to be

---

[338] Ibid., 16.1. "Though good acts can be meritorious of temporal reward for Thomas, he generally uses the term to refer to supernatural reward unless he states otherwise" (Denis R. Janz, *Luther and Late Medieval Thomism: A Study in Theological Anthropology.* Waterloo, Ontario, Canada: Wilfrid Laurier University Press, 1983, p. 46n50).

[339] Somme, "The Infallibility, Impeccability and Indestructibility of Synderesis," p. 416.

[340] "An Approach to a Key Theological Question," n.p.

balanced with "the embodied nature of the Christian hope."[341] The resurrection of the dead at least in part entails "the recovery of corporeity and the re-establishment of human life in its integrity by means of the union of the body with the soul"[342]:

> The resurrection had a key meaning for the formation of all theological anthropology, which could be considered simply as an anthropology of the resurrection. As a result of reflection on the resurrection, Thomas Aquinas neglected in his metaphysical (and at the same time theological) anthropology Plato's philosophical conception on the relationship between the soul and the body and drew closer to the conception of Aristotle [343]. . . . The truth about the resurrection clearly affirmed, in fact, that the eschatological perfection and happiness of man cannot be understood as a state of the soul alone, separated (according to Plato, liberated) from the body. But it must be understood as the state of man definitively and perfectly "integrated" through such a union of the soul and body.[344]

So it is "natural" for a human soul and body to be united; their temporary separation at death is just that—temporary. The hope of the immortal body is not an "irrational" hope, but neither is it an established fact. It is a "possibility" that can only be actualized by the miraculous resurrection of the body.[345] As second-century Church Father Athenagoras puts it, the resurrection of the body "takes place not for the sake of the judgment as the primary reason, but in consequence of the purpose of God in forming men, and the nature of the beings so formed. . . . For if no resurrection were to take place, the nature of men as men would not continue."[346] The human soul and body by nature belong together.

Third: *The soul is the form of the body.* The human soul within the body thus constitutes a human being; the soul is the animating principle of the body's matter. Without the soul, the body is dead and no longer a human being.

Fourth: *The rational soul, which is not transmitted by the parents, is infused by*

---

[341] Bruce Milne. *The Message of Heaven and Hell: Grace and Destiny.* Derek Tidball, ed. Leicester and Downers Grove: InterVarsity Press, 2002, p. 246.
[342] John Paul II. "The Resurrection and Theological Anthropology." The General Audience of Wednesday, December 2, 1981. *L'Osservatore Romano* (Weekly Edition in English) 7 December 1981: 3, p. 3.
[343] ST I.89.1.
[344] John Paul II, "The Resurrection," p. 3.
[345] Ric Machuga, *In Defense of the Soul*, p. 21.
[346] Athenagoras, *On the Resurrection of the Dead*, pp. 156-57, Chapters 14-15.

*God as soon as the body is ready to receive it.*[347] Although Aquinas mis-understands the timing of the body's reception of the organizing soul, due to his lack of scientific knowledge of genetics and embryology, the principle here stated is still valid: From the beginning, the body possesses the inherent shaping principle which directs the development of a human being. Because of its genetic code, the body also possesses all the material structure necessary to receive the animating principle of the soul. Therefore, Aquinas's error is scientific in nature, not metaphysical.

Fifth: *The human soul provides humans themselves with a* telos, *with ends specific only to humans.* Humanity's primary and overall end is happiness, leading up to and including Beatific happiness: "Final and perfect happiness can consist in nothing else than the vision of the Divine Essence."[348] This primary end of happiness is "easy to name but difficult to define," but there are also related ends for the various powers of the soul:

> There is a *telos* for human sociability, for example, for human thinking, for human sexuality, for bodily nourishment, for dealing with dangerous and painful things. There is also a *telos* for human bodily and psychological health. [Moral decisions arise when] sooner or later a conflict arises between what we want and what we truly are.[349]

These five points encapsulate the central principles of Aquinas's view of human nature relevant to our further discussion.

### 3. Adopting a Thomistic Anthropology

At the beginning of this work, the claim was made that Aquinas provides the definition of "human-ness" that best describes our complete humanity, even though a Thomistic anthropological framework would need to take into account certain factual advances in contemporary genetics and other fields. The framework of this claim for Aquinas's superior description was then provided through the following two arguments:

(1) First of all, materialistic views of human nature lack sufficient explanatory power for an adequate presentation of the animating principle behind human beings, especially those features of humans that are specifically intellectual in their operations. For example, the corporeal act of perception cannot include within itself the intellectual act of understanding, even as, for example, an image being formed on

---

[347] "An Approach to a Key Theological Question," n.p.
[348] ST I-II.3.8.
[349] Robert Sokolowski, "What Is Natural Law?" p. 511.

film within a camera (a physical operation) does not provide the camera with an "understanding" of the image (an intellectual operation). When once this rejection of wholesale materialism has been made, Aquinas's description of the human being is seen as being based in natural law's recognition of the human ontological difference of kind and the analysis of what that difference in kind entails for humans morally.

(2) Secondly, the attempt was also made from a Thomistic standpoint to rebut any view of human nature that overly emphasizes humans' spirituality. Without their corporeal nature, humans are incompletely human; even if for no other reason, humans require their bodily senses in order "to gather knowledge from individual things."[350] In Aquinas's *a posteriori* epistemology, a bodiless "human" would require a supernatural infusion of divinely granted knowledge to replace the natural procedures of learning "after experience." It is the natural state of a human being to be composed of both soul and body, and so "an adequate anthropology must be careful to prevent the development of any dualism. Humanity's material and bodily reality must not be severed from its capacity to express metaphysical meaning."[351]

The Thomistic/Aristotelian concept of the hylomorphic composite of form and matter, non-corporeal intellect and corporeal body, seems to fit the human experience most exactly and to possess the greatest explanatory power regarding human nature. As summarized by D.Q. McInerny:

> Should Thomistic ethics be seen as but one among many worthy ethical systems, vested with its own peculiar strengths and curiosities, but not to be taken, as a whole, as necessarily superior to any other system that could be singled out? No. From a purely historical perspective, Thomistic ethics can indeed be regarded as just one ethical system among many, but the philosophical position which is assumed here is that Thomistic ethics is to be given primacy of place by reason of the fact that its doctrine is universally applicable, and that is so because it is based upon a unified, coherent understanding of the nature of man. In the final analysis, what lends the commanding force and authority to Thomistic ethics is . . . the fact that it is thoroughly grounded in the objective order of things.[352]

Adopting a Thomistic anthropological stance can therefore be seen as

[350] ST I.76.5.
[351] Joseph C. Atkinson, *"Familiaris Consortio,"* p. 256.
[352] D.Q. McInerny. *A Course in Thomistic Ethics.* Elmhurst, Pennsylvania: The Priestly Fraternity of Saint Peter, 1997: pp. 9-10.

not only reasonable; it is in fact preferable both to scientific materialism and to either Cartesian or Platonic substance dualism, due to "its ability to combine ontological, epistemological, and ethical positions into a single balanced, coherent, and comprehensive whole. . . . [It possesses the] ability to unify numerous mundane and fairly obvious facts about humans and the world we inhabit into a single coherent and comprehensive theory of human nature."[353]

Of course, not all will agree. In the next chapter, we will take up some well-known objections to Aquinas's anthropology and ethics.

---

[353] Ric Machuga, *In Defense of the Soul*, pp. 11-12.

# Chapter 6:  Opposing Arguments

Much of this debate, as it is commonly set up, turns on the moral status of the embryo: is the embryo a person (where "person" is philosophical shorthand for a being with the moral status that we normally accord to adult humans), a potential person, or a bundle of cells with little moral significance in and of itself? If it is the first, so the argument often goes, then the destructive uses of embryos cannot be justified, any more than it would be to dissect a healthy baby in order to obtain spare parts for surgery. If it is no more than a bundle of cells, then its destructive use seems much less morally problematic. If it is regarded as a "potential person," or in some other way accorded a moral status intermediate between that of a person and that of a lump of tissue, then it is likely also to be accorded an intermediate level of protection: for example, restrictions but not an outright ban on embryo research, as in current British legislation.[354]

A ship, essentially a machine for floating on water, is still a ship when in dry dock.[355]

## 1.    Other Views of Personhood

Of course, the topics of personhood and human moral status have been widely explored by thinkers in different traditions or from different perspectives than the Thomistic, the explicitly Christian, or even the implicitly religious. A widely held secular philosophical tradition exists which claims that to be a "living human" or even a "living human being" is not the same as being a human "person," and hence humanness does not carry the same moral worthiness or rights to protections

---

[354] Neil Messer, *Selfish Genes and Christian Ethics*, p. 239.

[355] Brian Scarlett, "The Moral Uniqueness of the Human Animal." *Human Lives: Critical Essays on Consequentialist Bioethics*. David S. Oderberg and Jacqueline A. Laing, eds. New York and London: Macmillan, 1997: 77-95, p. 92.

as personhood. Therefore, other arguments against this interpretation of Thomistic metaphysical principles (that a living human being with moral worthiness and rights to protection exists from conception) might be raised at this juncture.

(1)  *Personhood and Its Implications*

For example, one might go back to John Locke's examination of human understanding, in which the claim is made that a *person* "has reason and reflection, and considers itself as itself":

> State of a child in the mother's womb. He that will suffer himself to be informed by observation and experience, and not make his own hypothesis the rule of nature, will find few signs of a soul accustomed to much thinking in a new-born child, and much fewer of any reasoning at all. And yet it is hard to imagine that the rational soul should think so much, and not reason at all. And he that will consider that infants newly come into the world spend the greatest part of their time in sleep, and are seldom awake but when either hunger calls for the teat, or some pain (the most importunate of all sensations), or some other violent impression on the body, forces the mind to perceive and attend to it—he, I say, who considers this, will perhaps find reason to imagine that a foetus in the mother's womb differs not much from the state of a vegetable, but passes the greatest part of its time without perception or thought; doing very little but sleep in a place where it needs not seek for food, and is surrounded with liquor, always equally soft, and near of the same temper; where the eyes have no light, and the ears so shut up are not very susceptible of sounds; and where there is little or no variety, or change of objects, to move the senses.[356]

In this tradition, the category of "human persons" is smaller than the category of "human beings." Even new-born children may not be considered "persons," and the unborn fetus "differs not much from the state of a vegetable"; specifically, Locke in this passage is rejecting the Cartesian notion of the infant's *a priori* "innate ideas." It would be interesting to speculate how much Locke's view might owe to the Aristotelian concept of the "vegetative soul" of the original conceptus.

On the other hand, from one Christian perspective, the opposite view of personhood may be true. From this perspective, the term "person" would actually encompass a *broader* spectrum of beings than

---

[356] John Locke. *An Essay Concerning Human Understanding* [1689]. Oxford: Oxford University Press, 1975. Book II.1.21. However, Locke himself in the same work mentions abortion as an example of obvious wrongdoing (I.2.19); his views will be further discussed later in this chapter.

simply human beings; that is, humans possess both rational and animal/corporeal natures, and the animal/corporeal nature might not strictly be required for personhood, except in the genus of humanity itself. For example, angelic beings are also "persons" without being "human," being "rational" but not "corporeal." God, as three Persons in one Substance, is also "personal" in nature, while remaining non-corporeal.[357] Human persons, however, are both rational and corporeal simultaneously.

However, to repeat a previous discussion for the purposes of this chapter, the specifically Thomistic point is that for Aquinas, one cannot be a human being without being a human person; in his thought, there is no clear distinction between the two. As Eleonore Stump puts it, "For Aquinas, there is no difference between a human person and a human being."[358] A "person" might not be a "human being" (as in the case of angelic intelligences), but a "human being" is always a "human person." A human *person* is "identical to a particular in the species *rational animal*"[359]; however, the exact same definition would for Aquinas suffice to define the human *being*. Since he accepts Boethius's definition of "person" as "an individual substance of rational nature,"[360] he would not accept the ethical distinction made by such writers as Dombrowski and Deltete when they differentiate between a "human being" as such, and "a human person in some morally relevant sense."[361] The definition "individual substance of rational nature" suffices both for personhood and human-ness, with the additional qualification in the case of human-ness that a human is also embodied. Further, Aquinas "contends that only the *potentiality* for rational thought must be present" to justify the claim of human-ness and hence personhood: "It is important to recall here that Aquinas, in his account of embryogenesis, never asserts that a fetus must *actually* think rationally in order for it to be a human being."[362]

---

[357] Some writers do not consider the existence of God or angels, but do consider the possibility of "alien beings" as persons; e.g., Mary Anne Warren in "On the Moral and Legal Status of Abortion," p. 100. However, as Jason Eberl puts it, "Aquinas recognizes different types of beings as persons [but] since my interest here is solely with *human* persons, I will not entertain any further discussion of such other types of persons" (*Thomistic Principles and Bioethics*, p. 128n3. Emphasis in original).

[358] Stump, *Aquinas*, p. 486n73.

[359] Ibid., p. 53. Emphasis in original.

[360] ST III.2.2.

[361] Dombrowski and Deltete, *A Brief, Liberal, Catholic Defense*, p. 7.

[362] Jason Eberl, "Aquinas's Account of Human Embryogenesis," p. 384. Emphasis in original.

As Stephen D. Schwarz has pointed out, being a person is not always exactly the same condition as being able to function as a person; the functional ability may fluctuate while the personal identity does not.[363]

Of course, this view of "human-ness" and human "personhood" as being identical runs directly counter to some modern arguments that the conceptus has not yet achieved "personhood" until birth (or after) and thus has no innate "right to life."[364] Two of the most prominent and influential arguments in favor of virtually unlimited rights to abortion were put forward in widely reprinted and discussed essays by philosophers Mary Anne Warren and Judith Jarvis Thomson. In dealing with Warren's and Thomson's essays, one is certainly covering well-trodden ground. However, their work is first of all admirably representative of the positions they wish to establish. Secondly, their writing is exceptionally clear and direct. Although other authors refine or defend some of the points made by Warren and Thomson, the force of the original arguments still comes through in the original essays; in fact, Thomson's is probably the most often reprinted essay in contemporary moral philosophy. More recent literature advancing similar positions include David Boonin's *A Defense of Abortion*, which is an explicit defense of Thomson's original essay against various responses[365]; John Harris's *The Value of Life*, which arrives at conclusions similar to Warren's[366]; Michael Tooley's *Abortion and Infanticide*, which defends both titular practices[367]; also Tooley's "Personhood," which argues that fetuses are not persons and have no special moral status as human fetuses[368]; Jonathan Glover's *Causing Death and Saving Lives*, which "positively encourages abortion of all seriously abnormal fetuses" in the effort to avoid "socially disastrous consequences"[369]; also Glover's "The

---

[363] Stephen D. Schwarz, *The Moral Question of Abortion*, p. 94.

[364] Interestingly, it also runs counter to some ancient arguments as well: "We cannot enter here into the long and fascinating history of how the meaning of 'person' developed and became distinct. The distinction developed partly as a social and legal term in Roman law, where 'person' meant a human being with full legal rights as a Roman citizen, as distinguished from slaves, who were indeed human beings, but not persons" (W. Norris Clarke, S.J., *Person and Being: The Aquinas Lecture, 1993*. Milwaukee: Marquette University Press, 1993, pp. 25-26).

[365] Cambridge: Cambridge University Press, 2003.

[366] London: Routledge & Kegan Paul, 1985.

[367] Oxford: Clarendon Press, 1983.

[368] In *A Companion to Bioethics*. Helga Kuhse and Peter Singer, eds. Oxford: Blackwell, 1998: 117-26, p. 124.

[369] New York: Penguin, 1977, reprinted 1981, p. 149.

Sanctity of Life"[370]; Peter Singer's *Unsanctifying Human Life: Essays on Ethics*[371] and *Rethinking Life and Death: The Collapse of Our Traditional Ethics*[372]; and Helga Kuhse's *The Sanctity-of-Life Doctrine in Medicine: A Critique.*[373] These last works cover more issues than abortion, but are in general agreement with Warren's and Thomson's conclusions.

The third reason that both Warren and Thomson are being considered here is that each of their arguments contradicts the thrust of this book, albeit in a separate way: Warren's argument follows from a rival anthropology, from the explicit rejection of the idea of personhood as rooted in "substance" and "genetic embodiment." Thomson, on the other hand, for the purposes of discussion concedes this idea of personhood and thus even the idea of "personhood at conception," but goes on to argue that even such a concession would not yield the bioethical implications (in the case of abortion) that the present work maintains it would. Therefore, both of these arguments, one anthropological in nature and one not, should be addressed using the Thomistic principles thus far adumbrated.

(2)   *Warren and Thomson on Personhood and Abortion*

In her essay "On the Moral and Legal Status of Abortion," Warren argues that only human "persons" possess rights others must respect, based on the moral status of "persons" as opposed to genetic humanity; further, she maintains that fetuses should not be viewed as "persons." She asks, "Can it be established that genetic humanity is sufficient for moral humanity? I think there are very good reasons for not defining the moral community in this way." Warren's suggestion is "that the moral community consists of all and only *people*, rather than all and only human beings," and she goes on to ask, "What characteristics entitle an entity to be considered a person?"[374] Almost immediately, Warren adds, "In searching for such criteria, it is useful to look beyond the set of people with whom we are acquainted."[375] Though it strikes the reader that seeking to define the term "person" by consulting "the set of

---

[370] In *Bioethics: An Anthology.* Helga Kuhse and Peter Singer, eds. Oxford: Blackwell, 2006: 266-75.

[371] Helga Kuhse, ed. Oxford: Blackwell, 2002.

[372] New York: St. Martin's Griffin, 1996. Originally published Melbourne: Text Publishing, 1994.

[373] New York: Oxford University Press USA, 1987.

[374] Mary Anne Warren. "On the Moral and Legal Status of Abortion." *The Monist* 57.1 (1973): 43-61. Reprinted in *The Right Thing to Do: Basic Readings in Moral Philosophy.* 3rd edition. James Rachels, ed. New York: McGraw-Hill, 2003: 97-106, p. 99. Emphasis in original.

[375] Ibid., p. 99.

people with whom we are acquainted" seems to lead to a form of begging the question,[376] Warren does provide a list of five basic criteria for personhood:

(1) Consciousness (of objects and events external and/or internal to the being), and in particular the capacity to feel pain;

(2) Reasoning (the *developed* capacity to solve new and relatively complex problems);

(3) Self-motivated activity (activity which is relatively independent of either genetic or direct external control);

(4) The capacity to communicate, by whatever means, messages of an indefinite variety of types, that is, not just with an indefinite number of possible contents, but on indefinitely many possible topics;

(5) The presence of self-concepts, and self-awareness, either individual or racial, or both.[377]

Regarding this list Warren asserts, "We needn't suppose that an entity must have *all* of these attributes to be properly considered a person; [the first and second] alone may well be sufficient for personhood. . . . Neither do we need to insist that any one of these criteria is *necessary* for personhood, although once again [the first two] look like fairly good candidates for necessary conditions." Any being satisfying none of criteria 1 through 5 "is certainly not a person," according to Warren; this claim is "so obvious" that "anyone who denied it, and claimed that a being which satisfied none of (1)-(5) was a person all the same, would

---

[376] Warren's search for the criteria of personhood seems to beg the question because to know a set of "people" one must already have a definition of "person," or at least one must assume that all conscious humans one knows automatically and unproblematically qualify as persons. The response from a defender of Warren might be something like, "Of course the conscious humans one knows unproblematically qualify as persons; they are conscious, after all, and self-directed, not dependent on other humans for their existence, and so on. This argument thus begins with one's everyday concepts of personhood and deriving one's criteria from those everyday concepts." However, these concepts constitute the very criteria of "personhood" for which Warren is arguing; thus one cannot appeal to a set of "people" for a definition of "personhood." One should remember that under Roman law "slaves . . . were indeed human beings, but not persons" (W. Norris Clarke, *Person and Being*, p. 26). The automatic identification of conscious humans with persons is not unproblematic, given the initial separation of humanity and personhood, and especially given that Warren explicitly divides some *unconscious* humans from personhood ("On the Moral and Legal Status," p. 101).
[377] Ibid., p. 100. The emphases are in the original quotations throughout this section.

thereby demonstrate that he had no notion at all of what a person is—perhaps because he had confused the concept of a person with genetic humanity."[378]

Warren is quite explicit in her delineation of what does and does not constitute personhood: "Some human beings are not people. . . . A man or woman whose consciousness has been permanently obliterated but who remains alive is a human being which is no longer a person; defective human beings, with no appreciable mental capacity, are not and presumably never will be people; and a fetus is a human being which is not yet a person, and which therefore cannot coherently be said to have full moral rights." Perhaps because the description of "defective human beings" who "never will be people" sounds rather chilling, Warren immediately opens her definition of personhood in a more inclusive direction: "Citizens of the next century should be prepared to recognize highly advanced, self-aware robots or computers, should such be developed, and intelligent inhabitants of other worlds, should such be found, as people in the fullest sense, and to respect their moral rights."[379] Although Warren may seem to some readers to be rather over-accepting regarding the personhood of robots and computers, she can also seem rather stringent in her application of "personhood" criteria in the case of the human fetus:

> Thus, since the fact that even a fully developed fetus is not personlike enough to have any significant right to life on the basis of its personlikeness shows that no legal restrictions upon the stage of pregnancy in which an abortion may be performed can be justified on the grounds that we should protect the rights of the older fetus [Warren has previously discussed and discarded "viability" as a morally significant watershed], and since there is no other apparent justification for such restrictions, we may conclude that they are entirely unjustified. Whether or not it would be *indecent* (whatever that means) for a woman in her seventh month to obtain an abortion just to avoid having to postpone a trip to Europe, it would not, in itself, be *immoral*, and therefore it ought to be permitted.[380]

Any arguments against this extreme position which are based on moral repugnance Warren dismisses as "mere emotional responses,"[381] not as

---

[378] Ibid., p. 101. John Harris's conclusion is similar: "The foetus is not a person and therefore cannot be wronged if its life is ended prematurely" (*The Value of Life*, p. 159).
[379] Warren, "On the Moral and Legal Status," pp. 101-102.
[380] Ibid., pp. 103-104. Emphasis in original.

any type of intuitive moral knowledge. Aquinas, of course, allows for an intuitive, pre-articulated apprehension of moral knowledge via synderesis; however, Warren does not consider this argument.[382] Neither the fetus's "resemblance to a person" nor its "potential for becoming a person" justifies any sort of restriction on abortion, one of "a woman's most basic moral and constitutional rights."[383]

Judith Jarvis Thomson, in her even better known essay "A Defense of Abortion," takes an approach differing from Warren's in that she even allows for the possible truth of the premise that a fetus is a human person. She writes, "I am inclined to think also that we shall probably have to agree that the fetus has already become a human person well before birth." However, she disagrees as to the personhood of the conceptus: "On the other hand, I think that the premise is false, that the fetus is not a person from the moment of conception. A newly fertilized ovum, a newly implanted clump of cells, is no more a person than an acorn is an oak tree."[384] After pointing out that most discussions of abortion, even those from opposed perspectives, revolve around the question of the personhood of the conceptus, she moves to the distinctiveness of her argument: "I propose, then, that we grant that the fetus is a person from the moment of conception."[385]

Even with the granting of this crucial premise, Thomson argues that the addition "and hence the fetus should not be aborted" is not a sustainable conclusion. David Boonin paraphrases the argument against which Thomson writes her essay as follows:

P1: The fetus is a person.
P2: Every person has a right to life.
C1: The fetus has a right to life.
P3: The woman has a right to control her body.
P4: The right to life outweighs the right to control one's body.
P5: Abortion kills the fetus.
C2: Abortion is morally impermissible.[386]

Against this argument Thomson devises some thought experiments, the

---

[381] Ibid., p. 103.

[382] See also Leon R. Kass's argument for "the wisdom of repugnance" in his and James Q. Wilson's work, *The Ethics of Human Cloning* (Washington, D.C.: AEI Press, 1998).

[383] Warren, "On the Moral and Legal Status," p. 105.

[384] Thomson, "A Defense of Abortion." *Philosophy and Public Affairs* 1.1 (Fall 1971): 47-66, pp. 47-48.

[385] Ibid., p. 48.

[386] David Boonin, *A Defense of Abortion*, p. 135.

two most famous being the "Violinist" and the "People-Seeds" examples. In the "Violinist" example, the readers are asked "to imagine this":

> You wake up in the morning and find yourself back to back in bed with an unconscious violinist. A famous unconscious violinist. He has been found to have a fatal kidney ailment, and the Society of Music Lovers has canvassed all the available medical records and found that you alone have the right blood type to help. They have therefore kidnapped you, and last night the violinist's circulatory system was plugged into yours, so that your kidneys can be used to extract poisons from his blood as well as your own. The director of the hospital now tells you, "Look, we're sorry the Society of Music Lovers did this to you—we would never have permitted it if we had known. But still, they did it, and the violinist now is plugged into you. To unplug you would be to kill him. But never mind, it's only for nine months. By then he will have recovered from his ailment, and can safely be unplugged from you." Is it morally incumbent on you to accede to this situation?[387]

Thomson's point is not necessarily that Premise 4 ("The right to life out-weighs the right to control one's body") is mistaken, although some have taken precisely this as her point.[388] Rather, she is arguing regarding the fetus's use of the mother's body, that "even though the fetus has a right to life, it need not have the right to use its mother's body to stay alive."[389] Boonin explains more fully: "Thomson's claim is precisely that there is no such conflict between these two rights [the right to life and the right to control one's body] in the case she has presented, that unplugging yourself from the violinist does not violate his right to life in the first place. Even though he has a right to life, that is, he has no right

---

[387] Thomson, "A Defense of Abortion," pp. 48-49.

[388] For example, Peg Tittle writes, "Thomson proposes this thought experiment in order to explore the ethics of abortion. Specifically, it puts to the test the argument that abortion is wrong because the fetus's right to life overrides the pregnant woman's right to decide what happens in and to her body" (*What If: Collected Thought Experiments in Philosophy*. New York: Pearson/ Longman, 2005, p. 175). Likewise, "[Thomson] rejects the idea that the fetus has a right to life which overrides the mother's right to her own body" (Louis P. Pojman and Francis J. Beckwith, eds. *The Abortion Controversy: A Reader*. Boston: Jones and Bartlett, 1994, p. 131). However, Thomson's argument more precisely is that the fetus's right to life does not include the right to *whatever keeps the fetus alive*.

[389] Sally Markowitz. "Abortion and Feminism." *Social Theory & Practice* 16.1 (Spring 1990): 1-17, p. 1.

to the use of your kidneys. So in unplugging yourself from him, you do nothing that conflicts with his right to life, even though you do something that brings about his death."[390] In the case of abortion, this thought experiment suggests that even if the fetus as a human person has an unqualified right to life from conception, the fetus's right to life does not entail the right to the use of whatever is necessary to keep the fetus alive—including the mother's body.

The surrealism of this thought experiment (surreal especially when the actual processes of conception and gestation are considered) pales in comparison to Thomson's "People-Seeds" argument, from the same essay: "Suppose it were like this: people-seeds drift about in the air like pollen, and if you open your windows, one may drift in and take root in your carpets or upholstery. You don't want children, so you fix up your windows with fine mesh screens, the very best you can buy. As can happen, however, and on very, very rare occasions does happen, one of the screens is defective; and a seed drifts in and takes root. Does the person-plant who now develops have a right to the use of your house?"[391] Tittle brings out the analogy: "This scenario is intended to parallel unwanted conception, and the issue Thomson is exploring is whether or not a fetus can be said to have acquired a right to the use of a person's body."[392]

To summarize Warren's and Thomson's positions before proceeding to responses: Warren argues that only human "persons" possess rights other persons must respect, based on the moral status of "persons" as opposed to genetic humanity; further, she maintains that human fetuses should not be viewed as "persons." Those who are genetically human, therefore (such as fetuses), should not be included in the moral community of those human persons possessing human rights. In order to qualify as a "person," a human would need to meet a set of functional criteria; Warren asserts that those who think a fetus could be a "person" simply reveal that they do not properly understand what a person is. On the other hand, even though she agrees with Warren that fetuses are not "persons," Thomson is willing to allow the premise that fetuses are in fact persons. She argues that even while allowing this premise, abortion should be permitted, because even if the fetus as a human person has an unqualified right to life from conception, the fetus's right to life does not entail the right to the use of whatever is necessary to keep the fetus alive, such as the mother's body. In order to

---

[390] Boonin, *A Defense of Abortion*, p. 137.
[391] Thomson, "A Defense of Abortion," p. 59.
[392] Peg Tittle, *What If*, p. 179.

illustrate this point, Thomson gives some thought experiments such as her "Violinist" and "People-Seeds" examples.

(3)  *Non-Thomistic and Thomistic Considerations and Objections*

At this point, some objections to Warren's and Thomson's arguments, from both non-Thomistic and Thomistic perspectives, are worth considering.

One of the first objections immediately occurring to many who read these arguments has been labeled the "Weirdness" objection. According to some writers, the "Violinist" and "People-Seeds" analogies are not truly analogous to the situation of conception in many ways; in fact, they are so non-analogous they are "irrelevant to reality," as one puts it. For example, unlike the case of the violinist, "In most abortions, the children aren't just 'unplugged' and removed from the womb—they are killed," as Doris Gordon writes. Gordon goes on to add:

> Since a prenatal child is where she is because of her parents, the child could be said to be acting as her parents' agent—which places her "guilt" squarely on her parents' heads. In Thomson's analogy the sequence is: The violinist develops a fatal kidney problem, his friends go to his aid; they capture an innocent stranger and plug the violinist into him; the stranger unplugs himself, which lets the violinist die. But what if the violinist is in the life-threatening condition because the stranger is not innocent? What if the stranger had hit the violinist with his car? This would make the situation closer to what's at issue in the abortion debate. The violinist has the right to defense, so why wouldn't he have the right to compel the stranger to keep him alive, especially since the stranger is able to prevent his death? If we put someone at death's door *and then take another step that brings about the death*, that's not letting him die; that's killing him. And that kills Thomson's defense, too. Conception and pregnancy are foreseeable consequences of even careful sex. By causing children to be, parents also cause them to need support; it's a package deal. When parents mutually enable their sperm and ova to join, the parents are not enslaved—they've volunteered. This may put the *needs* of a parent and child in conflict, but it creates no clash of rights between them. This is because parents owe their children support.[393]

Boonin argues against this idea by distinguishing between one's responsibility for "the needy person's *neediness*" and responsibility for

---

[393] Doris Gordon. "Abortion and Thomson's Violinist: Unplugging a Bad Analogy." Wheaton, Maryland: L4L.org/Articles/ThomViol: 1991. Updated 1999, n.p. Accessed 21 April 2007. Emphasis in original.

"the needy person's *existence*."[394] For example, if a doctor saves a dying patient and five years later the patient has another need, the doctor has no moral responsibility toward the patient simply by being the instrument of the patient's continued existence. However, as Francis J. Beckwith responds to this scenario, in the case of the doctor and the patient, "An already existing state of affairs was improved. On the other hand, in the case of pregnancy, net human neediness is increased, for a child-with-neediness, a joint condition, is actualized by an act which is ordered in such a way that its proper function (though not its only function) is to produce a child-with-neediness. In the case of the violinist, the physician *helps* a violinist to be less needy than he otherwise would have been. In the case of pregnancy, a needy being is brought into existence that otherwise would not exist if not for its progenitors engaging in an act ordered toward producing needy beings."[395] Although this argument may seem to be utilitarian in nature, with its references to "net human neediness" bearing a family resemblance to "net human happiness," the neediness to which Beckwith specifically refers is that of a "child-with-neediness." In other words, the emphasis is not on the quantitative analysis of a *response* to another's neediness, but rather on the qualitative difference between such a response, on the one hand, and the act which *brings into existence* a child (and hence the child's neediness), on the other. Beckwith allows for Boonin's point (that the doctor, though responsible for the existence of the patient, is not thereby responsible for the patient's subsequent neediness), while denying that the point has application to the case of pregnancy. The doctor's actions are not directed toward bringing into being the patient's subsequent neediness. However, in the case of the action of bringing into being a conceptus, the existence of the pregnancy and the subsequent neediness of the conceptus cannot be separated; they are, in fact, identical. Therefore, the abortion of the conceptus does not merely "allow" the conceptus to die by "unplugging" it from an "unjust use" of the mother's body; in reality, there is no such "unplugging" and no "unjust use," but rather an intentional mortal action directed against the very existence of the conceptus. As philosopher Philippa Foot writes:

> [When one unplugs oneself from the violinist] the fatal sequence resulting in death is not initiated but is rather allowed to take its course. [Abortion is] completely different. The fetus is not in

[394] Boonin, *A Defense of Abortion*, p. 170. Emphasis in original.
[395] Beckwith, "Defending Abortion Philosophically: A Review of David Boonin's *A Defense of Abortion*." *Journal of Medicine and Philosophy* 31 (2006): 177-203, p. 194.

jeopardy because it is in its mother's womb; it is merely dependent on her in the way children are dependent on their parents for food. An abortion, therefore, originates the sequence which ends in the death of the fetus.[396]

In other words, the case of abortion and the case of unplugging oneself from the violinist are not truly analogous. The violinist has a *previously existing condition* which leads eventually to death; unplugging oneself is not a direct mortal action. The conceptus, on the other hand, has no previously existing condition which the abortion allows eventually to lead to death; the abortion itself is the cause of mortality, the direct mortal action.

Nor, except in the case of rape leading to conception, does conception occur as in the Violinist example, by an uninvolved person's being kidnapped while sleeping. (The parallel to rape lies in the fact of non-consent on the part of the victimized person.) Moreover, Thomson herself clearly means the Violinist example to apply to the case of pregnancy resulting from consensual relations as well as from rape, and a defender of her position argues, "If her argument succeeds in rape cases, then it succeeds in non-rape cases as well."[397]

However, as one critic writes, "the violinist example is *weird*" and "pregnancy is the opposite of weird." He goes on: "The moralities we have represent some ways of dealing with the realities and regularities of human life; and they may not fit well the irregularities or impossibilities . . . . So what is appropriate for kidnapped kidney bearers and their violinist parasites might not be appropriate for mothers and the babes in their wombs."[398] As even Boonin (who defends Thomson strenuously) admits, "Hypothetical examples can indeed become so artificial that their practical significance vanishes."[399] Mortal assault against another cannot be equated with "unplugging" oneself from someone else, even if the "unplugging" means the other human will be allowed to die.

---

[396] Philippa Foot. "Killing and Letting Die." *Killing and Letting Die.* Bonnie Steinbock and Alastair Norcross, eds. 2nd edition. New York: Fordham Univ. Press, 1994: 280-89, pp. 282-83.
[397] David Boonin. "Death Comes for the Violinist: On Two Objections to Thomson's 'Defense of Abortion.'" *Social Theory and Practice* 23.3 (Fall 1997): 329-64, p. 329.
[398] John T. Wilcox. "Nature as Demonic in Thomson's Defense of Abortion" [1989]. *The Ethics of Abortion: Pro-Life vs. Pro-Choice.* Revised edition. Robert M. Baird and Stuart E. Rosenbaum, eds. Buffalo, New York: Pranetheus Books, 1993: 212-25, pp. 214-15. Emphasis in original.
[399] Boonin, *A Defense of Abortion*, p. 140.

Not only is Thomson's view contrary to the normal view of conception, it also persists in regarding the conceptus as a sort of "invader" or "parasite" which has no moral grounds to expect the use of the mother's body. However, first of all, such a view is not technically accurate; parasitism is a form of symbiosis which occurs only between members of separate species, and simple reproduction is neither parasitic nor symbiotic. Further, holding the view of "conceptus as parasite" runs contrary to all normal intuitions regarding the relationship between the conceptus and the expectant mother. For example, writer Thomas L. Johnson points out, "A parasite is generally detrimental to the reproductive capacity of the invaded host"; on the other hand, the conceptus appears to be the *sine qua non* of human reproduction: "A human embryo or fetus is absolutely essential to the reproductive capacity of the involved mother (and species)."[400] The conceptus is in the womb for nine months, while parasites are usually in the host organism until the death of the host. Like a conceptus, a parasite "obtains nutrients and enjoys protection" from its host, as a microbiological text puts it; however, the parasitic relationship is so typically negative, causing "damage to tissues (disease) or even death," that parasites are also commonly referred to as "pathogens."[401] Johnson concludes: "A parasite is an organism that associates with the host in a negative, unhealthy, and nonessential (nonessential to the host) manner which will often damage the host and detrimentally affect the procreative capacity of the host. . . . A human embryo or fetus is a human being that associates with the mother in a positive, healthful, essential manner necessary for the procreation of the species."[402] The objection might arise, "But of course the conceptus is not technically a parasite; the expectant mother is regarding it as such in a social and ethical sense, not in a biological." However, if in fact the conceptus is a human being and person, a premise Thomson allows in the presentation of her argument, the fact that the expectant mother (or anyone else involved) does not regard it as such, even if in a social and ethical sense, affects neither its right to life nor its right to exist within the mother. Finally, the arguments here presented against the view of the conceptus as a "parasite" may also be applied to the view of some, such as Dr. Warren M. Hern, that pregnancy may be seen as an "illness."[403]

---

[400] Thomas L. Johnson. "Why a Human Embryo or Fetus Is Not a Parasite." Wheaton, Maryland: L4L.org/articles: 1974, n.p. Accessed 21 April 2007.

[401] Kathleen Park Talaro. *Foundations in Microbiology*. 6th ed. New York: McGraw-Hill, 2008, pp. G-14 and 195.

[402] Johnson, "Why a Human Embryo or Fetus Is Not a Parasite," n.p.

One of Thomson's central claims has already been considered and rejected: namely, the claim that there is no real conflict between the right to life of the conceptus and the right on the part of the mother to control her own body (this right to control leading to the right to abortion because, even if the conceptus as a human person has an unqualified right to life from conception, that right to life does not entail the right to the use of whatever is necessary to keep the conceptus alive, including the mother's body). Another central claim may also be discussed profitably at this point: namely, the claim that humans, specifically mothers, do in fact have the right to control their own bodies. However, is this claim either obvious or unproblematic? Does this right actually exist? If so, to what does it extend—does it extend, for example, to the right to kill oneself? The theological point may be raised as to whether or not any humans actually do "control" "their own" bodies, or whether these bodies, as with everything else in life, are best seen as a stewardship granted by God, the rightful owner of all things, including human bodies. However, such a theological argument might not exert compelling power outside of the ranks of those predisposed to accept it. A better argument regarding this claim might address the question, "Whose body is it that is most directly involved in the abortion process?" Certainly the mother's body is directly involved, but the body of the conceptus itself may be seen as even more involved, as it is the ultimate object of the abortion.[404]

In other words, even if the right to control one's own body is granted as a premise, the mother's right to control her body would not apply in the case of abortion, since her right of control (in particular, her right to harm) does not extend to the body of the conceptus. According to Aquinas, any existing "right to control one's body" would not apply in the case of abortion: "An internal member of the mother is something of hers by continuity and material union of the part with the whole: whereas a child while in its mother's womb is something of hers

---

[403] Hern writes that society should "abandon the erroneous assumption that pregnancy is *per se* a normal and desirable state, and to consider instead a more accurate view that human pregnancy is an episodic, moderately extended chronic condition. . . . Accordingly, the open recognition and legitimation of pregnancy as an illness would be consistent with the individual self-interest of those experiencing pregnancy, good standards of medical practice, and the continued survival of human and other species" ("Is Pregnancy Really Normal?" *Family Planning Perspectives* 3.1 [January 1971]: 5-10, pp. 8-9).

[404] The argument that follows is specifically directed toward Thomson's position and not Warren's, since Thomson allows for the sake of discussion that "the fetus is a person" ("A Defense of Abortion," p. 48).

through being joined with, and yet distinct from her. Wherefore there is no comparison [between what happens to the body of the mother and what happens to the body of the conceptus]." The specific case under discussion by Aquinas concerns whether or not the conceptus is baptized when the mother is baptized. For the reasons given, Aquinas argues that the answer is no: "The child's soul, to the sanctification of which Baptism is ordained, is distinct from the soul of the mother; and because the body of the animated infant is already formed, and consequently distinct from the body of the mother."[405] Aquinas is speaking in particular of the "animated" or "quickened" fetus, which he considered to be "ensouled," but the same principle would apply to the conceptus at any stage of development (for reasons presented through-out this work). The relevant point is that for Aquinas the body of the conceptus is "distinct from the body of the mother." Therefore, even if a "right to control one's body" exists, such a right would not extend to the destruction of the body of another.

Two thought experiments might serve to illustrate this point. The first is taken from today's headlines: A sniper shoots at a pregnant woman, intending to murder her. The sniper hits the pregnant woman in the abdomen. The pregnant woman survives, but the unborn child is killed. The sniper is captured. Should the sniper be charged with murder or only attempted murder?

The thought experiment is not merely hypothetical. For example, in Decatur, Illinois, a man named Arthur Thomas Massey, on July 11, 2006, stabbed to death a woman and her eight-year-old son. In addition to the counts of first-degree murder pressed against Massey, prosecutors also sought convictions of intentional homicide based on the fact that the murdered woman was "about seven months pregnant at the time of her death."[406] Based on these charges, the state of Illinois sought the death penalty against Massey. Such a case (multiple other examples easily could be adduced) raises the obvious question: Was the charge of "intentional homicide" gratuitous, or was the charge based on the reality of the separate embodied existence of the conceptus? If the latter is the basis for the charge, in what way does the mother's "right to control her own body" change the reality of that separate embodied existence, especially to such an extent that the mother herself may intentionally and lawfully seek the death of the conceptus?

---

[405] ST III.68.11.
[406] Edith Brady-Lunny. "Psychologist Appointed to Help Massey Defense in Murder Case." Decatur *Herald & Review*. Updated 5 Jan. 2007. Herald-Review.com. Accessed 16 May 2007.

The second thought experiment is taken from Peter Kreeft and runs as follows[407]: If someone buys a new sofa for her house, the sofa would be *inside* the house, but it would be incorrect to say the sofa was therefore *part of* the house; in Aquinas's terms, it would not possess a "continuity and material union" with the house. On the other hand, if she then builds another room inside her house, complete with walls, door, doorknob, and so on, it seems she could then say, "This house now possesses another room, walls, door, and knob—the room is not just *in* the house, but is now part of the house; it possesses a continuity and material union with the house."

Could one, however, say the same thing of a pregnant woman? In other words, could one say of a pregnant woman that the woman, because of what she contains, now has two heads, four legs, possibly a penis, twenty fingers, and so on? If the conceptus is not yet physically developed, could one say that the mother has the *potential* to develop two heads, four legs, and so on? If one could not say this, what does that say of the relationship between the mother and the child? Would it not imply that, as Aquinas puts it, the conceptus is "joined with, and yet distinct from" the mother?[408]

Both of these thought experiments raise the issue of the "right to control one's body." Even if such a right is granted, is the body of the conceptus then merely a feature of the body of the mother, to be dealt with according to the mother's desires? Both examples indicate that the answer is no: the first because the conceptus can be addressed separately for legal purposes, and the second because the features of the body of the conceptus are not thereby features of the body of the mother; again, they may be addressed separately. Also, both examples have the advantage of being much closer to humanity's actual lived experience than, for example, Thomson's "violinist" or "people-seeds," and therefore they easily escape the "weirdness" objection. It could be argued that the fetus is not in fact much more like "a new sofa in the house" than it is like "an unconscious violinist," and that all such analogies have a somewhat strained, "weird" feeling to them, precisely because the relationship of mother and fetus is in a sense *sui generis*. However, most people would have at least some actual lived experience with the former analogy, as opposed to with Thomson's; a child in the womb may in most cases be recognized as more similar to "a new sofa

---

[407] The example is from Kreeft's *The Unaborted Socrates: A Dramatic Debate on the Issues Surrounding Abortion*. Downers Grove, Illinois: InterVarsity Press, 1983, pp. 45-47.

[408] ST III.68.11.

in the house" than as more similar to the artificially attached "violinist." Further, the "violinist" is not readily recognizable as a legitimate moral responsibility, in contrast to the child in the womb.

Finally, these examples serve to point out that the very idea of unqualified rights over one's own body is problematic in itself, especially when one is also dealing with a pregnancy. For one thing, the rights-to-one's-own-body argument implies that the woman's conception of the fetus within her own body gives her the unique right to harm the fetus in her own interest. However, the argument could easily be extended (as it has been in history) to permit parents to sell their children into servitude to further their (the parents') own interest, since the parents are the ones who brought the children into existence.[409] Because of this darker extension of the implicit reasoning behind the rights-to-one's-own-body argument, one could also argue against overly strenuous, technologically aided efforts to conceive children, for similar reasons: Eventually the children could well become viewed as the parents' property, and "the right to *possess* a child" as a "fundamental right."[410] The view of personhood for which this work argues would mitigate against such views: "The distinction that personhood is innate makes the idea of human rights plausible."[411]

To turn from Thomson's to Warren's arguments: Earlier I described Warren's famous "On the Moral and Legal Status of Abortion" essay as "chilling" in some of its explicitly stated conclusions, such as the statement that some "defective human beings . . . never will be people."[412] In fact, aspects of Warren's arguments have always been eerily reminiscent of the slightly older doctrine of *Lebensunwerten lebens*, "life unworthy of life,"[413] and several reasons exist for this "chilling" quality to the essay: First of all, the entire notion of establishing certain criteria for personhood that some human beings meet and others do not "leaves the matter of human rights open to arbitrariness and prejudice. .

---

[409] For a defense of this *reductio*, see Brody, *Abortion and the Sanctity of Human Life*, Chapter 2.
[410] James T. Burtchaell. "The Child as Chattel: Reflections on a Vatican Document." *Guaranteeing the Good Life: Medicine and the Return of Eugenics*. Richard John Neuhaus, ed. Grand Rapids, Michigan: Eerdmans, 1990: 89-121, p. 101. Emphasis added.
[411] Sheila Peters. "The Human Person, Freedom, and Moral Responsibility." *Sapientia et Doctrina* 1.1 (2004): 55-60, p. 56.
[412] Warren, "On the Moral and Legal Status," pp. 101-2.
[413] The phrase is taken from the influential work *The Permission to Destroy Life Unworthy of Life* [*Die Freigabe der Vernichtung lebensunwerten Lebens*], by Alfred Hoche and Karl Binding (Leipzig, 1920).

. . There are undoubtedly those who would claim that certain minorities fail to meet fully the criterion of humanity."[414] Leaving aside the question of majority/minority populations, one could point out, as does Peg Tittle, that "a newborn has none of the traits [Warren's listed criteria for personhood] mentioned either—does that mean that infanticide is also morally permissible?"[415] (Some public philosophers actually are considering the public acceptance of infanticide, as we will discuss.) Secondly, in many cases where the options of abortion or allowing a born child to die are considered due to birth defects in the child, even though the child's "quality of life" is nominally the prime consideration, the intrinsic right to life on the part of the child, should that right exist, does not change due to handicaps. More likely what is the prime consideration in these cases is the *family's* quality of life. In these cases, what is held to justify the action is "an inability to cope; the child's entitlement to life, or lack of it, does not enter into the matter."[416]

Occasionally the conceptus is labelled a "potential" person, not a person already in possession of human rights such as the right to life. As has been argued, the Thomistic view "interprets 'potential' as continuity and identity" and therefore sees no valid demarcating line between the human and the "person"; rather, it "ascribes personhood already to the zygote, i.e., the fertilized egg after the fusion of the nuclei of egg and sperm and before cell division."[417] However, this ascription of personhood to the zygote at conception (which is the position of the present work) is not actually even necessary to argue against Warren's and Thomson's claims.[418] For example, L.W. Sumner points out that the division of "no moral standing" on the one hand (the "liberal" view of the zygote, to use Sumner's term) and "full moral standing" of the zygote on the other hand (the most "conservative" view) are not the only two options. Rather, they comprise the two ends of a continuum formed of greater or lesser ascriptions of "moral standing"—to the

---

[414] Brody, *Abortion and the Sanctity of Human Life*, p. 69.

[415] Peg Tittle, *What If*, p. 183.

[416] Anne Maclean. *The Elimination of Morality: Reflections on Utilitarianism and Bioethics*. London and New York: Routledge, 1993, p. 30.

[417] Maureen Junker-Kenny, "The Moral Status of the Embryo." *Concilium: The Ethics of Genetic Engineering* (April 1998): 43-53, p. 43.

[418] As Stanley Hauerwas writes, even if one is not fully recognizable as a "person," one might still be recognizable as a "child" ("Must a Person Be a Person to Be a Patient? Or, My Uncle Charlie Is Not Much of a Person but He Is Still My Uncle Charlie." Hauerwas, David B. Burrell, and Richard Bondi. *Truthfulness and Tragedy: Further Investigations in Christian Ethics*. Notre Dame, Indiana: University of Notre Dame Press, 1977, pp. 127-28).

zygote, to the embryo, to the fetus.[419] One point which could be taken from this, although it is definitely not the point toward which Sumner proceeds, is that any ascription of "moral standing" to the zygote *at all* would surely entail at the least the protection of the zygote's basic right not to be destroyed at the will of another, even if that other is a human of "full moral standing." Therefore, Warren and Thomson must argue (as they do) either that the zygote has "no moral standing" at all (Warren), or that, even if the zygote has a right to life, it has no right to continued life by developing in the mother's womb (Thomson); in other words, according to Thomson, the "right to life" allowed to the conceptus for the sake of argument does not imply even a negative duty on the part of the mother, that of allowing the conceptus continued habitation in her body. The necessity of these claims should aid in recognizing the extremity of Warren's and Thomson's positions.[420]

Further, one might ask whether the motivation for these extreme claims is in fact a disinterested philosophical desire for truth and accuracy; as Andrew Peach argues, "It is difficult not to feel that such accounts of personhood have been engineered for no other reason than to justify abortions, and, not surprisingly, they play virtually no role, if any, in any other analyses in applied ethics":

> Gradualist and achievement accounts of personhood [the term that has been used in the present work is "functionalist" accounts] are not based upon generally valid moral distinctions and then applied to the problem case of abortion; they appear to have been devised exclusively to justify the practice of abortion, and that practice alone.[421]

Elsewhere Peach has written similarly:

> If this distinction [between "human being" and "person"], as used by pro-choice thinkers, does not appear anywhere except in defenses of abortion, one should question whether or not it was engineered for any other reason than to justify abortion, in which case it would be highly suspect to say the least. . . . *Indeed, there is not a single case of a human being outside the womb who is free to be killed because he or she is not a "person" in Warren's sense of the word; mere membership in the human race is a sufficient condition to be protected from harm.* Given this

---

[419] L.W. Sumner. *Abortion and Moral Theory*. Princeton: Princeton University Press, 1981, pp. 26-27.

[420] However, it must be admitted that, extreme or not, this is in fact the position of current (2014) United States law on abortion.

[421] Andrew J. Peach. "Late- *vs.* Early-Term Abortion: A Thomistic Analysis." *The Thomist* 75.1 (January 2007): 113-41, p. 140.

fact, there can be little doubt that the distinction between human and person has been engineered for no other reason than to justify abortion. Warren has not observed a generally valid moral distinction and then applied it to the problem case of the unborn child and abortion; she has determined that abortion should be morally permissible and then has created a distinction to justify that practice. To proceed in this fashion is the philosophical equivalent of gerrymandering.[422]

Perhaps Peach here is overly assured, particularly in his emphasized sentence, of the self-evidence of the conclusion to which his argument leads: Certainly some *would*, in fact, use the "human being/human person" distinction in the attempt to justify the killing of a human being outside the womb. However, the recognition of the personhood of the conceptus seems to help provide a sure theoretical foundation for the practical ascription of human rights, and so surely any functionalist account of personhood which denies the personhood of the conceptus should be based upon premises with a very strong presumption in their favor. Since such does not appear to be the case, the ascription of human rights itself (to fetuses, to the aged, to the mentally infirm, to the comatose, to the negligible or unwanted) is needlessly brought into question by any functionalist account of personhood, seemingly for the purpose of justifying the practice of abortion.

Actually, Warren herself seems to place her finger on a crucial problem when she asserts that anyone who rejects all of her listed criteria for personhood "would thereby demonstrate that he had no notion at all of what a person is."[423] One could make a similar assertion, but from the opposite perspective: Many in the contemporary world do not seem to know what is a person, since they insist on defining personhood in terms of human functionality rather than in terms of the innate, continuously developing human substance. To accept the latter terms in defining personhood would also entail accepting protections for the conceptus thus defined. As Peter Kreeft has written, the only conditions under which abortion would be justifiable *prima facie* would be those in which (1) the conceptus is not a person, and (2) society possesses knowledge that this is indeed the case. If (1) the conceptus is a person, and (2) society possesses knowledge of this, then abortion

---

[422] Andrew J. Peach. "Pro-Choice 'Personhood': An Abortive Concept." *Life and Learning XIII: Proceedings of the Thirteenth University Faculty for Life Conference.* Joseph W. Koterski, S.J., ed. Washington, D.C.: University Faculty for Life, 2003: 187-210, pp. 191, 193-94. Emphasis in original.

[423] Warren, "On the Legal and Moral Status," p. 101.

would be equivalent to murder. If (1) the conceptus is a person, but (2) society does not possess knowledge of this, then abortion is equivalent to manslaughter. At the very least, if (1) the conceptus is not a person, but (2) society does not possess knowledge of this, then abortion is equivalent to criminal negligence.[424] Since society does not in reality possess indisputable knowledge that the conceptus is not a person, which would seem to be the minimal standard to be met for abortion's justification, there exists no *prima facie* justification for abortion. Even should Warren's list of functional criteria for personhood be accepted, she has shown "only that a fetus does not function as a person, not that it lacks the being of a person, which is the crucial thing."[425]

Finally, the objection might be raised that Aquinas's definition of "person," as borrowed from Boethius, may be seen as a somewhat ambiguous phrase. If a person is an "individual substance of a rational nature," which of the following is meant by the definition?
1. The individual is a member of a class which is characterized by rationality.
2. The individual is itself actually rational.[426]
As has been seen, those holding to functionalist criteria for personhood would doubtless point to the second definition as the one that should be accepted. If the individual is not itself actually functioning as a rational being, it is not a person, according to this view. However, "if we consider the species label *homo sapiens, rational* man, it is clear that we understand that label in the first of these senses."[427] Humans may be characterized generically in many ways (e.g., as the species which makes non-practical, representational art, simply for the enjoyment of it), even though an individual human, selected randomly, may never in his or her life fulfill all of those characterizations. Nevertheless, "A ship, essentially a machine for floating on water, is still a ship when in dry dock."[428] Likewise, a member of a class which is characterized by rationality (the class of persons), even if not currently thinking rationally or even not currently capable of rational thought, is still a member of that class and is therefore an "individual substance of a rational nature." It enters that class, the class of persons, at the very time it comes into existence as an

---

[424] Peter Kreeft. "The Apple Argument Against Abortion." *Crisis* 18.11 (December 2000): 25-29, p. 28.
[425] See Chapter 7 of Stephen D. Schwarz's *The Moral Question of Abortion* for his defense of this claim, especially pp. 94-ff.
[426] Brian Scarlett, "The Moral Uniqueness of the Human Animal," p. 91.
[427] Ibid., p. 91. Emphasis in original.
[428] Ibid., p. 92.

individual substance.

Aquinas himself at least implicitly makes a similar argument in his *Quaestiones Disputatae de Anima*, "Whether the Soul Is Its Powers?" The powers of the soul "are certain properties of it," but cannot be the "essence" of the soul, since "a power is nothing but a thing's principle of operation." Although some maintain that the "essence itself of the soul is the immediate principle of all its operations" (such as when a human "understands, senses, and acts, and other things of this sort"), according to Thomas "this opinion cannot be maintained":

> Now it is evident that the powers of the soul, whether active or passive, are spoken of directly with respect to something substantial, but not with respect to something accidental. Similarly, to be understanding or sensing actually, is not a substantial mode of existing, but an accidental one to which the intellect and sense are directed. It is similar with respect to being large or small, to which the augmentative power is ordered.[429]

Therefore, whether or not a human is actually understanding or thinking at any given time has no more to do with the definition of the human essence than whether or not the human is large or small in size: "Now no accident of any kind ever constitutes part of the essence of a thing, and thus an accident is never found in a thing's definition. Hence we understand the essence [*quod quid est*] of a thing without thinking of any of its accidents." Even though "Man is said to be an intellect because the intellect is said to be the highest thing in man," still "this does not mean that the essence of the soul is the intellective power itself." One could readily extrapolate from this that the presence of the substantial form of the conceptus warrants describing the conceptus as a human person, apart from any current manifestation or lack of manifestation of its rational intellective power.

(4)  *The Possibility of Twinning*

Perhaps at this point it would be premature to agree completely with Robert P. George's assessment, "The arguments advanced for denying that embryos are human beings have been astonishingly weak." Certainly one could say that these arguments are remarkably repetitive, relying almost entirely on "functionalist" views of personhood in order to reach their conclusions. However, occasionally stronger and more original arguments do arise.[430] For example, some have questioned the

---

[429] *Quaestiones Disputatae de Anima.* John Patrick Rowan, trans. *The Soul.* St. Louis & London: B. Herder Book Co., 1949, Article 12.
[430] George, *The Clash of Orthodoxies*, p. 320. However, George does not think highly of the "possibility-of-twinning" argument either, merely labeling it "even

very early status of the zygote on the basis that the unified zygote has the potential to divide into monozygotic twins (or triplets, etc.) up until about the fourteenth day of its existence, and therefore "If the fecundated ovum can split into two beings which turn out to be two persons, it is difficult to admit that it was itself a person, hence fully human."[431] Anthony Kenny refers to this as the stage "before true individual development has begun" and places the beginning of individual personhood at somewhere around the fourteenth day of pregnancy:

> Before fertilization we have two entities (two different gametes) and after it we have a single one (one zygote). [However] the moment at which one entity (a single embryo) splits into two entities (two identitical twins) is equally a defining moment.

Kenny concludes that until the fourteenth day of its existence, the embryo "is not an individual human being." Interestingly, he follows up on this argument with his bluntly stated corollary: "After that time [i.e., the fourteenth day] it is an individual human being. If so, then late abortion is indeed homicide—and abortion becomes 'late' at an earlier date than was ever dreamt of by Aquinas."[432]

However, the possibility of twinning does not perhaps raise the ethical "defining moment" Kenny claims it does. For instance, David Albert Jones argues that the early embryo possesses a potential—that of developing into twins—that it loses within a few days, but that the mere fact of the early embryo's possessing this potential does not change the fact of its being a unitary human being up to that time:

> Scientists who deal with human embryos treat them as biological individuals. . . . . From a biological perspective, there is no difficulty in saying that, during the first stage of human development, some individuals divide to produce twins. For secular philosophers the occasional multiplication of human embryos in this way should be no barrier to counting the embryo as a human being, at least in the biological sense.[433]

Even in the fully mature adult human being, certain stem cells retain their pluripotentiality without changing in any way the unitary nature of the human in whom they may be found. The fact that the early

---

more esoteric" than other arguments (p. 322).

[431] Piet Schoonenberg, *God's World in the Making.* Pittsburgh: Duquesne Univ. Press, 1964, p. 50.

[432] Anthony Kenny. "The Beginning of Individual Human Life." *Daedalus* 137.1 (Winter 2008): 15-22, pp. 21-22.

[433] Jones, *The Soul of the Embryo*, pp. 225-26.

conceptus contains the capacity both for twinning and for toti-potentiality likewise does not bring into question the unitary nature of the conceptus.

In fact, whether or not the zygote separates into twins, it already possesses from conception all of the genetic material needed for its continued growth and self-organization as a human, with the innate potentials both of totipotency and of monozygotic twinning; neither this genetic material nor this potential seem especially problematic for the theory of immediate hominization.[434] As George has it, "The fact that a human individual in the embryonic stage can divide or be divided into two individuals is no cause for doubting whether the individual is a human being":

> Consider the parallel case of division of a flatworm. Parts of a flatworm have the potential to become a whole flatworm when isolated from the present whole of which they are part. Yet no one suggests that prior to the division of a flatworm to produce two whole flatworms the original flatworm was not a unitary individual and a whole living member of the species.[435]

On this point, Aquinas would perhaps not agree that the division of a flatworm is "parallel," as George puts it, with embryonic division. Thomas writes in *Quaestiones Disputatae de Potentia Dei* ("On the Power of God"), "The human soul is not capable of being multiplied in the same way as material forms which can be divided if their subject be divided: but remains in itself in its simplicity and unity."[436] However, regarding creatures such as flatworms, "In the case of those animals which live when cut in two, there is one soul in act and many in potency. Now through the act of cutting they are brought forth into actual manyness, as happens in the case of all forms which have extension in matter."[437] The form of the flatworm, in other words, ceases to exist when the flatworm is divided, for now two different flatworms exist; the flatworm's form or soul has been divided when its "extension in

---

[434] On this point see R. Koch-Hershenov, "Totipotency, Twinning, and Ensoulment at Fertilization." *Journal of Medical Philosophy* 31.2 (April 2006): 139-64. In fact, Koch-Hershenov argues that ensoulment at fertilization may itself provide a possible explanation for the puzzling mechanism of monozygotic twinning.

[435] George, "Sweet Reason." Review of *Human Life, Action, and Ethics: Essays by G.E.M. Anscombe*. Mary Geach and Luke Gormally, eds. *First Things* 159: Jan. 2006: 56-59, p. 58. See also George, *The Clash of Orthodoxies*, p. 322.

[436] *Quaestiones Disputatae de Potentia Dei*, V.10.ad6.

[437] *Quaestiones Disputatae de Spiritualibus Creaturis*. Mary C. Fitzpatrick and John J. Wellmuth, transs. Milwaukee: Marquette University Press, 1949: IV.ad19.

matter" is divided. The same, however, cannot occur with a human's rational soul, which has no extension in matter as such:

> A flatworm's division does not preclude its existence as an individual substance before its division. Nevertheless, a flatworm does not survive the division. Neither of the two resulting flat-worms is identical to the original; neither flatworm has the same soul as the original, for the original's soul ceased to exist when it was divided into many. . . . Aquinas thus distinguishes the possible division of a flatworm's soul from the impossible division of a rational soul.[438]

Thus in Thomistic terms one must conclude that a "unitary individual and whole living member of the [human] species" exists from its conception, even if this member of the human species also possesses the potential to become *two* or more unitary individuals and whole living members of the species. Probably George himself does not mean to imply that flatworm division and embryonic division are *precisely* parallel; as Eberl states, "The main point is that the potentiality to divide into two or more organisms does not preclude an organism's *previous* substantial unity; this is the same for both flatworms and embryos."[439] The relevant fact is not whether or not embryonic twinning is exactly parallel to other forms of division in other creatures, but rather that nothing that is not already a human being has any potential at all to develop further as a human being. Whether the early embryo is one human being or possibly more should make no difference to its protection.

Nevertheless, what about this question of the souls of twins? In other words, if the conceptus is a single unitary being until the time of twinning, does only one soul exist and therefore how does the twin receive his or her own soul? Jones states various options on this question concisely:

> The difficulty in telling a convincing "soul story" about twinning is due, at least in part, to uncertainty in regard to the precise biological mechanism of the process. Is twinning genetically predetermined or determined by the fertilization event? In which case, the early embryo could be thought of as conjoined twins. . . . Is twinning asymmetrical? In which case it could be understood as one embryo generating a second. . . . Is twinning symmetrical? In which case it could be thought of as the destruction of one individual to give rise

---

[438] Jason T. Eberl, "A Thomistic Perspective on the Beginning of Personhood: Redux," p. 285.
[439] Ibid., p. 286. Emphasis in original.

to two new individuals. . . . The problem with twinning seems less our inability to tell a "soul story" and more our inability to judge between these stories. Until more is known empirically, it is difficult to know what sort of story to tell.[440]

Despite this empirical difficulty, Jones does state his own view: "Twinning should probably be thought of as analogous to reproduction, with souls being multiplied according to bodies."[441] This Thomistic view is a direct paraphrase of Aquinas: "It is impossible that one individual intellectual soul should belong to several individuals. . . . For it is impossible for many distinct individuals to have one form, as it is impossible for them to have one existence, for the form is the principle of existence. . . . In like manner the multiplicity of souls is in proportion to the multiplicity of bodies."[442] Likewise Thomas argues elsewhere, "Souls are numerically differentiated according to the relation they have to different bodies."[443] Thus one soul exists for the single corporeal conceptus; if the zygote divides into twins, two souls now exist just as two corporeal entities now exist.[444] A more specific description of this process cannot yet be given, as Jones says, "until more is known empirically."

In *A Defense of Abortion*, David Boonin takes a different tack of opposition, arguing that there is some moral relevance in the fact that embryologists disagree over the precise point in the initial fertilization process at which a human being comes into existence.[445] For example, some embryologists argue "that a human being comes to be when the sperm penetrates the ovum, while others argue that this occurs when the pronuclei of the maternal and paternal chromosomes blend in the oocyte." On the other hand, in the latter stage, even before the diploid set of chromosomes has been formed, the sperm and ovum "have ceased to exist as distinct entities" and the oocyte "seems to behave like an individual living organism with an intrinsically-directed nature," as Francis J. Beckwith puts it.[446] Beckwith's response to Boonin may also be applied to the objection that the fertilized zygote has not yet become

---

[440] Jones, *The Soul of the Embryo*, pp. 226-27.

[441] Ibid., p. 234.

[442] ST I.76.2; see also *Quaestiones Disputatae de Spiritualibus Creaturis* IX.ad4.

[443] *Compendium Theologica* (hereafter CT), § 85. Cyril Vollert, S.J., trans. [1947]. New York: Sophia Institute Press, 1998.

[444] A detailed and helpful analysis of these matters may be found in Benedict Ashley and Albert Moraczewski's "Cloning, Aquinas, and the Embryonic Person" (*National Catholic Bioethics Quarterly* 1.2 [Summer 2001]: 189-201).

[445] Boonin, *A Defense of Abortion*, pp. 37-40.

[446] Beckwith, "Defending Abortion Philosophically," p. 180.

differentiated between embryo and placenta. We do not "personalize" the placenta; it may be considered merely as one more amazing aspect of the unfolding potential and self-direction of the zygote.[447]

However, even though due to these facts some embryologists think a new human being may have come into existence prior to completed syngamy (the point at which both sets of parental chromosomes form a diploid set), what seems "indisputable" is that "at syngamy a new human being, an individual human substance, exists and is in the process of development and is not identical to either the sperm or the ovum from whose unity it arose."[448] The fact that this new human being also possesses for a time the potential to become twins or even multiple humans does not change its character as an individual human substance of rational nature, a human person.

### 2.     The "Lethal Logic" of Peter Singer

Peter Singer, of course, disagrees with this conclusion, although he agrees with some of the premises behind it (e.g., he agrees that the typical pro-choice arguments fail to establish their position). For example, in a June 2005 letter to the New York *Times* he readily admits, "Even the earliest embryo conceived of human parents is alive and a member of *Homo sapiens*." However, he then goes on to say:

> The crucial moral question is not when human life begins, but when human life reaches the point at which it merits protection. . . . Unless we separate these two questions—when does life begin, and when does it merit protection—we are unlikely to achieve any clarity about the moral status of embryos.[449]

In a comment on this passage, Richard John Neuhaus points out that while Singer rejects the conclusions reached by those opposing abortion, he has surrendered the central premise of their argument without a qualm:

> Singer has an intellectually complexified answer to the question as to what human lives merit protection. He argues, for example, that the life of an adult pig deserves protection more than that of a newborn human baby, and that parents should be free to kill their young children already born if they deem them unacceptably disabled. So, while Singer comes up with barbarously wrong answers, he comes close to posing the right questions for public

---

[447] See Junker-Kenny, "The Moral Status of the Embryo," pp. 51-52.
[448] Beckwith, "Defending Abortion Philosophically," p. 181.
[449] Singer, "Science, Religion and Stem Cells" [response to editorial column "Not on Faith Alone," Mario Cuomo, 20 June 2005]. *The New York Times* 23 June 2005.

consideration: Given the biological fact that an embryo is a human being, what duty, if any, do we have to protect that life? And, if we say we have no such duty because that life is too small or too weak or too burdensome, how do we avoid extending that lethal logic to the monstrous conclusions espoused by Peter Singer?[450]

(1)  *Why Reject Singer's Arguments?*

One of the central arguments arising throughout this book is that any answer given to these questions posed by Neuhaus that minimizes the protection afforded to humans at any stage of their development has no really good arguments against that answer's extension—its "lethal logic," as Neuhaus has it. Once the human substance is accepted as, in fact, human (because of its innate form in the Thomistic sense), any argument disallowing its protection could also be used, as Singer does, to disallow protections for those even in far more advanced stages of development. Since "abortion violates the rational humanist tenet of the equality of human lives,"[451] its acceptance may lead inexorably to other denials of equality.

For example, consider what is implied in the following:

Thus the arguments of philosophers and physicians notwithstanding, anthropologic and theologic evidence suggests that notions of what constitutes a person in the strict sense range all the way from assignment of rights to zygotes on the basis of the potential for later development of full personhood to the with-holding of that designation until an individual has had formal teachings designed to make him or her a person at or near the age of puberty.[452]

Even this paraphrase on the part of Gerald T. Perkoff (the author of the quoted passage) does not accurately state the position. Zygotes may be assigned rights, not because of their "potential for later development," but because of what they already are: human beings at the earliest stage of human development. They will not develop into anything other than older, more developed humans. However, the important point here under consideration is that in a practical sense Perkoff holds the door open for the possibility of the denial of the

---

[450] Neuhaus, "While We're At It" 159, p. 74.

[451] John T. Noonan, Jr. "Aquinas on Abortion." *St. Thomas Aquinas on Politics and Ethics.* Paul E. Sigmund, ed. New York: Norton Critical Edition, 1988: 245-48, p. 248.

[452] Gerald T. Perkoff. "A Normative Definition of Personhood." *Abortion and the Status of the Fetus.* William B. Bondeson, H. T. Engelhardt, Jr., Stuart F. Spicker, and Daniel H. Winship, eds. Dordrecht, Holland: D. Reidel Publishing, 1983: 159-66, p. 163.

ascription of "personhood" (and hence the assignment of protective rights) until a child is "at or near the age of puberty," whether or not the author of this passage actually holds this view. The psychological effect of such reasoning is to suggest that perhaps as society recoils from the legalized killing of a twelve-year-old, infanticide (as a more reasonable "middle ground") may be seen as more permissible and even reasonable: "In the case of the one-month-old infant, however, there is no evidence that a person in a strict sense is present," as one author asserts.[453]

Singer's fundamental mistake in this matter is similar to Mary Anne Warren's, that is, the mistake of the initial separation of human-ness from personhood. For justification for this separation, Singer points back to the "impeccable philosophical precedents" of John Locke's functional definition of personhood,[454] as described earlier in this chapter. However, as Jenny Teichman has pointed out, Singer's position is only "quasi-Lockean," since Locke himself would have rejected Singer's use of his definition of "person" for the following reasons: "Firstly because he was a Christian, secondly because he believed in *natural* rights (and natural rights can only belong to a natural species), and thirdly (as implied in Chapter 27 of the *Essay*) because he held that it is important for justice that *neither* persons *nor* human beings (human bodies) be wrongly punished."[455] In fact, Locke himself writes, "It is part of the worship of God . . . not to procure abortion."[456] In context, Locke is presenting this as a truth not known innately, as part of his argument against innately known moral truths, but still as a truth positively known by other means; he explicitly refers to abortion as "among the most obviously immoral actions," a comment which "seems to have gone almost unnoticed by scholars."[457] Singer's

[453] H. Tristram Engelhardt, Jr. "Introduction." *Abortion and the Status of the Fetus.* William B. Bondeson, H. Tristram Engelhardt, Jr., Stuart F. Spicker, and Daniel H. Winship, eds. Dordrecht, Holland: D. Reidel Publishing, 1983: xi-xxxii, p. xv. (Engelhardt, to his credit, in later writings changed his position on this subject rather dramatically.)

[454] Singer, *Practical Ethics*, p. 87. Singer's discussion of personhood continues from this page.

[455] Teichman, "The False Philosophy of Peter Singer," pp. 28-29. Emphasis in original.

[456] Locke, *An Essay Concerning Human Understanding*, I.2.19.

[457] Eric Manchester. "Locke on Bodily Rights and the Immorality of Abortion: A Neglected Liberal Perspective." *Life and Learning XVI: Proceedings of the Sixteenth University Faculty for Life Conference.* Joseph W. Koterski, S.J., ed. Washington, D.C.: University Faculty for Life, 2007: 383-409, p. 384.

misappropriation of Locke and his consequent separation of human-ness from personhood lead directly to some of the positions he has adopted for which he has become infamous. For instance, he argues from the stance of "a conscious disavowal of any assumption that all members of our own species have, merely because they are members of our species, any distinctive worth or inherent value that puts them above members of other species. . . . To prohibit any cross-species comparisons would be philosophically indefensible."[458] However, Singer's reason for this stance is at least partially derived from the basic premise that *some humans are not persons*—since infants, for example, lack rational functionality, they according to Singer are not to be seen as persons.[459] But as soon as Singer's basic premise is rejected in favor of the Thomistic definition of a person as an "individual substance of rational nature," one immediately perceives that humans do have "distinctive worth" and "inherent value" because they are members of a species that is also and already made up of *persons rather than things*.

But why should anyone reject Singer's premises in favor of the Thomistic definition? In fact, since Singer works and writes from a completely secular preference-utilitarian stance (these are his own labels), it may seem as if this discussion comprises merely a "talking past" each other; as MacIntyre might put it, it may seem an "interminable" ethical argument between positions that share no common vantage points or foundational elements:

> The most striking feature of contemporary moral utterance is that so much of it is used to express disagreements; and the most striking feature of the debates in which these disagreements are expressed is their interminable character. I do not mean by this just that such debates go on and on and on—although they do—but also that they apparently can find no terminus. There seems to be no rational way of securing moral agreement in our culture.[460]

However, there do appear to be sound reasons to prefer the Thomistic account of human personhood over Singer's. Primarily, (1) the Thomistic account of personhood should be accepted because it is scientifically more accurate, and (2) Singer's account of preference-utilitarianism contains internal logical inconsistencies which should disqualify its acceptance.

First, in order to adopt Singer's "quasi-Lockean" shift from "human

---

[458] Singer, *Practical Ethics*, p. ix.
[459] *Rethinking Life and Death*, p. 210.
[460] Alasdair MacIntyre. *After Virtue: A Study in Moral Theory*. 2nd edition. Notre Dame, Indiana: University of Notre Dame Press, 1984, p. 6.

being" to "human person," one would have to pinpoint an ontological change similar to Aquinas's antiquated description of the change from the vegetative to the animal to the intellectual soul. Such an ontological change in human status genetically does not and cannot occur; the human "person" eventually manifested at a certain level of functional abilities is exactly the same genetically as the human "being" brought into existence at conception. The development which takes place from conception onwards does not change the human ontologically but only in terms of the human's functional abilities and organic development. Aquinas, at least, given his own metaphysical principles of the human's "organic" hylomorphic unity, would today acknowledge the *scientific* point—in Thomistic language, that since there is no change in the embryo's substantial form there is also no change in the embyo's embodiment and genetic endowment—and modify his account of the embryo's ontological status. Singer acknowledges the genetic description of the embryo as a human being, but asserts that this scientific point makes no difference to his argument since he has already accepted a different definition of personhood. Again, however, how and when does this ontological distinction of "personhood" arise, except as a simple presupposition? If one decides upon rational functioning and self-awareness as the marks of personhood, what is the scientific basis for such a decision? It seems rather that such a decision and definition is based upon other considerations, considerations with no scientific warrant whatsoever.

Secondly, Singer's account of preference-utilitarianism should be rejected because of its internal logical inconsistencies. For Singer, the "non-moral goods to be sought" are the interests or preferences of sentient beings, "and the non-moral evils to be avoided are the corresponding *frustration* or *thwarting* of such interests or preferences."[461] However, Singer's account of "goods" and "evils" depends, as do all such consequentialist accounts, upon the intuitive commitments of those prescribing the goods to be maximized and the evils to be minimized. For Singer, the basic goods appear to be readily summarized: Human persons should seek their own fulfillment by following their interests or preferences, and should as much as possible allow other human persons (note: *not* mere human beings) to do the same. Further, since other animal species at least have the basic interest or preference of not feeling pain, human persons should treat other

---

[461] Andrew Sloane. "Singer, Preference Utilitarianism and Infanticide." *Studies in Christian Ethics* 12.2 (January 1999): 47-73, p. 54. Emphasis in original. See also Singer's *Practical Ethics*, p. 13.

species with kindness and respect to the greatest degree possible, by allowing them to pursue their own interests and preferences. Out of these basic goods, Singer extrapolates also the philosophical commitment to political and economic equality between human persons.

This leaves, however, an important series of questions to be answered (as, again, do all consequentialist systems of ethical theory). As Andrew Sloane points out, Why should we be concerned with others' preferences? "Why do any of these things [the "goods" previously listed] matter? How can Singer claim that it is 'better' to live this way rather than that?" Sloane continues: "I suspect that, once again, we come upon Singer's fundamental ethical intuitions. Many of them are sound; some are not. None of them have any real justification within the context of his theory."[462] Even though some of Singer's intuitions regarding the good appear coherent and practicable, why should his readers accept his intuitions concerning the fundamental ends toward which humans should aim? Ironically, some of Singer's basic intuitions do appear to have some justification once the idea of an objective moral order is acknowledged: "Many (but not all) of these intuitions can be justified in the context of belief-systems, such as Christian ones, which affirm the objective nature of morality. But that is cold comfort for Singer."[463]

Singer's campaign in moral theory seems to have two essential ends: first, that human persons should as much as possible allow for the maximal fulfillment of others' preferences within the context of an overall utilitarian good; and secondly, that this preference-utilitarian stance should be universalized across all societies within their varied systems of moral discourse.[464] However, in what way could these essential ends possibly be seen as normative or "objective" for all human persons (especially considering the principle of "universalizability"), or even as describing the ethical state of affairs? If Singer is not actually describing the ethical state of affairs, his arguments may be disregarded as simply another form of intuitionism; but if he is in fact objectively describing the ethical state of affairs and what humans universally "should" do given this state of affairs, such a description "has unacceptable consequences for Singer's preference utilitarianism, for if that principle stands, then why not others?"

Indeed, if it stands as a substantive principle *per se*, then Singer's

---

[462] Ibid., pp. 70-71.
[463] Ibid., p. 71.
[464] See on these points Singer's *The Expanding Circle*, especially pp. 105-ff. (*The Expanding Circle: Ethics and Sociobiology*. Oxford: Clarendon Press, 1981).

system falls, for this ethical principle, at least, refers to an objective moral order. Singer cannot have it both ways. Either there is an objective moral order, in which case universalisability may be a valid *substantive* ethical principle. But in this case other principles cannot be ruled out of court: indeed, a case must be made against other principles arising from similar fundamental moral intuitions. Or there is no such moral order, in which case the principle does not hold. But if the principle does not hold, then Singer's theory falls. Either way, Singer's theory falls.[465]

This argument may at first be seen as an elaborate form of *tu quoque*, that is to say: "Believers in an objective moral order might ground their actions in simple intuitionism, but so does Singer!" However, such is not the case. In ordinary life, the moral intuitions of most humans (such as the intuition that infanticide is morally wrong and to be rejected) are grounded in belief in the objective moral order, not the other way around. For example, *contra* Singer, the moral intuition of most appears to be that a species has a certain inherent worth and value if the members of the species in question are persons simply due to their membership in that particular species. In the natural world, the only creatures known without question to be persons are humans. The meaning of the word "person" in ordinary life, according to Teichman, "is governed by the fact that its extension is in practice the same as the extension of the term 'human being.' In other words, in ordinary life 'person' and 'human being' refer to the same things." This is of course Aquinas's position as well,[466] as is also the moral point Teichman draws:

> For this reason the *ordinary* sense of the word "person" does not, indeed cannot, detach moral import from the concept of the human. The case is otherwise with the Singerian view of personhood, because when Singer draws his distinction between human beings and persons he carefully detaches moral import from his idea of the human and transfers it to his idea of the person. . . . [This operation] is arbitrary indeed: it does not mirror ordinary use (because ordinary use equates persons with human beings), it does not mirror legal use (ditto, roughly), it does not describe a naturally existing class of natural objects (such as a species), and it does not

---

[465] Sloane, "Singer, Preference Utilitarianism and Infanticide," p. 68. Emphasis in original.

[466] As was brought out earlier, Aquinas does think of a human being as a human person, even though due to his wrongful biological notions he does not think of the early conceptus as a human being and hence does not think of the early conceptus as a person.

144

even mirror Locke (for the reasons explained above).[467]
Although Singer effectively wants to exclude ontology from the
discussion altogether and focus exclusively on the functionality of the
human being in order to determine the human's personhood, such a
move should be rejected. Any sort of determination of the appropriate
functionality of a "person" is "arbitrary indeed," to use Teichman's
term. The complementary facts, that formally the substance of the
conceptus does not change, and that materially the DNA structure of
the conceptus does not change, should be enough to prefer acceptance
of the definition of the conceptus as an individual substance of rational
nature, and hence a person. In this case, the moral intuition leading to
the protection of humans at their earliest stage of development turns
out to be both scientifically and logically validated.

(2) *Singer's Two Fundamental Mistakes*

In sum, the two most crucial mistakes made by Singer are also the
philosophical stances for which he has become most well known: the
separation of personhood from humanity, and the consequentialist-
based ethical implications of such a separation. First, Singer separates
the human person from the human being. Although other philosophers
argue for the same separation, Singer is certainly the most public
proponent of the "person/human" distinction; however, suffice it to
say that the validity of the "person/human" distinction is far too often
presumed rather than proven.[468]

On the other hand, it should again be acknowledged on Singer's
behalf that he does not flinch from the unsavory implications of this
distinction. Theologian John Jefferson Davis lists some of the more
obvious of these implications:

> Proponents of the abortion-on-demand and abortion-on-indica-
> tions positions generally take the fetus to be less than a full
> "person" or "human being" because of the lack of fully developed
> consciousness. It is dangerous, however, to equate the *fact* of
> personhood with certain *psychological states*. Personhood is a meta-
> physical reality out of which arises, during the normal course of
> human development, the psychological manifestations of the
> person. A newborn baby does not possess the adult's powers of
> speech or thought, but in due course the baby will develop these
> powers, because they are inherent in the child's nature. The same
> argument that justifies abortion because of the lack of conscious-

---

[467] Teichman, "The False Philosophy of Peter Singer," p. 29. Emphasis in
original.
[468] Gilbert Meilaender, *Bioethics*, p. 36.

ness in the unborn could also justify infanticide after birth. The equation of personhood with certain states of consciousness could also be extended to argue for the killing of the comatose, the senile, and the mentally retarded.[469]

However, as stated, Singer recognizes this potential extension—the "lethal logic" of his position—and accepts it. According to Teichman's summary of Singer's conclusions as expressed in Chapter 2 of his *Practical Ethics*, "The kinds of human beings who have no right to life [include] not only disabled newborn infants but also month-old hemophiliac infants not wanted by their parents or adopters, any young infant not wanted by its parents or adopters, and all human beings who do not know they are persons." This last phrase arises out of Singer's dictum "that children who do not yet understand they are persons are not persons, and can be killed if they are not wanted by their parents."[470] One of the tests for this self-knowledge on the part of persons is awareness of the potential fate of unwanted children, which then somewhat ironically serves to exclude one from this fate; as Singer allows, "Those old enough to be aware of the killing of disabled infants are necessarily outside the scope of the policy."[471] In Chapter 2 of *Practical Ethics*, hemophilia is used by Singer as a primary example of a disability thought to allow logically for the killing of an infant; hence Teichman's specific mention of that disease in her summary of Singer's views.

Singer's second crucial mistake follows from this first. Since in his view certain groups of human beings exist who are not equivalent to human persons, these humans also are not qualitatively different from nor in any sense superior to non-human animals, who also are not persons. As a secular preference-utilitarian, Singer thus thinks the basis for making ethical decisions regarding the lives of both human beings and non-human animals is the same—the degree to which these humans and animals can feel pleasure or pain, or the degree to which the ethical decision interferes with the preferences of the ones affected by it.[472] Although Singer usually argues from the latter preference-based form of utilitarianism, he has also linked the simple Benthamite pleasure/pain calculus to the concept of preferences or "interests": "If

---

[469] John Jefferson Davis. *Evangelical Ethics: Issues Facing the Church Today.* Phillipsburg, New Jersey: Presbyterian and Reformed Publishing Company, 1985, p. 153. Emphasis in original.

[470] Teichman, "The False Philosophy of Peter Singer," pp. 27-28.

[471] Singer, *Practical Ethics*, p. 192.

[472] Ibid., pp. 89-ff.

you recognize that other animals are sentient beings, then they have interests—for example, they have an interest in not feeling pain. . . . [Is] the pain suffered by that animal less significant than the pain suffered by a member of the species *Homo sapiens?*. . . . The answer is no."[473] Since an adult dog (for instance) can probably feel pleasure or pain (one aspect of the utilitarian calculus occasionally used by Singer) or have certain preferences (the other aspect) to a greater degree than can a human being in a coma, or a newborn human infant, the adult dog would also possess greater moral rights than the comatose human or human infant. The dog would possess, for example, a greater right to life than the humans, since for Singer no good reasons exist for preferring the humans over the animal: "When we are comparing similar interests—of which the interest in avoiding pain is the most important example—[the] principle of equal consideration of interests demands we give equal weight to the interests of the human and the [animal]."[474] More recently Singer, with the ruthless logicality known only to those in the grip of an erroneous theory, has extended this equivalence of humans and non-humans into arguments for the acceptance of inter-species sexual relationships, arguments presented in rather graphic detail.[475]

However, perhaps given his premises Singer *must* extend his thinking into realms such as this, for granting any superiority to human beings *qua* human beings (in other words, as rational creatures who thereby should come to be recognized as *persons* rather than things) would undermine the entire logical structure of his argument; as Joseph Fletcher, who agrees with Singer, writes, the central point at issue throughout this and related debates is "whether a fetus is a person or not."[476] Singer must therefore insist on a strict human being/human person distinction, rejecting absolutely the older view of personhood as

---

[473] Peter Singer. Interview: "Does the End Justify the Means?" *The Examined Life*. DVD. Pasadena, California: Intelecom, 2002.
[474] Singer, *The Expanding Circle*, p. 121. For other typical examples of Singer's arguments in this regard, see his *Animal Liberation* [1975] (New York: Harper Perennial Reprint, 2001); *In Defense of Animals: The Second Wave* (Oxford: Blackwell, 2005); and his essay "All Animals Are Equal" (*Philosophic Exchange*. Brockport, New York: Center for Philosophic Exchange, 1974: 103-16).
[475] Peter Singer. "Heavy Petting." *Nerve* (March 2001), n.p. Nerve.com/ Opinions/Singer. Accessed 4 January 2008.
[476] Joseph Fletcher. *The Ethics of Genetic Control*. Garden City, New York: Anchor Press, 1974, p. 135. Of course, the present discussion presses the question further back in the development of the conceptus than the "fetus" stage.

inherent in any individual substance of a rational nature. A cogent statement of this older view of personhood, from Davis, will serve to conclude this discussion: "A 'person' in the proper sense exists from the earliest moments of human existence. Personhood denotes not merely conscious, postnatal humans, but all members of the human species, those who are genetically distinct human entities with their own unique life trajectory and developmental futures. Rather than saying that the unborn represent 'potential human life,' it is more accurate to say that the unborn represent *actual* human life with *great potential*."[477] Singer's rejection of this view of personhood, his insistence on the "human being/human person" distinction, is the initial error leading gradually to more obvious and even bizarre errors as his arguments have progressed throughout his career.

Although one might wish Singer's views were much other than what they are, he at least has the distinction of being one of the few proponents of abortion-on-demand who point out the logical implications of "potential-person" rhetoric. Since the arguments based on the distinction between "potential" and "actual" humanity tend to apply "just as much after birth as [they] do before," Singer, as has been seen, does not shy away from the open embrace of infanticide as public policy: "I do not deny that if one accepts abortion on the grounds provided . . . the case for killing other human beings, in certain circumstances, is strong. As I shall try to show in this chapter [on infanticide], however, this is not something to be regarded with horror."[478] Singer usually qualifies such arguments when he further discusses the killing of adults, by incorporating the adults' considered wishes; however, as Davis points out, the acceptance of "potential-person" rhetoric may extend much further into human life, perhaps even into adulthood, without necessarily considering the adults' wishes in the matter, since in some situations some adults may not be aware of being killed and may have no means of expressing their preferences in the matter. Likewise, Norman Kretzmann writes in his discussion of Aquinas on potentiality and activity, "The mere fact that human existence is temporal rather than eternal already entails that the actual existence of any human person at any time is mixed together with countless unactualized potentialities."[479] Therefore, since according to Singer only those humans at certain levels of functionality, or with

---

[477] Davis, *Evangelical Ethics*, p. 153. Emphasis in original.
[478] Singer, *Practical Ethics*, p. 175.
[479] Norman Kretzmann. *The Metaphysics of Creation: Aquinas's Natural Theology in Summa Contra Gentiles II*. Oxford: Clarendon Press, 1999, p. 39.

expressed preferences, have any real rights to be considered "human persons" with basic human rights, it seems plausible that others involved in human-life ethical discussions should discontinue the use of "potential-person" rhetoric altogether, unless they are prepared to press their case as far as Singer has pressed it. Usually those using the phrase "potential person" mean by it only the human being in the womb. However, it could be argued that the conceptus must already possess some sort of actualization, or it would be literally nothing at all; the question is what sort of actuality the conceptus possesses: If "we could call growth a kind of unfolding . . . of already-present potential [then] is not the zygote simply the first stage of this unfolding? . . . Its potential is not to become a different species or essence, but a potential to unfold the essence. The essence is already there, guiding the unfolding."[480] A different way of phrasing the same basic idea is to say "the potentialities of a thing are rooted in the form it actually [already] has."[481]

At the very least, the concept of infanticide should be used "as a starting point for the evaluation of other positions," as Anthony Kenny points out: "Any argument used to justify abortion, or in vitro fertilization (IVF), or stem cell research must undergo the following test: would the same argument justify infanticide?" Kenny concludes, "If so, then it must be rejected."[482]

(3)    *The Question of Utilitarian Benefits*

As can be seen in the case of Singer, much of the justification for the functionalist view of personhood relies substantially on a sort of consequentialist calculus, aiming for the greatest societal good for the greatest number, in particular the greatest good for the greatest number of people in dire medical need or in dire social circumstances. However, one problem with this sort of justification is the same foundational problem one might find in any discussion of utilitarianism in general: The concept of "greatest good" does not itself define the "good" toward which one should strive. If one substitutes any specific quality, such as the goal of enhanced clinical knowledge or the biotechnological goal of "medical benefits," too much of what makes human life worthwhile may readily be left out of the calculation:

> Many public policy discussions about bioethical issues seem to take place within a purely consequentialist framework—they exclude moral arguments other than those concerned with outcomes (such as attempts to weigh up the likely risks against benefits). . . .

---

[480] Peter Kreeft, *The Unaborted Socrates*, pp. 64-65.
[481] David Albert Jones, *The Soul of the Embryo*, p. 22.
[482] Kenny, "The Beginning of Individual Human Life," p. 16.

[However] there is more to be said than this.[483]

Even in utilitarian ethics, the "good" for which one should strive must be seen as a total human flourishing rather than as Bentham's hedonic or Singer's "preference" calculus; however, this total human flourishing must be defined as a flourishing according to human *nature*. And, of course, any sort of discussion of a flourishing according to human nature leads one directly back into the discussion of Thomistic anthropology. Only by maintaining sight of first-order anthropological principles may one maintain sight of the natural goods one might legitimately seek to maximize: "The conviction that a little evil may rightly be done for the sake of a greater good, or for the sake of preventing a greater evil, puts human beings on the path to losing their grip on good and evil altogether."[484]

### 3. Concluding Thoughts Regarding Personhood: Two Views

Throughout this work, the position taken regarding personhood has been two-fold in nature: (1) No legitimate division exists between a "human being" and a "human person," and certainly no difference that would imply a "human being" lacks the innate right to life that a "human person" possesses; and (2) a human being/human person exists from conception. The contrary argument *against* these two claims and *for* the separation of human-ness and personhood may be summarized as follows (in the words of H. Tristram Engelhardt, Jr.)[485]:

---

[483] Neil Messer, *The Ethics of Human Cloning*, p. 22. See also Messer's "Human Cloning and Genetic Manipulation: Some Theological and Ethical Issues" (*Studies in Christian Ethics* 12.2 [January 1999]: 1-16).

[484] Robert P. George, "Sweet Reason," p. 57.

[485] This quotation from Engelhardt was chosen for its admirable clarity and concision. However, in fairness to Engelhardt, it should be noted that since 1983 (the year of the quote's publication) his position seems to have shifted to a considerable extent. In fact, in the second edition of his *The Foundations of Bioethics* (New York: Oxford Univ. Press USA, 1996), Engelhardt confesses of the first edition, "Many of the conclusions to which I had found myself drawn were (and still are) abhorrent" (p. viii). For example, in his follow-up work *The Foundations of Christian Bioethics* (Lisse: Swets & Zeitlinger, 2000), Engelhardt asserts that ethically "one may not use abortion to avoid having a child.... All violence against human zygotes, embryos, and fetuses must be recognized as freighted with grave spiritual peril" (p. 235). He goes on, "Any act to kill a zygote or early embryo should count as murder.... One must condemn . . . any action taken to expel an embryo from the womb, as equivalent to murder" (pp. 280-81). He disagrees with the position of the present work, that "persons" should be protected and that the formal animating principle qualifies one as a person, but argues for protection despite this: "The requirement is that one must give recognition to new human life, even if the soul may not have

150

"Zygotes, embryos, and fetuses, like brain-dead but otherwise alive human beings, give no evidence of being persons. Nor will it help to say they are potential persons. *Y*'s that are potential *X*'s are *a fortiori* not *X*'s. If fetuses are to be treated with respect greater than that accorded to non-human animals of similar development, it will be because of the value of such a practice, not because of the intrinsic value they possess (at least insofar as general, secular arguments are concerned)."[486]

On the other hand, to summarize the most pertinent of the arguments against functionalist definitions of humanity: Aquinas clearly asserts in several places that the actual operation of a potentiality is accidental to the existence of the soul containing these potentialities.[487] Therefore, whether or not sentience is a "capacity in hand" or simply a potential to develop a capacity in hand seems to lack moral significance. What is important is that the rational soul may inform a developing conceptus even apart from actual sentience: "Since a rational soul is a human body's substantial form. . . . it is inconsequential whether such operations are actually exercised in a body for a rational soul to inform it."[488] The ongoing development toward sentience and eventual fully fledged rational thought indicates the presence of the human rational soul, even if that soul is not currently rationally thinking, cannot currently undertake rational thought at all, or cannot even experience sensory input, i.e., is non-sentient. Such development indicates as well the presence of a person: "Persons cannot be potential, because they are, logically and ontologically, the foundation of potentiality. Persons are the transcendental condition of possibilities or potentialities."[489] What is more, the functionalist definition of personhood would serve immediately to exclude from personhood many categories of humans already born.

(1) *"Potential Persons" and the "Moment of Conception"*

For example, one could easily question the "value" of practicing greater regard for fetuses than that accorded to non-human animals, as Peter Singer has done. Why would this practice possess value if the fetuses

---

entered. Killing that life will involve being implicated in a person's not having life" (p. 305n136). In other words, Engelhardt now argues that the human should be protected from conception *whether or not* the zygote is ensouled and *whether or not* the zygote is (yet) a person.

[486] Engelhardt, "Introduction," *Abortion and the Status of the Fetus*, p. xv.

[487] E.g., in ST I.76.4.

[488] Jason T. Eberl, *Thomistic Principles and Bioethics*, p. 28.

[489] Anselm Ramelow, O.P. "Review of *Persons: The Difference Between 'Someone' and 'Something'* by Robert Spaemann (Oliver O'Donovan, trans. Oxford: Oxford Univ. Press, 2007)." *The Thomist* 72.2 (April 2008): 317-21, p. 320.

themselves have no greater "intrinsic value"? Such a greater regard, *if it has no rational basis*, would be little more than humanity's preference for its own kind ("speciecism," in Singer's term), a preference which appears to have little if any moral justification.[490] Of course, I am pressing the position that this greater respect does have a rational basis and therefore a moral justification.

Singer and a few other similar philosophers have actually been of enormous practical benefit in bioethical discussions. Open discussions and recommendations of infanticide and involuntary euthanasia are no longer seen as the fantasies of overheated pro-life rhetoric, since they are contained within the respectably published and widely circulated writings of well-known living philosophers. Also, practically speaking, no longer is the "slippery-slope" argument used by the pro-life cause considered quite so much of a "fallacy"; the slippery slope seems to have become more of a free-fall. However, Singer is correct in pointing out the further implications of many pro-choice arguments. As Peter Kreeft points out, those many who say, "I am personally opposed to abortion, but I don't want to impose my values on others" are either being disingenuous or careless in their thinking:

> Why are you personally against abortion? . . . If you think a fetus is a human being, you surely ought to protect it by law against its potential murderers, just as we protect all other human beings. But if you think it is not a human being, why are you personally against abortion?[491]

Singer's stance seems the inverse of Kreeft's: If the conceptus is not a person, but only a "potential person," this categorization not only provides grounds for the abortion of the conceptus, but also for the killing of others who would seem more clearly to be human beings, such as handicapped children or terminally ill adults. These children and adults also seem to lack enough "actualized potential" that they could be disqualified from personhood, and hence from natural human protections: "The philosophical premises from which Singer derives his justification of infanticide are not confined to the deformed and the suffering. They consist in the theses that infants are not persons and that only persons have significant moral status and a serious right to life."[492] Kreeft's assumption, therefore, that "by law . . . we protect all

---

[490] On the other hand, according to Robert Spaemann, the emphasis on the personhood of human beings does not constitute "speciecism," since personhood in other creatures would warrant their protection as well; he mentions dolphins as a possible example (*Persons*, p. 248).

[491] Kreeft, *The Unaborted Socrates*, p. 99.

other human beings" is perhaps both premature and overly sanguine. However, as has been pointed out, a "potential person" is *a fortiori* not a person. The "potential-person" categorization thus accomplishes really nothing regarding the moral status of the conceptus; if no good reasons exist to be against abortion as such and in actual law, no good reasons exist to be "personally opposed" to abortion, except perhaps squeamishness. In Singer's words, "We have seen that liberals have failed to establish a morally significant dividing line between the newborn baby and the fetus."[493] At least thanks are due to Singer for clarifying this point, even though the net effect of his argument is to extend the range of candidates for killing; as his position as described in his *Practical Ethics* may be summarized, Singer "insists that there is nothing wrong with killing infants if they are either (a) severely deformed or brain-damaged or (b) simply not wanted by parents or adopters."[494] For popular consumption and in his "defending against attack" mode, Singer generally focuses on criterion (a) rather than (b).[495]

Further, it serves no purpose to argue, as does Christine E. Gudorf, that the moment of conception has no real meaning and thus there is no "moment" at which a human being comes into existence:

> The nineteenth-century discovery of the ovum and the process of fertilization, together with the rudimentary science of genetics, were almost immediately seized upon in the Catholic church as evidence that completely individuated human life—a person—is present from fertilization of the ovum. The church therefore decreed that human life begins at the "moment" of conception. This has led to some irreconcilable differences with later scientific discoveries, especially the discoveries that fertilization, and therefore conception, is an extended process, not a moment, and that individuation is not necessarily complete for weeks.[496]

This argument serves no purpose because firstly it seems to suggest that because conception does not necessarily occur at any single "moment," conception is thereby not to be considered a valid demarcation for the

[492] Jenny Teichman. "Dr. Jekyll and Mr. Hyde." *The New Criterion* 19.2 (October 2000): 64-67, p. 66.
[493] Singer, *Practical Ethics*, p. 149.
[494] Teichman, "Dr. Jekyll and Mr. Hyde," p. 64.
[495] For an example of this "defensive" mode, see Singer's "A German Attack on Applied Ethics" (*Journal of Applied Philosophy* 9.1 [1992]: 85-91).
[496] Gudorf, "Contraception and Abortion in Roman Catholicism." *Sacred Rights: The Case for Contraception and Abortion in World Religions*. Daniel C. Maguire, ed. New York: Oxford University Press USA, 2003: 55-78, p. 69.

beginning of human life. However, the word "moment" can be and often is used to mean an extended period of time; for example, a political speaker may say to an audience, "This is our moment in history." Secondly, just because a process may be gradual does not negate the real transformation occurring within the process. Consider the following diagram as representing a spectrum of color shading from black to white:

**Black---Various shades of grey lightening to---White**

The observer of this spectrum cannot put his or her finger on any specific color gradation and say, "At this exact point the black has shaded to white." On the other hand, when one looks from the left side of the spectrum to the right side, one can definitely say, "The black has shaded to white." The color change is real and substantive. Likewise, conception may also require "an extended process," as Gudorf rather indefinitely puts it (this "extended process" actually takes less than a day), but when the process has taken place, a real transformation has also taken place. The process may be gradual, but it is also real and substantive. Gudorf's stance illustrates what Francis Beckwith has called the "fallacy of the beard": "Just because I cannot tell you when stubble ends and a beard begins, this does not mean that I cannot distinguish bearded faces from clean shaven ones."[497]

In fact, given the need for conceptual clarity in these topics, here is a proposed change in terminology, designed to do away completely with the distinction between "human being" and "human person." Consider as a thought experiment what would happen in current public reasoning and debates if one simply replaces the phrase "human being" with "human who may not possess self-awareness and sentience and who may not be self-sustaining"; likewise if one replaces the phrase "human person" (and the distinctions and conferred rights implied by that phrase) with "human who does possess, to a greater or lesser degree, self-awareness and sentience, and is self-sustaining, again to a greater or lesser degree." As has been discussed, something like the following is commonly argued: "Persons have rights, including the right to life, that must be protected, but human beings as such do not necessarily have rights, including the right to life, that must be protected." The effect of this sentence changes, however, when one gives the terms their proposed substitutions: "Humans who do possess, to a greater or lesser degree, self-awareness and sentience, and are self-sustaining, again to a greater or lesser degree, have rights, including the right to life, that must be respected and protected by other humans like them; however,

---

[497] Beckwith, "Defending Abortion Philosophically," p. 181.

humans who may not possess self-awareness and sentience and who may not be self-sustaining do not necessarily have rights, including the right to life, that must be respected and protected by other humans in more favorable circumstances." What is now obviously spelled out is that one group of humans with certain capacities and "privileged" circumstances is claiming power over another group of humans that may not possess the same capacities or privileges, at least not to the same degree of actualization. To be even more blunt, the "power" that the privileged group of humans is claiming is the power to take the lives of those in the non-privileged group of humans, more or less at the privileged humans' own discretion.

(2) *The Burden of Proof*

Surely the burden of proof for the position that "human persons" are sufficiently qualitatively superior to mere "human beings" to have such life-or-death power over them must lie with those, like Warren, Thomson, and Singer, who argue for such power. Such a burden of proof does not appear to have been relieved by their arguments. To the contrary, the syllogism for which a Thomist could argue appears to run counter to the trend toward distinguishing between "humans" and "persons." Given today's empirical knowledge, one could argue as follows:

(1) A "person" is any individual with a rational intellectual soul, such as a human being.

(2) This rational intellectual soul, as has been argued throughout the present work, is infused into the zygote at conception; otherwise the zygote would not begin its development into anything with a *clearly recognizable* rational intellectual soul. As Oliver O'Donovan writes, those yet unborn are persons because "they become *known* to us as persons when they are children."[498] The fact of their becoming known to us as persons indicates the ontological status they actually possess all along, since there seems to be no ontological "moment" of personhood to which the functionalist can point with any certainty. Moreover, as has been shown, for Aquinas the human intellectual soul is not defined by its intellective functioning.[499]

(Conclusion) Therefore, the zygote at conception is not only a developing human being, but a developing person, deserving of any protections to which any other human person is entitled by virtue of

---

[498] Oliver O'Donovan. "Again, Who Is a Person?" *On Moral Medicine.* Stephen E. Lammers and Allen Verhey, eds. Grand Rapids, Mich.: Eerdmans, 1998: 380-86, p. 384. Emphasis in original.
[499] *Quaestiones Disputatae de Anima*, Article 12.

that human's very personhood.

Given the argument maintained throughout the present work, its proposed Thomistic definition of "human person" still stands: A human person is a rational, embodied member of the species *Homo sapiens* (the species being determined by the genetic structure of its embodiment), created in God's image but fallen, at any level of development, from conception to death. "Functionalist" criteria for personhood seem to serve only to obscure this conclusion and to limit its protections, and should therefore be rejected.

Further, the three criteria presented earlier seem both more plausible and more humane than any criteria for human-ness or personhood which depend upon the human's abilities. To reiterate these three criteria, one is a human being if all of the following apply:

(1) One must possess a DNA code from the species *Homo sapiens*.

(2) One must possess a separate and uniquely expressed DNA code.

(3) One must possess the potential, under normal circumstances, to develop into a mature example of *Homo sapiens*. (This potential for development points to the presence of the human DNA code, the primary efficient cause of human development; the actual fact of the animated, unitary being undergoing development points to the impelling presence of the human substantial form or soul, the formal cause of the actual human.)

Humans thus possess rational intellectual souls (the human substantial form); as persons they are created in God's image, even though fallen; and they are embodied members of the species *Homo sapiens*, as indicated genetically by their DNA.

These attributes characterize the human being/human person, from conception to death.

### (4)    Can Moral Consensus Be Recovered?

Early on, in Section 2 of the Introduction, this work's overall project was laid out. From the start the central questions of this work have been two in number: (1) What is Aquinas's definition of a human being? (2) How might this definition aid in addressing contemporary bioethical issues? Throughout this work, the discussion has made its way gradually through the first question and into the second. It is true that Aquinas "clearly could not have even imagined the issues of embryonic stem cell research, cloning, withdrawal of artificial life support, or organ donation." On the other hand, Aquinas's basic principles are applicable to these issues: "He did, however, write about the inherent value of human life, the individual nature of human persons, the complex nature of human intentionality, and the moral imperative to be charitable; each of which, respectively, bears on the ethical evaluation of these issues."[500]

Therefore, this second question involving contemporary issues must also be taken up by addressing some of the more detailed bioethical implications of Aquinas's anthropological analysis.

Despite having gone through many attacks, Thomistic anthropology remains a vital view of human nature and presents pertinent and convincing public reasoning on these and other contemporary ethical issues. The natural law principles underlying Aquinas's view of human nature hold much promise of fruitful application, especially in the realm of bioethics. Upon considering the likelihood of a societal return to shared moral views, MacIntyre in his *After Virtue* is dubious; he thinks the best one could hope for is "the construction of local forms of community within which civility and the intellectual and moral life can be sustained through the new dark ages which are already upon us."[501] J. Budziszewski holds a similar view regarding history's judgment on contemporary society:

> Historians will write that by the last decade of the twentieth century, great numbers of men and women in the most pampered society on the earth had come to think it normal and desirable that their sick, their weak, and their helpless should be killed. When they were a poor country, they had not so thought; now in the day of their power and prosperity, they changed their minds.[502]

However, stranger events have transpired in human history than the ethical seismic shift the application of natural law principles would bring about in today's culture; even MacIntyre himself in his later work appears to have become considerably more hopeful for the advancement of Thomistic principles in society: "We can take courage from the thought that, in the life of the mind as elsewhere, there is always more to hope for than we can reasonably expect."[503] So also does Budziszewski: "Moral consensus can be recovered even in corrupted societies like our own, because people in general know more about the moral law than they realize—or more than they admit. The task of the moral persuader is not so much to explain to people what they don't know at all, as to dredge up and clarify their common moral sense. . . . The immediate task isn't to convince people of the theory of the natural law—something they have probably never heard of. Rather it is to put

---

[500] Jason Eberl, *Thomistic Principles and Bioethics*, p. 3.

[501] MacIntyre, *After Virtue*, 2nd edition, p. 263.

[502] J. Budziszewski. *The Revenge of Conscience: Politics and the Fall of Man*. Dallas: Spence Publishing, 1999, p. 125.

[503] MacIntyre, *God, Philosophy, Universities*, p. 180. See also his *Three Rival Versions of Moral Enquiry*, especially Chapters VI-ff.

them in touch with their own dim awareness of the natural law—something they already have."[504]

It seems that anyone, whether Roman Catholic or not, could find reason to rejoice in the truth of the words of Pope John Paul II:

> Even in the midst of difficulties and uncertainties, every person sincerely open to truth and goodness can, by the light of reason and the hidden action of grace, come to recognize in the natural law written in the heart the sacred value of human life from its very beginning until its end, and can affirm the right of every human being to have this primary good respected to the highest degree. Upon the recognition of this right, every human community and the political community itself are founded.[505]

As Jason T. Eberl puts it, "One does not have to be a Roman Catholic, a Christian, or even a theist to consider Aquinas's philosophical accounts of human nature and morality, and their relevance to certain bioethical issues at the margins of human life."[506] If Aquinas's teachings on synderesis and the practical intellect are correct, some moral truths may need only to be re-stated and re-explicated in the public square in order to be re-recognized as true—for example, the truth of "the sacred value of human life from its very beginning until its end."

Although this sacred value of innocent human life may seem today to be threatened on many fronts, we must never lose hope, even in the face of inevitable setbacks; as Walter Farrell writes in another context of Aquinas, "He understood well that if we completely succeed it is because we have aimed too low."[507] Therefore, we must continue to re-think and re-defend the culture of life, and to work toward its implementation in ourselves and in our societies.

In the next chapters, we will consider some specific topics related to this overall moral project.

---

[504] Budziszewski, *Natural Law for Lawyers*, p. 19.

[505] John Paul II. *Evangelium Vitae*. London: Catholic Truth Society, 1995, p. 4.

[506] Eberl, *Thomistic Principles and Bioethics*, p. 22.

[507] Walter Farrell, O.P. *A Companion to the Summa. Volume III—The Fullness of Life.* New York: Sheed and Ward, 1945, p. viii.

# Part Two: Aquinas and Contemporary Bioethical Issues

# Chapter 7: Bioethics, Abortion, and Infanticide

I will neither give a deadly drug to anybody who asks for it, nor will I make a suggestion to this effect. Similarly I will not give to a woman an abortive remedy. In purity and holiness I will guard my life and my art.[508]

I will maintain the utmost respect for human life from its beginning even under threat and I will not use my medical knowledge contrary to the laws of humanity.[509]

If it is given me to save a life, all thanks. But it may also be within my power to take a life; this awesome responsibility must be faced with great humbleness and awareness of my own frailty.[510]

I do not deny that if one accepts abortion on the grounds provided . . . the case for killing other human beings, in certain circumstances, is strong.[511]

## 1.    Bioethics and Biotechnology

When one considers the above introductory quotations, which range chronologically from about 400 B.C. to A.D. 1993, a definite progression may be noted: The classical Hippocratic Oath begins with the physician's flat denial of aid in assisted suicide, euthanasia, and abortion; the Declaration of Geneva modifies this flat denial to the maintenance of the "utmost respect for human life"; the "new" Hippocratic Oath accepts, seemingly with humble resignation, the

---

[508] From the Hippocratic Oath, c. 400 B.C. Ludwig Edelstein, trans. Baltimore: Johns Hopkins Press, 1943.
[509] From the Declaration of Geneva, adopted by the General Assembly of the World Medical Association at Geneva, 1948.
[510] From a "new" Hippocratic Oath, used in many medical schools today, written in 1964 by Louis Lasagna, Academic Dean of the Medical School at Tufts University.
[511] Peter Singer, *Practical Ethics*, p. 175.

"power to take a life"; lastly a contemporary ethicist (Peter Singer) prepares to provide society with a "strong" assertion of "the case for killing other human beings" which follows from the case for the acceptance of abortion. This "case for killing other human beings" is not the case to be made for killing in self-defense, in war, or in state-sanctioned execution; this is rather the case for killing decided upon by the judgment of private individuals, most notably physicians, and in context this case for killing refers specifically to infanticide. A decade earlier (1983), another philosopher had written similarly, "One will have to determine whether the competing moral issues at stake in abortion are in any fashion similar to those that would allow (or forbid) infanticide of children."[512] Perhaps one should be grateful for the two parenthetical words. Meanwhile, as G.K. Chesterton states, the "march of human progress through abortion to infanticide" continues apace.[513]

More recently other philosophers have argued that the killing of infants is not to be considered as morally equivalent to "murder."[514] Philosophers who have endorsed various forms of direct infanticide include Jonathan Glover, Jeffrey Reiman, Joseph Fletcher, Michael Tooley, and of course Peter Singer.[515] In her book *Social Ethics*, Jenny Teichman refers to Glover and Singer, among others, as "personists"— those who, like Mary Anne Warren, think only "persons" have rights to life that must be respected, and who also think that born infants do not qualify as persons, even for several months of their lives.[516] Singer himself has flatly stated, "Killing a disabled infant is not morally equivalent to killing a person. Very often it is not wrong at all."[517] One can readily see, therefore, that the discussions of the previous chapters over the nature of "personhood" are not at all disconnected from

---

[512] H. Tristram Engelhardt, Jr., "Introduction," *Abortion and the Status of the Fetus*, p. xv.
[513] G.K. Chesterton. "Where Is the Paradox?" *The Well and the Shallows* [1935]. San Francisco: Ignatius Press, 2006: 198-203, p. 200.
[514] The reference is to Jeffrey Reiman's *Abortion and the Ways We Value Human Life*. Lanham, Maryland: Rowman and Littlefield, 1999, pp. 92-ff.
[515] This endorsement may be found in, among other publications, Glover's *Causing Death and Saving Lives* (1977); Reiman's *Abortion and the Ways We Value Human Life* (1999); Tooley's *Abortion and Infanticide* (1983); Singer's *Practical Ethics* (second edition 1993); and Fletcher's *Situation Ethics: The New Morality* (1966).
[516] Teichman, *Social Ethics*. Oxford: Blackwell, 1997, p. 31.
[517] Singer, *Practical Ethics*, p. 191. This is quoted from the second (1993) edition; in the first (1979) edition, "disabled infant" is actually "defective infant" (p. 138). The editorial touch is interesting.

practical bioethical recommendations for medical practice. Such bioethical applications should be explored in the light of the Thomistic
anthropological stance described thus far.

(1)  *Anthropology and Bioethics*
In the opening chapters of this work, the connections between anthropology and ethics were explored, since "our understanding of ourselves
as human beings is related to our understanding of the good and
virtuous human life."[518] However, these connections can be traced in
finer detail, from anthropology to ethics and now to the applied
sciences, particularly to the biological and medical sciences. Discussions
in these fields may then have even further ramifications in political
philosophy and for the sake of public political actions, although specific
policy recommendations for these actions lie outside the scope of this
present work. This logical connection (from anthropology to ethics to
medicine to public policy) has occasioned the rise of the sub-category of
ethics known as "bioethics."

Although, of course, ethical prescriptions have from antiquity been
applied to human biological selves and their medical conditions, as may
be seen in the Hippocratic Oath itself, the term "bioethics" was "first
coined in the early 1970s by the cancer researcher Van Rensselaer
Potter."[519] A basic definition of the topic has been offered by James
Childress: Bioethics is "the application of ethics to the biological
sciences, medicine, health care, and related areas as well as the public
policies directed towards them."[520] Standard accounts of the theory and
history of bioethics have also been written, for instance by H. T.
Engelhardt, Jr., and by Albert R. Jonsen.[521] However, as Oliver O'Donovan points out, one should not "think of bioethics as a new intellectual
discipline. . . . It is an unfinished discussion among representatives of
many disciplines and none."[522] In today's world, given the concaten-
ation of social issues related to biology and medicine (abortion, cloning,
stem cell research, assisted suicide, and euthanasia, to name merely the
most prominent topics), this "ill-defined discipline of bioethics"[523] is a

---

[518] Sokolowski, "What Is Natural Law?" p. 527.
[519] Neil Messer, *Theological Issues in Bioethics*, p. 1.
[520] James Childress. "Bioethics." *A New Dictionary of Christian Ethics*. John
Macquarrie and James Childress, eds. London: SCM Press, 1986, p. 61.
[521] Engelhardt, *The Foundations of Bioethics* (New York: Oxford University Press,
1986); Jonsen, *The Birth of Bioethics* (New York: Oxford University Press, 1998).
[522] O'Donovan, *Begotten or Made?* p. vii.
[523] Richard John Neuhaus. "The Politics of Bioethics." *First Things* 177 (Nov.
2007): 23-28, p. 23.

widely and intensely debated field. Since technological advances in the biological sciences and medicine have occurred so rapidly in recent years, it seems plausible that contemporary anthropological and ethical views must also change to accommodate themselves to the new biotechnological procedures available. However, the opposite view, the view for which this present work argues, seems at least as plausible and perhaps more so: Given the rapid changes in biotechnology, perhaps the technology itself may require all the more vigorous regulation from established anthropological and ethical positions, from long-standing and stringently preserved principles of social conduct. Society, in other words, must insist "that science accommodate itself to moral principle, rather than the other way around."[524] This ethical regulation may (and probably must) be then extended *mutatis mutandis* into political regulation.

What would be examples of these "principles of social conduct" seemingly mandated by a Thomistic anthropology? One principle might be phrased in the following way: In order for a human morally to receive a different treatment than the treatment all humans *qua* humans deserve, or in order for a human to give up the human rights other humans claim as their own, that human would have to go through one of two changes in situation: (1) The human would have to forfeit the treatment other humans deserve by his or her actions—e.g., by committing a crime deserving of punishments other humans, who are innocent of the crime, do not morally deserve. These punishments may even include the infliction of death. (2) The other change that could cause a different treatment would be a *substantial* change—e.g., the human changes in such a way that he or she is no longer a human, and therefore does not automatically possess the same human rights that those who *are* humans possess. In the case of an embryo, the substantial change would proceed in the opposite direction, not *from* humanity *to* non-humanity, but from non-humanity to humanity. In other words, the embryo would not be a human until a certain time elapses, at which point the substantial change would take place, converting the embryo into full-fledged human-ness and granting it human rights to life and protection. Until that substantial change takes place, the embryo would not possess these human rights (as some would maintain).

(2) *Against Killing Innocent Persons (Substances of Rational Nature)*
Despite its seeming abstraction, this line of argument does have practical bioethical points, the points pressed in earlier chapters of this

---

[524] Richard John Neuhaus. "While We're At It." *First Things* 180 (February 2008): 61-72, p. 67.

work: When does a human being *become* a human being? In the terms used thus far, at what point is a human substance formed, a substance with the innermost shaping principle which impels the substance onward toward the mature example of human-ness? As already argued, the separate developments of personality traits, the actual practice of rational thought, the ability to survive on one's own, or any other functional abilities, do not seem to transform the substance of the human; i.e., these developments do not effect a substantial change. Rather, they are incidental changes, rather like getting taller, or gaining in knowledge, or moving out from one's parents' house to one's own. As has been seen, the construction of Boethius, that a person is an individual substance of a rational nature, is the definition adopted by Aquinas; this definition is opposed to the much later innovation of Locke, that a person in order to be a person must possess the functional abilities of reason, reflection, and self-consideration.[525] In other words, being a human "person" is for Aquinas a quality granted merely by being a member of the human species, an individual substance of rational nature. Therefore, even though that personhood may develop and be more fully expressed by means of incidental change, the development and expression of personhood is not part of a substantial change from "non-human being" to "human being," or from "human being" to "human person."

In his commentary on Aquinas's *On Being and Essence* (§ 18), Joseph Bobik makes a similar point regarding a thing's "essence":

> It is clear from the inductive analysis of change that when matter acquires form, a natural substance comes to be and comes to be what it is. Hence, anything superadded to the substance would presuppose the substance as already constituted by its matter and its form; anything superadded would be *per accidens* or extraneous to what the substance is.[526]

In the case of the human substance, the fact of its human-ness is presupposed, in Bobik's term, because whatever else that may occur to it or whatever else may be added to it would be added to an already existing substance—an embodied soul, matter that has already acquired a form. This substance may become a pianist or a plumber or a professor or a pilot, but only because of what it already is. The incidental characteristics are "superadded" and "extraneous" to its previously given definition.

---

[525] Locke, *An Essay Concerning Human Understanding*, II.1.21.
[526] Joseph Bobik. *Aquinas on Being and Essence*. Notre Dame, Indiana: University of Notre Dame Press, 1965, p. 73.

The point here is that *any function or training or skill*, even if it flows directly from the essence of what a thing is, cannot be used as part of the *definition* of what that thing is in itself; it is superadded. Therefore, any definition of human-ness which includes a function or skill or maturation of latent potential must presuppose "the substance as already constituted by its matter and its form," in Bobik's words. Even defining humans in Aristotelian terms, as "rational animals," does not necessarily entail the ongoing activity of rational thought or rationality on the part of the human thus defined. The ongoing activity of rational thought is a "second actuality," as opposed to the "first actuality" of the essence of human-ness itself,[527] a view stated elegantly by Teresa Iglesias:

> *The act of being human*—or of being a human being—by its very nature temporal and physical with a beginning and an end, encompasses of necessity, for each one of us, our beginning as a cell, then development as an embryo for a time, then becoming foetus, child, and so on. In other words, part and parcel of being human is bearing and sharing in the total human condition with all other human beings, in all its dignity and vulnerability, its littleness and greatness, its materiality and immateriality, its obviousness and mysteriousness; a condition which requires it to come from human parents and at one stage to be an embryo.[528]

In November of 1951 (and seemingly presciently, considering the changes in American abortion law over the next few decades), Pope Pius XII pressed for a similar understanding: "Innocent human life, in whatever condition it may be, from the first moment of its existence, is to be preserved from any direct voluntary attack." He then linked this statement to the idea of inherent human rights, possessed by the conceptus just as by any others:

> This is a fundamental right of the human person, of general value in the Christian concept of life; valid both for the still hidden life in the womb and for the newborn babe; and opposed to direct abortion as it is to the direct killing of the child before, during, and after birth. No matter what the distinction between those different moments in the development of the life, already born or still to be born, for profane and ecclesiastical law and for certain civil and

---

[527] ST I.48.5.

[528] Iglesias, "Review of *Conceiving the Embryo: Ethics, Law and Practice in Human Embryology*, and *Creating the Child: Ethics, Law and Practice of Assisted Procreation*. Donald Evans, ed." *Studies in Christian Ethics* 11 (1998): 83-90, p. 86. Emphasis in original.

penal consequences—according to the moral law, in all these cases it is a matter of a grave and illicit attempt on inviolable human life.[529] The term "direct abortion" used here by Pius raises the distinction between "direct" and "indirect" abortion, a distinction which has provoked much heated discussion, especially within Christian theology.[530] However, leaving aside the vexed question of what constitutes a morally permissible "indirect" abortion, for the purposes of this work it is enough to point out that any action which *intends the death* of the conceptus is to be considered a "direct" abortion, what Pius calls a "direct voluntary attack." According to Pius this type of abortion, which of course comprises the overwhelming majority of all abortions, remains morally equivalent to the direct killing of a born child, and should therefore be outlawed.

## 2. Some Pro-Choice Arguments Considered

### (1) *A First Contrary Argument: Size*

Of course, many writers disparage the arguments granting the conceptus any sort of moral status or fundamental human rights. It is instructive to note how often these writers comment on the mere *size* of the conceptus as morally significant. For example, Robert Pasnau expresses explicitly the implicit thought of many when he writes, "It is surely absurd to think that a few unformed cells count as a human being."[531] Another writer points out for a more popular audience that the three-day-old blastocyst is composed of only about 150 cells, while the brain of a fly contains over 100,000 cells: "The human embryos that are destroyed in stem-cell research do not have brains, or even neurons."[532] Again, the implication is that anyone thinking of the zygote as possessing an "intellectual nature" or "form" of any sort is not to be taken seriously. Likewise, Daniel Dombrowski and Robert Deltete think of the position of immediate hominization of "a microscopic speck of matter" as "ridiculous."[533]

Peter Kreeft, who would disagree with the rhetorical intent behind these statements, nonetheless summarizes well their implicit primary

---

[529] See Thomas J. Welsh, "Catholic Faith and Reverence for Human Life." *Linking the Human Life Issues.* Russell Hittinger, ed. Chicago: Regnery Books, 1986: 9-19, p. 12.

[530] For a summary of this discussion, see David Albert Jones, *The Soul of the Embryo*, Chapter 12, "Probable Sins and Indirect Exceptions."

[531] Robert Pasnau, *Thomas Aquinas on Human Nature*, p. 120.

[532] Sam Harris. *Letter to a Christian Nation.* New York: Knopf, 2007, p. 29.

[533] Dombrowski and Deltete, *A Brief, Liberal, Catholic Defense of Abortion*, pp. 33 and 129.

idea:

> Whenever a person begins, it just can't be as early as fertilization. Just look at that zygote: a single cell with no brain, no nervous system, no consciousness, no heart, no face. . . . no differentiation of cells or functions or systems, no organs. . . . Don't you feel the utter absurdity of calling *that* a human being?[534]

Likewise, ethicist Maureen Junker-Kenny points out the significance of the "size" issue in the minds of many (though she herself also disagrees with this ascription of significance): "How can one suggest reflection on the moral status of something that is smaller than a speck of dust? For some, the question of moral status would already be answered by this observation, and dismissed as impossible."[535]

However, it seems an obvious question should immediately spring to one's mind: Why is this so? Certainly there may exist some pre-philosophic wisdom in the reluctance to grant personhood to "a microscopic speck of matter." On the other hand, if one wishes not to appeal to pre-philosophic sense as a moral guide, especially if one is making what is after all supposed to be a philosophical argument, one is left with the question: What does the size of a developing human have to do philosophically with that developing human's moral status? In Thomistic terms, what does the "substance" of human-ness have to do philosophically with the "accidents" of the human's size and appearance? What does the human "form" have to do with the human's "shape" or size?

> As debates over stem-cell research and cloning roil on, proponents ask: How can you care about these clumps of cells, no bigger than the period at the end of this sentence? But why is size an issue when there is so much inherent developmental capacity? Surely size in a world of quarks, quantum events, Planck's Constant, and neutrinos is relative. Scientists who describe the Big Bang claim that at its beginning the whole universe was many times smaller than a single human cell.[536]

In fact, while considering the notion of pre-philosophic wisdom, one might also mention the rather obvious point that humanity tends to think of a violation of a human victim as all the more a violation as the victim is the more helpless to resist. Abuse of a baby, for example, is commonly seen as worse than abuse of a twelve-year-old, abuse of a

---

[534] Kreeft, *The Unaborted Socrates*, pp. 62-63. Emphasis in original.

[535] Maureen Junker-Kenny, "The Moral Status of the Embryo," p. 43.

[536] Sidney Callahan. "Zygotes and Blastocysts." *Human Life Review* 28.3 (Summer 2002): 81-82, p. 81.

twelve-year-old as worse than abuse of a thirty-year-old, and so on until age renders the victim once more helpless. If the size of the conceptus is actually morally significant, it would seem to be so only in the sense that humanity should sympathize even more with the very helplessness of the victim of abortion.

"Some commentators say that human embryos don't 'look like' human beings," as Robert P. George writes. "[However] the answer is that they look exactly like the human beings they are, that is, human beings in the embryonic stage of their existence."[537] The size, shape, or appearance of the conceptus would seem to have no moral significance at all in the determination of when the conceptus should be accepted as a human person, as an individual, developing substance of rational nature.[538] The issue of size is discussed here solely because it continues to be brought up in bioethical disputations as if the mere mention of the microscopic size of the zygote or blastocyst does in fact convey some morally significant defense of the practice of abortion.

(2)  *A Second Contrary Argument: Location*

The related topics of the *location* of the conceptus and its *viability* outside of the mother's womb may occasionally arise as well in these disputations. The logic behind the "location" argument relies on a transitive relation among objects: If A is part of B and B is part of C, then A is part of C. For example, if a fingernail is part of the hand and the hand is part of the body, then the fingernail is part of the body. The analogy as applied by the abortion-rights advocate would then run as follows: If the conceptus is part of the mother's body and the mother's body is under the control of the mother's choices regarding it, then the conceptus is also under the control of the mother's choices regarding her own body. The mere fact of the location of the conceptus inside the mother's body is seen as morally significant, as it is hence rightfully under the control of the mother's choices: "Keep your laws off my body," as the pro-choice slogan has it.

First of all, however, the premise that "the mother's body is under the control of the mother's choices regarding it" is itself questionable.

---

[537] Robert George, *The Clash of Orthodoxies*, p. 320. George and Tollefsen expand this thought in a later work: "To claims about the size and appearance of the embryo, we must say that it simply begs the question about the humanity (and the rights) of the embryo to say that it does not resemble (in size and shape) human beings in later stages of development. For the five-day-old embryo looks exactly like what human beings look like at five days old" (*Embryo: A Defense of Human Life*, p. 159).

[538] ST III.2.2.

Many of one's choices regarding one's own body are both legally and rightfully circumscribed—the choice of suicide, for example, or self-mutilation, or the use of some drugs, or the amputation of healthy limbs. In theological terms, one's body is best seen as a stewardship granted by God, a stewardship for which one must ultimately give account. Secondly, the transitive relation does not seem to work well with regard to the separate entity of the conceptus; for instance, if ten toes are part of the conceptus and the conceptus is part of the mother's body, then the additional ten toes are part of the mother's body and the mother may be said to possess twenty toes (along with two different circulatory systems, two different DNA structures, possibly both sexes, and so on). Some of these features develop gradually (and so the mother would be said to possess the "potential" to develop twenty toes), while others such as the DNA structure are established at conception. Thus the transitive relation of location does not seem to warrant the moral significance attributed to it; as Aquinas writes, "An internal member of the mother is something of hers by continuity and material union of the part with the whole: whereas a child while in its mother's womb is something of hers through being joined with, and yet distinct from her."[539] Since the child is "joined with" the mother and yet a "distinct" human being as well, one could make the case that there exists "the continuity of human development from conception to adulthood" and that "a mere change in location (in this case, a movement from inside to outside the uterus) cannot result in a change in the inherent nature or dignity of that developing being."[540]

Even Peter Singer, who is emphatically pro-choice regarding abortion, agrees that "the location of the fetus/infant—inside or outside the womb—cannot make a crucial difference to its moral status."[541] From this insight, however, Singer draws the wrongful inference that infanticide as well as abortion is also permissible, an inference to be addressed later in this chapter.

(3)   *A Third Contrary Argument: Viability*

This argument from "location" may also be combined with the concept of "viability"; i.e., the argument may be modified to state that the embryo is under the control of the mother's choices, including the

---

[539] ST III.68.11.

[540] Richard Stith. "Abortion Is More Than 'Murder.'" *Life and Learning XV: Proceedings of the Fifteenth University Faculty for Life Conference.* Joseph W. Koterski, S.J., ed. Washington, D.C.: University Faculty for Life, 2006: 105-11, p. 107.

[541] Peter Singer. "Sanctity of Life or Quality of Life?" *Pediatrics* 72.1 (July 1983): 128-29, p. 128.

choice to abort, until it reaches the developmental stage of viability, at which stage it could probably survive more or less independently, or at least outside of the mother's womb. Since the fetus would not at this stage be directly dependent upon the nutrition and protection supplied by the mother, the fact of its likely survival even if separated from the mother (by premature delivery, for example) is seen as morally significant and as guaranteeing certain rights and protections not belonging to the conceptus until this watershed stage is reached. However, suspicion may be stirred immediately by the very notion of a basic human right, such as the right to life, which fluctuates in its application depending upon medical advances which lower the time of viability. According to data collected in 2004 and published in 2006, around one in eight babies in the United States are considered premature. The problem is that the concept of "premature" varies from birth at 37 completed weeks of pregnancy to the "extremely premature" birth at 22 completed weeks of pregnancy or even less time.[542] If human rights and human-ness go into effect at viability, at what point in this gap of almost four months does the fetus become viable and hence human?

Other problem areas open up as the concept of viability is explored. For instance, many babies born today, especially premature babies, could not survive past their initial medical difficulties without the aid of an incubator; however, given that aid, they overcome their difficulties, recover, and eventually flourish. Their time in the incubator is not seen as unusually heroic or extraordinarily life-prolonging care, but as typical medical treatment for many conditions. Now, since this typical medical treatment did not exist in its current form even a few decades ago, does this mean that a developing fetus today reaches "personhood" at an earlier stage of development than a similar fetus a few decades ago, simply because the threshold of viability after birth has been lowered by recent medical and technological advances? This conclusion seems both ridiculous and unavoidable, given the initial premise that viability determines human moral status. It seems, then, that this initial premise should be rejected.

Related to the issue of viability, the high mortality rate of pre-implantation embryos has also caused some difficulties with the assigning of hominization at conception. For example, Karl Rahner asks if the moral theologian could or should find acceptable the fact "that 50

[542] J.A. Martin, B.E. Hamilton, P.D. Sutton, S.J. Ventura, F. Menacker, and S. Kirmeyer. "Births: Final Data for 2004." *National Vital Statistics Reports* 55.1. Hyattsville, Maryland: National Center for Health Statistics, 2006.

per cent of all 'human beings'—real human beings with 'immortal' souls and an eternal destiny—will never get beyond this first stage of human existence."[543] However, the problem raised by this question seems not intrinsically to be a moral problem, but a problem in imaginative capacity—that is, humans are not in a position to understand or even visualize the immortal state and conditions of the afterlife. Further, it seems that this imaginative deficiency could also apply just as well to the problem of the deaths of new-born infants: "As Christians are required to say that there are very many new-born infants in the life of the world to come, then they should remain open to the possibility that there will also be many human embryos. If they are human and they have died, then they will be raised from the dead, though we cannot say what that will be like."[544] If the current physiological fact of the loss of pre-implantation embryos seems an insurmountable theological obstacle, then so also should the historical fact of infant death: "The Creator seems to provide in abundance 'seeds' that never bear fruit. But are we to say that historically, when more than half of the infants born died during childbirth, they were never living human beings?"[545] As location and viability do not seem to be significant moral factors in assigning personhood, so likewise the current high mortality rate of pre-implantation embryos does not seem to prevent the recognition of the personhood of the newly conceived human.

(4)   *A Fourth Contrary Argument: Sentience*

In the early 1980s, when faced on the one hand with the ascription of full personhood at conception and on the other hand with the withholding of personhood, rights, and protections until at least birth and possibly beyond, L.W. Sumner proposed his well-known "Third Way," the granting of personhood at sentience. "Sentience" means "the capacity for feeling or perceiving":

> A creature that is capable of experiencing any of the five senses or pain or sensations of pleasure is sentient. Synonyms for sentience include *awareness* and *consciousness*. Sentience is not the same as self-consciousness, which involves reflection on oneself and one's sensations. L.W. Sumner has defended sentience as the basis for the right to life.[546]

[543] Karl Rahner. *Theological Investigations.* Volume IX. G. Harrison, trans. London: Darton, Longman & Todd, 1972, p. 226.

[544] David Albert Jones, *The Soul of the Embryo*, p. 229.

[545] Kevin D. O'Rourke, "The Embryo as Person." *Life and Learning XVI: Proceedings of the Sixteenth University Faculty for Life Conference.* Joseph W. Koterski, S.J., ed. Washington, D.C.: University Faculty for Life, 2007: 281-96, p. 292.

"There is no doubt that a newborn infant is sentient," according to Sumner; likewise "There is also no doubt that a zygote, and also an embryo, are presentient."[547] Since the threshold of sentience appears to fall somewhere within the second trimester of pregnancy, abortion up to at least that time is permissible: "We are therefore inevitably confronted with a class of fetuses around the threshold stage whose sentience, and therefore whose moral status, is indeterminate."[548]

However, Sumner's "Third Way" may not be as much of a third way as it is claimed to be. If Sumner is seeking to balance on the one hand the ascription of full personhood at conception and on the other hand the withholding of personhood, rights, and protections until at least birth and possibly beyond, then the "Third Way" may be seen as a genuine attempt at a compromise solution. If the proposed solution, however, simply attempts once more to rebut the ascription of full personhood at conception by claiming that human moral significance is achieved only by means of some capacity or functional ability (in this case, the sentient ability to experience sensory input), then the proposed solution is merely another attempt at "functional" definition and runs headlong into the common problems with functionalist definitions of humanity. These problems have already been discussed earlier in this chapter, and elsewhere throughout this book.

### 3.   The Prohibition of Abortion and/or Infanticide

The logical conclusion to this chapter, and to the extended discussion leading up to this chapter, might be stated in a syllogistic fashion:

First premise: In natural law ethical reflection, the deliberate killing of an innocent human person is morally wrong and should not be legally allowed. Since natural law ethics is not generally utilitarian in nature, this first premise would hold true regardless of the good or bad consequences of its acceptance.

Second premise: Abortion (or infanticide), at any time from the developmental stage of the pre-implanted zygote, to the developmental stage of a born infant, is the deliberate killing of an innocent human person ("person" being defined in the Thomistic sense as an individual substance of rational nature).

Conclusion: Therefore, abortion (or infanticide), at any time from the developmental stage of the pre-implanted zygote, through the develop-

---

[546] Carson Strong. *Ethics in Reproductive and Perinatal Medicine: A New Framework.* New Haven, Connecticut: Yale University Press, 1997, p. 48. Emphasis in original.

[547] Sumner, *Abortion and Moral Theory*, p. 148.

[548] Ibid., p. 150.

mental stages of a born infant, is morally wrong and should not be legally allowed.

Those who have followed the argument to this point will notice that behind this syllogism lies another unstated premise: namely, that no moral or metaphysical rights held by other individuals or institutions overrule or outweigh the right to life held by an innocent human person, no matter that person's size, location, level of active sentience or other functional abilities, or level of dependence. These latter criteria are not morally relevant, and seemingly only arise in discussions of these matters in order to allow for the deliberate killing of an innocent human person, a killing based precisely on non-relevant factors.

This last point seems important enough to be repeated. As pointed out by Andrew Peach (and discussed in the previous chapter of this book), the ongoing debate over what does or does not constitute a "person" does not seem to have as its motivation any sort of real philosophical interest in human nature or its definition.[549] The motivating force seems precisely to be the desire to justify taking the lives of the innocent human persons thus defined out of the realm of "personhood." However, the criteria brought up as demarcating actual personhood from non-personhood do not in fact seem to do any such thing; these criteria serve only to demarcate one level of maturity and dependence from a different level of maturity and dependence. They seem to be, as stated, non-relevant factors whether considered morally, anthropologically, or scientifically.

The conclusion reached by Robert P. George, while strongly stated, is also warranted: "The pro-life position is superior to the pro-choice position precisely because the scientific evidence, considered honestly and dispassionately, fully supports it."[550] Furthermore, one might look beyond the scientific evidence alone and also add that the logical arguments proposed in support of the pro-choice position do not

---

[549] Andrew J. Peach. "Pro-Choice 'Personhood': An Abortive Concept," pp. 191 and 193-94.

[550] Robert P. George, *The Clash of Orthodoxies*, p. 69. Chapter 3 of George's book comprises an essay written by George in response to a claim made by Stanley Fish that "a pro-choice advocate sees abortion as a decision to be made in accordance with the best scientific opinion as to when the beginning of life, as we know it, occurs," while a pro-life advocate sees abortion primarily as "a sin against God" and opposes abortion on religious grounds (p. 66). George, of course, disagreed forcefully with this statement. Rather amazingly, especially considering Professor Fish's academic stature, Fish immediately conceded the strength of George's position and changed his own, even thanking George for correcting him (*First Things* 90 [February 1999], p. 78).

accomplish what that position's advocates seem to think they do. Hence the argument advanced in this work—that the human being is also a human person which exists from conception—is not only scientifically, but also logically, preferable to contrary "functionalist" positions. It is also a Thomistic position, when Thomas's metaphysical principles are properly applied to the biological facts currently known of conception.

# Chapter 8: Cloning and Stem Cell Research

The decisions people come to on philosophical matters are partly shaped by social, political and cultural influences. . . . In the case of embryo experimentation . . . scientists did not want to close off promising avenues of research and those suffering from medical illnesses looked to medical progress in search of hope. Such strong social and cultural forces make it difficult to give serious and unprejudiced thought to the ethical status of the human embryo.[551]

We are learning to do a great many clever things. Unless we are much mistaken the next great task will be to learn not to do them.[552]

## 1. The Uses of Cloning and Stem Cells

To clone something means to produce a "genetically identical copy of an animal or plant," by reproducing its "genetic blueprint" or DNA structure in another living organism.[553] Genetically identical individuals brought about by this process would therefore be clones (the word may be used as a verb or a noun). The birth of monozygotic identical twins or multiple births, after the naturally occurring split of the zygote within the mother, is a natural form of cloning, but even identical twins "are not truly physically identical," as Neil Messer writes: "For example, they have different finger-prints, thought to be the result of subtle differences in each twin's environment in the mother's womb."[554] These twins or multiple births share identical DNA but not identical phenotypes (the physical expression of one's genotype); further, their shared DNA is different from every other human's and therefore differentiates them as unique human beings. However, this discussion of identical twins is somewhat beside the point, for usually this type of natural process (i.e., giving birth to multiple siblings) is not what most

---

[551] David Albert Jones, *The Soul of the Embryo*, p. 241.
[552] G.K. Chesterton. *Varied Types*. New York: Dodd and Mead, 1903, p. 228.
[553] Neil Messer, *The Ethics of Human Cloning*, p. 3.
[554] Ibid., p. 16.

people have in mind when the topic of "cloning" is discussed. Nor do people usually have in mind the botanical processes involved in plant grafting, although this is a form of cloning as well; in fact, the word "clone" itself comes from the Greek *klôn*, meaning "twig."

(1)  *Moral Duties and Embryo Experimentation*

Discussions of cloning more usually refer to the technologically induced, asexual process by which a new human is brought into existence which is "at all stages of development, genetically virtually identical to a currently existing or previously existing human being." Although some mammals have been successfully cloned (for example, mice, sheep, goats, cows, horses, pigs, rabbits, rats, cats, dogs, mules, and a gaur), humans as of this writing have not; nor has *any* species of primate. (Much-heralded rhesus monkey "clones" have been produced, but these are actually the result of artificial twinning—the splitting of an embryo at its eight-cell stage into multiple embryos which are genetically identical.) The basic technique of primate cloning, however, would be similar to the technique used for other animals: "The nuclear material of a human somatic cell (donor) [would be introduced] into an oocyte (egg) whose own nucleus has been removed or inactivated, yielding a product that has a human genetic constitution virtually identical to the donor of the somatic cell (this procedure is known as 'somatic cell nuclear transfer,' or SCNT)."[555] This type of cloning could be used not only for human reproductive purposes, but also for therapeutic ends. Embryonic cells are "pluripotent"; that is, they possess an amazing plasticity encompassing the potential to become any of the cells found in humans at later stages of development. Thus these cells, known as "embryonic stem" (ES) cells, hold the possibility to be used as a supply of cells and tissues for clinical treatment; they also may be used for research into the mechanisms both of reproduction and of disease.

Two primary purposes exist, therefore, in favor of the production of cloned human embryos: the purpose of initiating a pregnancy "with the (ultimate) goal of producing a child who will be genetically virtually identical to a currently existing or previously existing individual"; and the purpose of using the embryo "in research or for extracting its stem cells" with the goal of "developing cures for human diseases."[556] These stem cells may be derived from cloned embryos or from embryos

---

[555] The President's Council on Bioethics. *Human Cloning and Human Dignity: An Ethical Inquiry.* Washington, D.C.: Government Printing Office, July 2002, p. xxiv.

[556] Ibid., pp. 229-30.

obtained by other means, such as *in vitro* fertilization (IVF), since in the usual IVF process "surplus" eggs are fertilized to help ensure the egg donor's (usually the mother's) successful pregnancy.[557] Lines of healthy pluripotent cells could conceivably be generated from ES cells so that these newly generated cells could then be transplanted back into humans, in order to restore the function of damaged or diseased tissues. If this research were to turn out successfully, these "generated" cells might someday be able to repair brain damage, nerve damage, Alzheimer's, damaged hearts and other organs, and so on. ES cell research thus seems to hold marvelous promise for the treatment of various medical conditions.

However, as Messer points out with regard to this latter purpose, whether these cells are obtained from SCNT or from IVF "surplus" embryos:

> Many of these applications would involve the creation of a human embryo to be used in research or as a source of cells. The end result of either would be the destruction of the embryo. If, for example, a human embryo is a person with the same moral status as an adult human being from the moment of conception, such uses of embryos will clearly be unacceptable.[558]

There may be some allowances for some use of cloning-related technology and techniques, as will be discussed later. However, these allowances must not be "slipped into" like falling into a river; it then becomes too easy to be carried along by a seemingly irresistible current. Rather, any allowances to cloning must be carefully thought out, precisely specified, and strictly limited at that point. Two extreme reactions to this biotechnology would be on the one hand to forbid it altogether, "refusing to intervene in the world at all" (although many forms of biotechnology are already in use and have been successfully implemented for years), and on the other hand to cast off restraint, "'playing God' and forgetting our human limitations."[559] If one seeks to use the special kind of powers embryonic cells possess, one must also

---

[557] "The ethics of overproducing embryos that will either be discarded or used in scientific experiments depends on the ethical status of the human embryo. In this respect IVF raises some of the same issues as abortion" (David Albert Jones, *The Soul of the Embryo*, p. 216).

[558] Messer, *The Ethics of Human Cloning*, p. 7. Messer also points out that such research on human embryos, up to fourteen days after fertilization, became legal in the United Kingdom in 1990 under the Human Fertilization and Embryology Act.

[559] Messer, *Christian Ethics*. London: SCM Press, 2006, p. 114.

keep foremost in mind the special kind of organism an embryo is.

Moreover, other types of less-problematic cells besides ES cells seem to have a similar potential and may be used in similar types of research. What are popularly called "adult stem cells" (although these cells are also found in children and even fetuses) and "cord blood stem cells" (collected from the umbilical cord at birth) also present possibilities to the researcher. Adult stem cells, or more precisely "non-embryonic" stem cells, although partially differentiated into their own broad categories of tissue, are possible sources of stem cells both for research and clinical treatment. Some controversies and also some remarkable new developments involving the use of adult stem cells will be discussed toward the end of this chapter; in the meantime, it is enough to suggest that "adult stem cells are less controversial than embryonic ones . . . because the former can be collected without lasting harm to the donor,"[560] which is not true in the case of ES cells.

On the other hand, some seem to have few or no doubts or qualms regarding the type of experimentation done in cloning and ES cell research. For example, the following is taken from a speech by former British Prime Minister Tony Blair: "Some people are opposed in principle [to embryo research]. . . . But . . . when stem cell research has huge potential to improve the lives of those suffering from disease, there are also strong ethical arguments in its favor."[561] Similarly, Ian Wilmut, formerly of the Roslin Institute near Edinburgh, who led the team which produced the cloned sheep Dolly in 1996, writes, "Although the arguments in support of embryo experimentation fall short of the rigor of a mathematical proof, there are also morally weighty reasons to continue. I respect the early embryo and have duties to it, but I passionately believe these are overridden by *the duty we have to people*."[562] However, Dr. Wilmut's recommendations for continuation of embryo experimentation seem to be based almost entirely on his oft-repeated contention that the early conceptus lacks personhood because it lacks rational consciousness.[563] This contention has been discussed and argued against extensively in previous chapters; therefore, my negative conclusion on this point remains the same. Functional abilities

---

[560] The President's Council on Bioethics. *Monitoring Stem Cell Research*. Washington, D.C.: Government Printing Office, January 2004, p. 11.
[561] See Arlene Judith Klotzko's *A Clone of Your Own? The Science and Ethics of Cloning* (New York: Cambridge University Press, 2006, p. 71).
[562] Ian Wilmut and Roger Highfield. *After Dolly: The Uses and Misuses of Human Cloning*. New York and London: Norton, 2006, p. 213. Emphasis added.
[563] Ibid., Chapter 6, "Is the Blastocyst a Person?"

should not be thought of as the relevant issue regarding personhood.

To further buttress this conclusion, it may also be argued that defining personhood by personal, rational consciousness is overly reductionistic. For example, John F. Crosby points out the interesting parallels between this type of definition and portions of the discussion in Plato's dialogue *Theaetetus*. In that dialogue, Socrates considers and refutes the central Sophist claim, that "man is the measure of all things," especially in the area of the possession of accurate knowledge: "Against Protagoras Socrates argues that we can err, and with the help of a teacher can correct our error and can enlarge and deepen our knowledge, and that this presupposes an object of thought which is not measured by our thinking but is the measure of our thinking." In other words, one's thinking may certainly fall short of the reality of the object of thought, and can therefore be corrected and expanded. Crosby then brings out the bioethical application:

> Now I want to argue that the human being *qua* person is just as little reducible to consciousness, or to conscious self-presence, as the objects of our thinking are, for Socrates, reducible to their being thought by us. Just as Socrates distinguishes between the being of an object and its being thought by us and does so by arguing that the latter can fall short of the former, so I will distinguish between the being of ourselves as persons and our being consciously present to ourselves, and will argue for this thesis by showing that the latter can fall short of the former.[564]

If even mature, flourishing human beings (as Crosby goes on to argue) can occasionally "fall short" of being "consciously present" to themselves, without thereby losing their identity as persons, such could certainly also be true in the case of a pre-conscious human being such as the conceptus. Whether or not this human being is consciously self-aware does not change his or her identity as a human person.

Therefore, although Ian Wilmut's expressed concern for "the duty we have to people" is undoubtedly genuine, it is also mistaken in that it places the good of some persons with certain specified functional abilities ahead of the good of other persons not yet able to exercise those abilities. Considerations of the good of persons and "the duty we have to people," in other words, must include the good of and the duty society has toward the conceptus, not as a "potential person," but as a

---

[564] John F. Crosby. "The Personhood of the Human Embryo." *Life and Learning III: Proceedings of the Third University Faculty for Life Conference*. Joseph W. Koterski, S.J., ed. Washington, D.C.: University Faculty for Life, 1993: 177-93, pp. 178-79.

pre-conscious person:

> We are not only patients, and easing suffering is not our only moral obligation. As much as we wish to alleviate suffering now and to leave our children a world where suffering can be more effectively relieved, we also want to leave them a world in which we and they want to live—a world that honors moral limits, that respects all life whether strong or weak, and that refuses to secure the good of some human beings by sacrificing the lives of others.[565]

Possibly the topic of cloning, or of ES cell research, is not high on most people's "priority issue" lists. For many, if they think about it at all, this controversy lurks somewhere down in the murky currents of "religious" topics or "moral" problems; therefore, they do not see the possibility of any clear-cut resolution to the controversy. However, even though the prohibition against killing innocent substances of rational nature, even from conception, does not directly draw from religious principles, it has its corollary in the biblical wisdom of Zechariah: "Do not despise this small beginning, for the eyes of the Lord rejoice to see the work begin" (4:10).[566] Every oak begins its life as a sprouted acorn; every human begins his or her life as an embryo. Is a researcher, and is society in general, warranted to end the "small beginnings" of some humans just for the potential benefit to other humans? Although many seem to think such research is in fact warranted, it at least seems worthwhile to explore with great deliberation the objections to such actions, rather than allow oneself to be swayed immediately by the admittedly remarkable possibilities of the research.

(2) *Some Preliminary Objections to Human Cloning*

On the other hand, many *do* see, and are swayed by, the possibility of "silver-bullet" advances in medical practice should the research be continued. The widow of deceased actor Christopher Reeve, for example, toured the United States in 2004 with the John Kerry presidential campaign, promoting ES cell research. There are numerous other high-profile celebrities, such as Michael J. Fox, who are also pushing for the research to continue. Given the current state of the science involved, these people are raising false hopes for rapid and miraculous recoveries in many who are sick. Still, the hopes are there. For example, on Election Day 2004 (U.S.), the voters of California passed a referendum, Proposition 71, budgeting three billion dollars for

---

[565] The President's Council on Bioethics, *Human Cloning and Human Dignity*, p. xxxiv.

[566] Taken from Kenneth Taylor's *The Living Bible*. Carol Stream, Illinois: Tyndale House Publishers, 1974.

further ES cell research in their state. This funding would not have passed without the prospect of major biomedical returns on the voters' investment. The first instances of this funding occurred seventeen months later, as the California Institute for Regenerative Medicine awarded over twelve million dollars in research and educational grants to sixteen universities and nonprofit research facilities throughout the state.[567]

Under U.S. presidents William Clinton and George W. Bush, separate committees were formed to explore and report upon the bioethical questions surrounding cloning and stem cell research. The earlier committee, the National Bioethics Advisory Commission, issued its report on human cloning in 1997. The later committee mandated by President Bush, the President's Council on Bioethics, under the leadership of Dr. Leon Kass, issued a number of publications. The first of these publications is probably also the most important, *Human Cloning and Human Dignity: An Ethical Inquiry* (2002). Although the committee was unanimous that reproductive cloning to produce children "is unethical, ought not to be attempted, and should be indefinitely banned by federal law," it narrowly split (by a vote of ten members to seven) on the subject of using ES cells, whether cloned or otherwise, for biomedical research. By way of compromise, the report ultimately recommended a four-year moratorium on all forms of cloning, whether federally funded or not.[568] With regard to stem cell research, stem cells could still be gotten from adults, and even embryonic stem cell lines generated before August 2001 could continue; the moratorium only affected the generation of new ES cell lines. (This moratorium was later lifted under President Barack Obama in 2009.)

The Council's recommendation regarding a total ban on human reproductive cloning, as explained in the publication, was based on five objections: First, cloned children may have "problems of identity and individuality"; their lives could be "shadowed by constant comparisons" to their original. Secondly, cloning raises "concerns regarding manu-facture," about which more will be said in the next section, since this objection seems crucial enough for a separate discussion. Thirdly, committee members expressed concerns regarding "the prospect of a new eugenics," including the use of cloning "to perpetuate genetically engineered enhancements." Fourthly, cloning might bring about

[567] "California Institute Funds Stem Cell Research." Associated Press release, 11 April 2006.
[568] The President's Council on Bioethics, *Human Cloning and Human Dignity*, p. x.

"troubled family relations," including the idea of parents becoming twin siblings to their children. Finally, cloning's "effects on society" were mentioned: "Even if practiced on a small scale, [cloning] could affect the way society looks at children and set a precedent for future nontherapeutic interventions into the human genetic endowment or novel forms of control by one generation over the next." Given these objections, the Council concludes, "In the absence of wisdom regarding these matters, prudence dictates caution and restraint."[569] The Council's objections to reproductive cloning and its ultimate conclusion were virtually identical to a 1997 conclusion made by a similar council in France, the National Consultative Ethics Committee for Health and Life Sciences:

> There is therefore not a single conceivable variation of reproductive cloning of human beings, be it cloning of an adult or of an embryo, which is safe from an accumulation of intractable objections. For all of these reasons, it can only provoke vehement, categorical, and absolute ethical condemnation. Such a practice . . . would be a grave moral regression in the history of civilization.[570]

In his testimony before the 1997 U.S. Advisory Commission, Kass himself anticipated many of the objections offered by the President's Council and urged even more stringent regulations: "We should do all we can to prevent human cloning from happening, by an international legal ban if possible, by a unilateral national ban, at a minimum. . . . One cannot presume a future cloned child's consent to be a clone, even a healthy one. Thus, we cannot ethically get to know even whether or not human cloning is feasible."[571] Although some scientists disagree with this last point, believing that animal testing will eventually produce results which will allow for human cloning as well,[572] Kass's primary thought is still valid: At some stage the leap would have to be made from cloning animals to cloning humans, and this leap would still be

---

[569] Ibid., pp. xxviii-xxix.
[570] The National Consultative Ethics Committee for Health and Life Sciences. "Reply to the President of the French Republic on the Subject of Reproductive Cloning." Section II.3. 22 April 1997. Ccne.ethique.fr/docs.pdf. Accessed 2 Feb. 2008.
[571] Leon R. Kass. "For an International Ban on Human Cloning." Testimony presented to the National Bioethics Advisory Commission, Washington, D.C. 14 March, 1997. Mindfully.org/GE/Human-Cloning-Ban-Kass, n.p. Accessed 21 January 2008.
[572] Aaron D. Levine. *Cloning: A Beginner's Guide.* Oxford: Oneworld Publications, 2007, pp. 118-19.

highly experimental in nature, no matter if the previous results for animal cloning had turned out positively. As Aaron Levine, who is generally quite favorable to cloning research, puts it, "Approximately three percent of children born in the United States and other developed countries suffer from serious birth defects, but this rate would likely be much higher for children produced asexually through cloning technology."[573] Ethically, such results could not be risked.

Kass's views, and especially his leadership role in the President's Council on Bioethics, have been attacked as overly "conservative" by many.[574] For example, Arlene Judith Klotzko refers to "gloomy prognosticators such as Leon Kass," since Kass has written that "cloning will lead to the commodification and consequent devaluation of human beings." Klotzko responds somewhat dismissively: "He said virtually the same thing about IVF twenty-five years ago and his grim vision of the future has not come to pass."[575] However, one might ask upon what Klotzko bases her view that no devaluation of human beings has in fact taken place, since she cites no empirical evidence to that effect. Certainly the concepts of assisted suicide and euthanasia are widely accepted by many today, and, as has been discussed in the previous chapter, even the concept of infanticide is openly publicized and promoted by some as a medical practice advancing the public welfare. Who would have imagined this devaluation of human life even a few short years ago?[576] Other "devaluation" symptoms abound; for example, the United States has experienced a dreary but devastating series of seemingly random, meaningless mass murders, usually committed by young men with no apparent motive.[577] Television

---

[573] Ibid., p. 118.
[574] In Levine's *Cloning*, Kass is the only scientist, researcher, or ethicist mentioned whose name is modified in any way by an adjective: "conservative" (p. 128).
[575] Klotzko, *A Clone of Your Own?* p. 122.
[576] Again, compare the words of the Hippocratic Oath (Edelstein's translation): "I will neither give a deadly drug to anybody who asked for it, nor will I make a suggestion to this effect."
[577] For example, on February 2, 2008, five women were randomly murdered in a Lane Bryant clothing store in Tinley Park, Illinois, a small community where several friends of mine attend church. On the very next day (February 3), a fifteen-year-old in Cockeysville, Maryland, confessed to murdering his father, his mother, and his two younger brothers. On February 14, an award-winning former graduate student randomly killed six other students and then himself at Northern Illinois University, DeKalb, Illinois. Other examples could be multiplied; these, however, were noteworthy because of their close proximity in

programming, even from standard broadcasting networks, has become increasingly violent and remarkably graphic in its depictions of humans as both victims of and perpetrators of assorted brutalities, under the guise of portraying "crime scene investigations." *Body Worlds*, an exhibition of two hundred or so "plastinated" human bodies, some of them apparently the victims of execution or murder, has been drawing large crowds since it began touring in 1995 in Germany (where it has now been banned).[578] Further, it seems, at least by casual but extended observation, that many in the rising generation do spend more time and manifest more commitment to interaction with various new technological devices than to social interaction with other human beings. Other examples both philosophical and anecdotal could be adduced. This is not meant to attribute these tendencies solely to trends in biomedical and technological research; it is meant merely to suggest that the "commodification and consequent devaluation of human beings" could be taking place in reality without occasioning a great deal of notice or comment, even as one might experience a slow drop in temperature without immediately recognizing that one has in fact become cold.

Moreover, Klotzko at times seems to betray a profound and even startling lack of concern for the objections to cloning raised by Kass and the other members of the Council. Regarding the "spare" embryos left over from IVF research, she writes, "Because I do not believe embryos to be persons . . . I believe that using them to derive ES cells is not only morally defensible, it is morally required." Regarding therapeutic cloning, she writes, "I believe that the practice is morally acceptable and even morally required." Regarding the possibility of disruptions in familial and societal relationships brought about by cloning technology, she writes, "There have been many dire predictions about the social consequences of cloning. . . . I don't believe any of this for a minute." Regarding a possible change in attitudes toward children brought about by the "manufacture" of babies, she writes, "I don't believe this either."[579] Perhaps a steadfast refusal even to entertain the possibility of the validity of objections to cloning itself manifests a

---

time.

[578] In 2010, this exhibition began including arrangements of "plastinated" human corpses in sexual postures. Discussing the relationships between the culture of death, reductionistic portrayals of physically dead humans, pornography, rejection of the naturally occurring results of sexual activity, and so on, could require another book in itself.

[579] Klotzko, *A Clone of Your Own?*, pp. 86, 101, 120, and 122.

measure of the "devaluation of human beings" already in place! Others who are in favor of the advancement of cloning technology, such as Levine, will at least admit regarding the possible change in attitudes toward children, "Even some supporters of human reproductive cloning agree that cloned children might face more specific expectations than children produced the old-fashioned way" (although Levine ultimately rejects the significance of this objection).[580]

Because of all these potential problems, many objectors to and even supporters of human reproductive cloning begin with the technological barriers and risks involved, in a sort of utilitarian analysis. Given the current lack of knowledge of "the precise causes of the many abnormalities afflicting cloned animals," according to Klotzko, "any attempt at human [reproductive] cloning is patently immoral."[581] Of course, even a utilitarian analysis might lead one to establish a firm *nolle prosequi* in the area of human cloning, since the current risks might be deemed too great and the current benefits not sufficiently tested on other organisms. As D. Gareth Jones writes:

> Under no circumstances should we contemplate cloning other humans at present. The enormous risks currently associated with attempting to clone laboratory and farm animals tell us that cloning would be incredibly dangerous. In no way can one even attempt to justify the procedure in humans, either now or in the foreseeable future. At present, the chasm of unknowns is prodigious, and no one acting in an ethical manner would even contemplate cloning humans.[582]

However, to base one's objections to cloning on this sort of utilitarian analysis is in my judgment a mistake. Even without these utilitarian objections, which will surely fade away as cloning technology improves, it has been shown that there exist several better reasons to limit at the outset the technology which could lead to human cloning. In the next section, the most fundamental of these reasons will be examined in greater detail.

## 2.   The Primary Objection to Reproductive Cloning

The most important objection to reproductive cloning (brought up as its second objection by the President's Council on Bioethics) has to do

[580] Levine, *Cloning,* p. 125.

[581] Klotzko, *A Clone of Your Own?* p. xxi.

[582] D. Gareth Jones. *Designers of the Future.* Oxford: Monarch Books, Lion Hudson, 2005, pp. 157-58. Interestingly, Jones is open to the possibilities of both reproductive and therapeutic cloning once cloning procedures are more finely honed.

with the overall relationship of the parents as "maker" to their potential child as "object made." Reproductive cloning's use "as one of a battery of reproductive techniques" would assuredly "lead gradually to a widespread expectation of the 'quality control' of children which, as well as being theologically and ethically objectionable in other ways, could turn out to be highly discriminatory," according to Messer.[583] Not only could parents "control for" their baby's overall health, but also for other "therapeutic" characteristics as well. Once the technology and opportunity are in place, the arguments against the technology's use would correspondingly weaken and the pressure to use the opportunity would correspondingly increase:

> The decisions people come to on philosophical matters are partly shaped by social, political and cultural influences. . . . In the case of embryo experimentation . . . scientists did not want to close off promising avenues of research and those suffering from medical illnesses looked to medical progress in search of hope. Such strong social and cultural forces make it difficult to give serious and unprejudiced thought to the ethical status of the human embryo.[584]

If a degree of success is obtained in the treatment of illness by way of advances in cloning technology and applications, would not the desire to expand such applications also itself expand? For example, could not an overly enthusiastic football fan seek to obtain (under a more praiseworthy guise, of course) the potential for a slightly denser muscle mass in his son (this would also presuppose the request for a son)? If this example is thought to be unlikely, one should consider that when the *Roe v. Wade* decision was handed down by the United States Supreme Court in 1973, partial-birth abortion was unthinkable, too. This is not necessarily to employ a "slippery-slope" argument; this is merely to state a fact. The use of cloning for enhancement could very well expand as surely as has the use of cosmetic surgery for enhancement rather than for remedial care, and as surely as has the rationale for abortions of all types.

Another example: If one supposes for a moment that some homosexual-rights activists are correct and that the tendency toward homosexuality is genetically determined, would not many or most potential parents take advantage of the medical opportunity to nudge their child's genetic structure in a heterosexual direction? (Of course, such manipulation would be hotly contested by sexual-identity organizations.) The control of genotypes seems to open almost limitless

[583] Messer, *The Ethics of Human Cloning*, p. 10.
[584] David Albert Jones, *The Soul of the Embryo*, p. 241.

possibilities "for parents to choose whatever they find desirable in a child and do whatever the technology allows to incorporate such characteristics into their progeny."[585] Any characteristic at all, in other words, could very well eventually come to be seen as "therapeutic" for a child, and the child merely raw material for the parents' imposition of creative desires: "The instrumentalization of human embryos—the seeds of the next generation—might tend to coarsen the sensibilities of our society toward future generations. . . . Since human suffering and disease will never come to an end . . . the resort to extreme and potentially exploitative methods is unlikely to find a logical stopping point."[586]

These possibilities would seem inevitably to lead to a profound change in the relationships of parents and children, from that of "begetter/begotten" to the Frankenstein-like image of "creator/creation" or "maker/artifact."[587] Rather than a "Thou," the child would become an "it"; fellow human beings, even those nearest and dearest to us, would be seen as "an artifact or a commodity rather than as an Other."[588] These possibilities "force us to reflect upon the meaning of the bond between parents and children,"[589] since such a bond would have been taken out of the hands of natural processes and placed firmly in the hands of human designers, designers who are perhaps not necessarily the cloned child's parents or even genetically related at all. The seeds of this transformation in attitude began to sprout during the beginnings of the abortion debate. Most readers will probably remember pro-abortion marches in which parents had their own children carry placards reading "I Am a Choice." From the start, this sentence struck the keynote attitude of those protesting: Their children were not seen as gifts, whether of nature or of God, to be humbly and gratefully received, but rather as "choices." Becoming a parent of another human being *who only exists as a choice* may well be seen as something like deciding whether or not to have a home in town or in the country, or what options to include in one's automobile purchase.[590] However, the

---

[585] Messer, *The Ethics of Human Cloning*, p. 13.

[586] The President's Council on Bioethics, *Monitoring Stem Cell Research*, p. 93.

[587] See Meilaender, *Bioethics*, Chapter 2; also Oliver O'Donovan, *Begotten or Made?* Chapter 1.

[588] Messer, *The Ethics of Human Cloning*, p. 11.

[589] Meilaender, *Bioethics*, p. 12.

[590] In case the reader thinks the "choosing a home" example trivial, allow me to relate an actual conversation I had with a young female academic, on the subject of abortion. Since she steadfastly refused to even consider the

attitude of reception, of seeing one's children as gifts rather than as choices, highlights the children's intrinsic worth and identity separate from that of the parents; it sees them as equally human with the parents, placing both parents and children on equal footing as human beings, even though the parents possess a further supervisory status over their children for a time. As Stanley Hauerwas puts it, this attitude "is based on the regard of the other as an entity that is not in my control but who is all the more valuable because I do not control him." He concludes, "Children are gifts exactly because they draw our love to them while refusing to be as we wish them to be."[591]

*They draw our love to them.* What happens to this unconditionally loving relationship when the parents become not the recipients of a gift, but the designers of an accessory to their lifestyles—even in the cases of couples desperately seeking children? Would the children "draw our love to them" in quite the same way if it is known that any displeasing characteristics or behaviors on their part could well have been changed or prevented simply by the refusal to accept those characteristics or behaviors in a pre-natal selection process? This parent/child relationship may be further complicated by the fact that the child would not be genetically related to at least one of the parents involved, which could have disruptive long-term effects on the natural loving bond of commitment felt by the parents: "Parents of a cloned child may not experience as strong a natural inclination to care for the child. . . . because the child is genetically unrelated to at least one of the parents— if not both in the case of donated genetic material—and the child's relationship to its parents is the result of choice, selection, and artifice,

---

possibility that the unborn child might have its own human existence and rights, I finally asked her directly, "So the fetal tissue inside the mother is no more important than any other scrap of tissue—say, the tomato the mother had with her lunch?" "That's right," came the response, "and it possesses no more importance than that. The only importance of the fetus is the importance the mother attaches to it." Thinking either that she misunderstood me or that I misunderstood her, I asked again: "So the woman's choice to have an abortion is no more important, and no more anyone else's business, than her choice whether or not to have tomato on her sandwich at lunch?" Again the response was the same: "That's exactly right; there is no significant difference." At least in this instance, the choice of where to locate one's home was probably seen as *more* important than the choice of whether or not to abort one's child. However, illustrative of the deep ambivalence in most people's thinking on the matter, this same young woman also said to me in another conversation, "I myself would never have an abortion."

[591] Hauerwas, *Truthfulness and Tragedy*, p. 153.

rather than openness to whatever sort of child may result from natural procreative activity."[592]

> To understand what it would mean to clone a child, we do well to consider most generally what it means to bring a child into this world, and with what attitude we should regard his or her arrival and presence. . . . Though their conception is the fruit of our activity, and though we are responsible for saying "yes" to their arrival, we do not, in normal procreation, command their conception, control their makeup, or rule over their development and birth. They are, in an important sense, "given" to us. Though they are *our* children, they are not our *property*. Though they are our flesh and blood, and deeply kin, they are also independent "strangers" who arrive suddenly out of the darkness and whom we must struggle to get to know. Though we may seek to have them for our own self-fulfillment, they exist also and especially for their own sakes. Though we seek to educate them, they are not like our other projects, determined strictly according to our plans and serving only our desires.[593]

By way of analogy, one might consider a writer working at a computer. Many times during the writing process, a displeasing sentence or phrase is erased forever with the flick of a computer key. The writer feels no compunctions about doing so, for after all, the chapter is his or her own creation, to do with as he or she pleases. Is it not possible, or even likely, that a similar attitude might begin to creep into parental relationships with cloned children?

"What we 'make,' then, is alien to our humanity," as O'Donovan writes:

> In that it has a human maker, it has come to existence as a human project, its being at the disposal of mankind. It is not fit to take its place alongside mankind in fellowship, for it has no place beside him on which to stand: man's will is the law of its being. That which we beget can be, and should be, our companion; but the product of our art—whatever immeasurable satisfaction and enjoyment there may be both in making it and in cherishing it—can never have the independence to be that "other I," equal to us and differentiated from us, which we acknowledge in those who are

---

[592] Jason Eberl, *Thomistic Principles and Bioethics*, p. 91.

[593] The President's Council on Bioethics, *Human Cloning and Human Dignity*, p. 7. As Leon Kass bluntly states, "Our children are not our children. They are not our property, they are not our possessions" ("For an International Ban on Human Cloning," n.p.).

begotten of human seed.[594]

Of course, this transformation in attitudes would not occur overnight. If it occurred, it would more probably be a result of what Robin Gill terms "crossing a line" or a "procedural deterioration."[595] Gill uses the example of the transformation in attitudes towards abortion in the United Kingdom since 1968, as a limited abortion license has turned effectively into abortion-on-demand: "We now have abortion on demand in Britain, and all of the safeguards built into the Abortion Act have been bypassed."[596] (In fact, Paul Ramsey points out that even conscientious objection to abortion on the part of medical doctors and nurses is now tacitly nullified in practice even when specifically granted in theory.[597])

A less serious example, but one that is similar in principle, involves the use of Viagra in the United States. Originally Viagra was designed to help treat clinical impotence on the part of men who could not otherwise enjoy genital sexual relations with their wives; however, the drug is now commonly used by men who do not have clinical impotence, but who merely desire to improve and enhance their sexual performance. The change in sales marketing for Viagra, from "thera-peutic treatment" to "enhancement," took less than one year from the time it was introduced on the market for sale. Gill points out the similar attitude shift in the United Kingdom regarding abortion, from "regrettable necessity" to "positive right." How long would it take for a similar shift to occur in the case of reproductive cloning—a shift from "last resort and aid for infertile couples" to "the right to design one's own baby as one sees fit"? A corresponding sea change in the parent/child relationship would seem inevitable.

Messer offers a summary of this line of argument:

> There may . . . be a moral structure to human parenthood that has to do with love, unconditional belonging, and the recognition that our children come to us as gifts whom we are called to receive and rejoice in, not to attempt to control. This moral structure may be distorted by the practice of cloning, even if done with the most innocent and understandable of motives.[598]

This seems the primary objection to reproductive cloning—that it

---

[594] O'Donovan, *Begotten or Made?* pp. 1-2.
[595] Robin Gill. "The Challenge of Euthanasia." *Euthanasia and the Churches.* Robin Gill, ed. London: Cassell, 1998: 15-38, pp. 37-38.
[596] Ibid., p. 37.
[597] Ramsey, *Ethics at the Edges of Life*, pp. 50-53.
[598] Messer, *The Ethics of Human Cloning*, p. 23.

almost inevitably and necessarily distorts the "moral structure" of the relationship between parents and children. "If these observations are correct, certain things follow regarding the attitudes we should have toward our children," as a governmental report on cloning puts it. "We treat them rightly when we treat them as gifts rather than as products, and when we treat them as independent beings whom we are duty-bound to protect and nurture rather than as extensions of our selves subject only to our wills and whims."[599]

Some writers see the point of this objection (that "If we set conditions on which child we get, we are setting conditions on our love for whatever child we get") and yet attempt to circumvent the objection by arguing that genetic manipulation is compatible with "unconditional love." Philosopher John K. Davis refers to this genetic manipulation as "selection drift," the tendency to select for children "whose genetic traits are above average." Given this tendency, Davis asserts that "the standard for acceptable children is creeping upwards as we get better at selecting potential children on genetic grounds." Nevertheless, Davis argues firstly that "selection drift is not inconsistent with unconditional parental love" and secondly that unconditional parental love might even require parents to select for genetic traits in their children, in the children's own best interest: "Contrary to what proponents of the parental love objection seem to believe, the ideal of unconditional parental love implies that we should practice selection drift—that is, we should try to select potential children with the best genetic endowments."[600]

However, despite Davis's extensive argument toward these two conclusions, he seems to begin amiss simply by mis-defining the word "unconditional." According to Davis, "The ideal of unconditional parental love implies that parents should want their children to be as well off as possible," and therefore children below the genetic ideal would be selected out of existence due to the potential children's parents' "unconditional" love.[601] But this is not at all what most people would think of as an "unconditional" type of love. Of course, parents want their children to be as well off as possible; however, the clear implication in this statement would be that parents want their children to be as well off as possible *given their genetic endowment*, which the parents

[599] The President's Council on Bioethics, *Human Cloning and Human Dignity*, pp. 7-8.
[600] John K. Davis. "Selecting Potential Children and Unconditional Parental Love." *Bioethics* 22.5 (June 2008): 258-68, p. 259.
[601] Ibid., p. 264.

unconditionally receive as a unique, unselected, non-designed gift, independent of the parents' particular will for their children. Any other definition of "unconditional" renders the term almost meaningless.

### 3. The Primary Objection to Therapeutic Cloning

Of course, supporters of continued research in and application of the technology of cloning human beings do so for more reasons than aiding reproduction; perhaps even more importantly, they also see the possible therapeutic and biomedical research advances to be made by cloning technologies. Earlier supporters of this research made reference to the "functional" definitions of personhood already discussed and argued against in previous chapters; for example, in 1998 a Congressional Research Report stated, "Supporters of embryo research believe that very early embryos, those up to the implantation stage of development, do not have the same moral and legal status as persons. While they acknowledge that embryos are irrefutably genetically human, they believe embryos do not have the same moral relevance, because of the lack of specific capacities, including consciousness, reasoning, and sentience."[602] Since all of these points have been dealt with in previous chapters, the arguments presented against the use of "specific capacities" to demarcate personhood should be considered as given.

However, more recently a different variety of this argument has arisen, one that acknowledges the personhood of the conceptus but still considers its destruction permissible if properly motivated in the interests of research. As previously mentioned, seven members of the seventeen-member President's Council on Bioethics argued in favor of cloning to produce embryonic stem cells for biomedical research; as these members put it, "In both cases—creating embryos to aid fertility or creating embryos for biomedical research—the ultimate goal is something humanly good."[603] This approach, with its implicitly utilitarian rationale, would seem to be negated simply by arguing for the personhood of the embryo as has been done throughout the present work, but such is not the case. According to these members in the Council's report, even if the personhood of the embryo be granted, the destruction of this embryo may be permitted if the destruction of the embryo is not the *intention* of the researcher: "Thus, in the case of cloning-for-biomedical-research, it is wrong to argue, as some do, the

[602] Irene Stith-Coleman. "Human Embryo Research." Library of Congress Congressional Research Service. Research Report Number 95-910 STM. Updated 29 January 1998. Accessed 22 November 2005.
[603] The President's Council on Bioethics, *Human Cloning and Human Dignity*, p. 141.

embryos are being 'created for destruction.' Certainly, their destruction is a known and unavoidable effect, but the embryos are ultimately created for research in the service of life and medicine."[604] The united Council does conclude against research on embryos in the blastocyst stage or beyond; however, as has been argued throughout this work, such a dividing line seems arbitrary and groundless, especially since this argument as appearing in the Council's publication states that "the cloned embryo has only an intermediate moral status."[605]

Ironically, this discussion in favor of therapeutic cloning immediately gives rise to the primary *objection* to therapeutic or research-oriented cloning, for the argument from the seven member of the Council seems to hinge on a simple factual misstatement. It cannot be said that the destruction of the embryos is not directly intended by the researcher, for the act of the research itself, at least initially, is directly constituted by the destruction of the embryo; the act of research "does not merely *cause* some distinct harm but *constitutes* the destruction of the embryo"; likewise, "Cloning-for-biomedical-research. . .involves creating embryos with the intention of destroying them for medical use."[606] Therefore, as Jason Eberl matter-of-factly concludes in his discussion of this point, "Therapeutic cloning involves the creation of embryos *with the purpose of destroying them.*"[607] Consider the analogy of one performing tests upon glass windows with a mechanized metal hammer in order to discover the shattering point of various types of glass; one could not then say, "The object of this exercise is knowledge of the potential strength of various glass materials; the actual shattering of the glass is incidental to the process." To the contrary, the shattering of the glass cannot be thought of as incidental to the process; it *is* the process. Likewise one could not say, "The materials of the embryo are being used in the furtherance of medical knowledge, but the actual destruction of the embryo is incidental to the process." Again to the contrary—the using of the embryo's "materials" is identical to the destruction of the embryo, for whatever purpose or for whatever benefits.

Perhaps Aquinas's understanding of "hypostasis" should again be brought up at this point. Human cells in themselves, or even human organs or other bodily parts in themselves, are not necessarily deserving

---

[604] Ibid., pp. 141-42.

[605] Ibid., pp. 142-43.

[606] William FitzPatrick. "Surplus Embryos, Nonreproductive Cloning, and the Intend/Foresee Distinction." *Hastings Center Report* 33.3 (May-June 2003): 29-36, pp. 29 and 34. Emphasis in original.

[607] Eberl, *Thomistic Principles and Bioethics*, p. 89. Emphasis in original.

of special moral consideration: "Not every particular substance is a hypostasis or a person, but that which has the complete nature of its species. Hence a hand, or a foot, is not called a hypostasis, or a person."[608] No one worries over the possible moral objections to getting a haircut or clipping one's fingernails. However, special moral consideration is due the conceptus not because of any quantitative factors, but rather the qualitative distinction possessed by the zygote from conception, which no other organ or bodily part possesses: The zygote is a hypostasis, just as is an adult human. Whether "implanted" or not, whether characterized by "potentiality" or not, the fertilized ovum is the same substance of rational nature as the adult human, at a different level of development. When the embryo is implanted or when the fetus is capable of life outside of the womb does not change its basic substance. For example, should technology allow researchers to sustain a developing embryo outside of the womb, up to the time of the embryo's "birth," would that technological advance in itself change the embryo's moral status or make it any more or any less "human"? No, for it does nothing to change the embryo's individual substance of qualitatively rational nature.

This seems to be a point some ethicists may grasp (the idea of the rational substance) while still misunderstanding its full implications. For example, Michael Tooley proposes a thought experiment regarding a hypothetical chemical injection; this injection into a kitten's brain "would cause the kitten to develop into a cat possessing a brain of the sort possessed by humans, and consequently into a cat having all the psychological characteristics of adult humans." After arguing that the cat would then possess a right to life like a human's (if humans them-selves possess such a right), Tooley then attempts his bioethical application:

> It would not be seriously wrong to refrain from injecting a newborn kitten with the special chemical, and to kill it instead.[609] The fact that one could initiate a causal process that would transform a kitten into an entity that would eventually possess properties such that anything possessing them *ipso facto* has a serious right to life does not mean that the kitten has a serious right to life even before

---

[608] ST I.75.4.

[609] If an editorial comment may be inserted here: This seems quite odd to me. If one has no good reason to kill the kitten, why would it not be morally wrong to do so, even if the kitten is not itself a substance of rational nature? What would be the typical moral attitude toward one who kills kittens for no good reason?

it has been subjected to the process of injection and transformation. . . . [Furthermore] if it is not seriously wrong to refrain from initiating such a causal process, neither is it seriously wrong to interfere with such a process. Suppose a kitten is accidentally injected with the chemical. As long as it has not yet developed those properties that in themselves endow something with a right to life, there cannot be anything wrong with interfering with the causal process and preventing the development of the properties in question.[610]

Tooley then concludes: "If it is not seriously wrong to destroy an injected kitten which will naturally develop the properties that bestow a right to life, neither can it be seriously wrong to destroy a member of *Homo sapiens* which lacks such properties, but will naturally come to have them."[611]

However, Tooley's argument stands or falls on at least three problematic points: (1) First of all, he insists on describing the injection as initiating a "causal process" which eventually will cause the cat to develop "those properties that in themselves endow something with a right to life." The first mistake here lies in assuming that the right to life is gained only through the addition of "properties" and is the end result of a "causal process." In other words, Tooley implicitly relies on, again, a "functionalist" view of personhood and its rights, in which personhood depends on the achievement of certain functional abilities. However, in the case of individual substances of rational nature, there is no "causal process" which leads to personhood or a gradual gaining of human rights—or, if such a causal process does exist, that causal process is simply conception itself. Therefore, contrary to Tooley's explicitly stated assumption, there is no such thing as a "member of *Homo sapiens* which lacks such properties, but will naturally come to have them." If one is a human being, one possesses a "serious" right to life, even apart from any subsequent process of development. Tooley's second problem follows from this one: (2) He assumes that the process of injecting the cat and changing its own substantial development is relevantly similar to conception. Of course, this is not the case. The process of injecting the cat makes the cat a *different substance*—it would not otherwise develop its rational, human-like characteristics. The unborn human, however, *would* develop under normal circumstances into full rationality, in a way that the non-injected cat would not. The

---

[610] Michael Tooley. "Abortion and Infanticide." *Philosophy and Public Affairs* 2.1 (1972): 37-65, pp. 60-61.
[611] Ibid., p. 61.

conceptus is not yet functionally rational, of course, but it is a "rational creature at an early stage of its development," from the time of its conception, in a way that the non-injected cat is not and could never be under normal circumstances. In order for the cat to develop rationality, it would have to undergo a substantial change through the injection; on the other hand, in order for the human embryo to develop rationality, nothing would have to be done to it except to allow it to develop normally. The human embryo, in other words, is qualitatively different in kind from the non-injected cat, and even different from the injected cat (which leads to Tooley's third mistake): (3) The embryo is different from the injected cat because the cat has had its substance changed in a way that the human embryo does not require for its continued development. Further, since the injected cat has in fact had its substance changed, Tooley is wrong to maintain that it would still be allowable to destroy the cat before its process of "transformation" is complete. Tooley tries to avoid this point by seamlessly eliding "injection" and "transformation" together as one phrase, "the process of injection and transformation." However, if the injection has already changed the substance of the cat into that of a being possessing a rational nature, but not yet rational capabilities, then the cat's new potential for trans-formation is not really the morally relevant element in the decision to destroy it. The same is true regarding the embryo's innate, self-directed potential for transformation. It is wrong to destroy the embryo not because of what it could become, which is more or less irrelevant, but because of what it is in itself.

Thus (to return to this section's topic) the process of obtaining embryonic stem cells for research purposes, what Tooley euphe-mistically would call "interfering with" the embryo, in its essence is equivalent to the process of early-term abortion, discussed in the previous chapter, and may be opposed for a similar reason: that the process ends the continued life of an innocent human substance of rational nature, a person. This constitutes the primary objection to therapeutic cloning: The cloned embryo is brought into existence, as an innocent individual substance of rational nature, for the purpose of disaggregation/destruction. The additional purpose of gaining know-ledge does not mitigate this initial purpose; nor does the fact of the embryo's functional lack of rational capabilities.

## 4. The Prohibition of Human Cloning: Some Other Possibilities

### (1) *Some Conclusions*

The logical conclusions to this chapter, and to the extended discussion leading up to this chapter, might be stated in syllogistic fashion:

198

*Against reproductive cloning:*

First premise: Any individual substance of rational nature of the species *Homo sapiens* is a human person.[612] All humans are therefore morally equal at least in the fact of their shared human-ness: "Moral equality may legitimately be predicated of three different human subjects: one who exercises the use of reason, one who has lost its exercise through mental dysfunction, and one (a fetus) who has not yet begun to exercise the use of reason. This means that from conception onwards, all human fetuses may claim moral equality with all other living human beings."[613]

Second premise: Even though human persons beget other human persons, they do not "make" or "manufacture" them. Such a making or manufacturing would change the relationship of equality between human persons in a morally harmful way, from the relationship of "human person/human person" to that of "human person/manufactured artifact." Reproductive cloning would entail such a making or manufacturing.

Third premise: Human persons should not be allowed to change the relationship of equality between themselves and other human persons in a morally harmful way. Since natural law ethics is not generally utilitarian in nature, this third premise would hold true regardless of the good or bad consequences of its acceptance.

Conclusion: Therefore, reproductive cloning would be morally harmful to the relationship of equality between human persons and should not be allowed.

This argument takes into account only the most important objection to reproductive cloning; as has been seen, several other persuasive objections may also be put forward. The cumulative case made by these objections still points to the conclusion that reproductive cloning should be banned.

*Against therapeutic cloning or cloning for research:*

First premise: In natural law ethical reflection, the deliberate killing of an innocent human person is morally wrong and should not be legally allowed. Since natural law ethics is not generally utilitarian in nature, this first premise would hold true regardless of the good or bad consequences of its acceptance.

Second premise: Both embryonic stem cell research and other uses

---

[612] ST III.2.2.
[613] Donald G. McCarthy and Albert S. Moraczewski, eds. *An Ethical Evaluation of Fetal Experimentation: An Interdisciplinary Study.* St. Louis, Missouri: The Pope John XXIII Medical-Moral Research and Education Center, 1976, p. 73.

of cloned embryos in biomedical research (insofar as they destroy the embryo) directly entail the deliberate killing of an innocent human person ("person" again being defined in the Thomistic sense as an individual substance of rational nature).

Conclusion: Therefore, both embryonic stem cell research and other uses of cloned embryos in biomedical research (insofar as they destroy the embryo) are morally wrong in that they involve the killing of an innocent human person, and therefore should not be legally allowed.

(2)   *Some Other Possibilities: Non-Embryonic Cells*

One may be thankful for the fact that a large part of this discussion, particularly in the realm of ES cell research, may by now be virtually a moot point. Researchers have long held out promise of stem cells manipulated from "non-embryonic" cells,[614] although some critics think of these attempts as thus far creating only "disabled embryos." These researchers faced the question: Could pluripotent stem cells (cells with the plasticity to become various differentiated cells) be produced without the use of embryos and without the cells passing through any stage of being totipotent (embryonic cells with the innate means of continued development as a human being), and thus avoid the moral pitfalls inherent in ES research?[615] While all human cells in each individual contain the same genetic information, each cell's information is expressed quite differently, resulting in different "epigenetic" states for the various types of cells:

> With few exceptions all human cells contain a complete human genome, i.e., the complete DNA sequence characteristic of the human species. Specifically, one-celled human embryos, pluripotent human embryonic stem (or ES) cells, multipotent human adult stem cells, and differentiated (specialized) adult human cells such as neurons all contain a complete human genome. Thus, possession of a human genome is a necessary but not sufficient condition for defining a human embryo with its inherent dignity. Rather the

---

[614] For example, see Christen Brownlee's "Do Not Harm: Stem Cells Created Without Destroying Healthy Embryos" (*Science News* 168.17 [22 October 2005]: 259).

[615] Another serious moral pitfall involved in ES cell research has not even yet been mentioned: namely, that the oocytes used are "hard-to-obtain eggs surgically harvested from women," and therefore potentially exploitative especially of poorer women who might be more likely to undergo the chemical stimulus required to induce the body to produce more eggs (Nidhi Thareja, M.D. "Human Embryonic Stem Cells—Without an Embryo" [Abcnews.com, n.p. 20 Nov. 2007. Accessed 20 Nov. 2007]).

nature of each cell depends on its epigenetic state, i.e., which subset of the approximately thirty thousand human genes is switched on or off and, if on, at what level.[616]

A pluripotent cell is "genetically" human, but its epigenetic state is not that of a full-fledged human being—that is, it is not a cell "such that it is oriented to develop toward maturity as a member of the species,"[617] which is in fact the case with totipotent cells. In other words, pluripotent cells do not necessarily have to be embryonic in origin or nature.

In fact, in a 2005 publication, the President's Council on Bioethics examines four possible sources for pluripotent cells, the last two claiming to be non-embryonic processes. The first of these possible non-embryonic sources is Altered Nuclear Transfer (ANT), a process originated by Dr. William Hurlbut in 2005. ANT attempts to produce non-embryonic stem cells with the plasticity and potential of ES cells, by "extracting cells from artificially created non-embryonic but embryo-like cellular systems." The second possible non-embryonic process involves "dedifferentiation of somatic cells [ordinary body cells from children or adults] back to pluripotency."[618] The Council statement ultimately rejects ANT on ethical grounds, because of dubiety regarding the claim that the "non-embryonic artifact" produced by the process is in fact non-embryonic. So that it will not become totipotent, the cell in this process "has, from the beginning, a built-in genetic defect that prevents it from developing normally." However, some critics of the ANT process claim it is difficult to know with certainty whether this results in "the production of a non-human entity" or "the deliberate creation of a doomed or disabled human embryo,"[619] with certain epigenetic elements in the embryo simply "switched off." The Council's conclusion is quite tentative:

Because this proposal [ANT] raises many serious ethical concerns,

---

[616] "Production of Pluripotent Stem Cells by Oocyte Assisted Repro-gramming—Joint Statement." Alterednucleartransfer.com, n.p. 20 June 2005. Accessed 5 Feb. 2008. The numerous well-known signatories to this joint statement include Hadley Arkes, Robert P. George, Maureen L. Condic, Kevin Flannery, Germain Grisez, Markus Grompe, William Hurlbut, Patrick Lee, and many others.

[617] Ryan T. Anderson. "Faithful Reason about Stem Cells." Firstthings.com, n.p. 7 June 2007. Accessed 7 June 2007.

[618] The President's Council on Bioethics. *Alternative Sources of Human Pluripotent Stem Cells*. Washington, D.C.: Government Printing Office, May 2005, p. 3.

[619] Ibid., p. 38.

we do not believe that it is *at this time* ethically acceptable for trials with human material. . . . We find no insuperable ethical objections to pursuing this proposal in animal models. . . . The possibility of any future endorsement of trying this approach in humans will depend upon a more thorough ethical analysis made possible in part by animal experiments.[620]

By way of response, Dr. Hurlbut originated a variation on the Altered Nuclear Transfer process known as Oocyte Assisted Reprogramming (ANT-OAR). This variation alters "the somatic cell nucleus or the egg cytoplasm or both . . . before the nucleus is transferred." According to Grompe and George, "These genetic alterations would permit the egg to reprogram the somatic cell nucleus directly to a pluripotent, but not a totipotent (i.e., embryonic) state."[621] The genome of a somatic cell would first be altered before being transferred into an enucleated oocyte, forming a new cell. The cytoplasm of this cell "would work to reprogram the cell to a pluripotent state":

How can we know? Because the transcription factor cdx2 is necessary for the epigenetic state of a cell to be totipotent, and transcription factors like nanog and oct3/4 are responsible for instructing a cell to be pluripotent. Since the cell never had any cdx2 but had nanog, it could never have been totipotent, only pluripotent. In fact, nanog is never found in oocytes or zygotes, but it is always found in pluripotent stem cells. When its expression is forced *from the very beginning* of a cell's existence, we can be sure that the new cell is not totipotent but pluripotent. It's not an embryo; it's a non-embryonic, highly plastic cell.[622]

Despite ANT-OAR's attractiveness as a possible source of non-embryonic stem cells, some criticisms of it still exist, primarily regarding the definition of "totipotency." If certain transcription factors are suppressed in the development of this newly-made cell, the cell would not be totipotent in the sense that it could not develop normally as an embryo, but perhaps this would simply mean that the cell would be a defective or disabled embryo. However, one of the primary goals of ANT-OAR is specifically to prevent any embryonic phase at all in the reprogrammed cell; if it turns out in animal experimentation that the forced expression of nanog does not accomplish this goal, many other

---

[620] Ibid., p. 59. Emphasis in original.
[621] Markus Grompe and Robert P. George. "Creative Science Will Resolve Stem-Cell Issues." *The Wall Street Journal* (20 June 2005): A14, p. A14.
[622] Ryan Anderson, "Faithful Reason about Stem Cells," n.p. Emphasis in original.

transcription factors are also available for testing. Given this, some who were initially skeptical of the original ANT proposal now support ANT-OAR, believing that ANT-OAR "eliminates the risk of creating a defective embryo, rather than a truly non-embryonic artifact."[623]

(3)     *New Developments in Dedifferentiation*

The debate regarding ANT-OAR, however, may at this point have been rendered unnecessary, since a truly remarkable advance from two separate research teams was announced simultaneously in two scientific journals in late 2007,[624] regarding the second of the President Council's stated alternatives in non-embryonic stem cell production. This second alternative, "dedifferentiation of somatic cells," seems to involve "neither the creation nor the destruction of human embryos," and thus runs into no ethical obstacles: "There would seem to be nothing to object to ethically if procedures were developed to turn somatic cells into pluripotent stem cells, non-embryonic functional equivalents of embryonic stem cells." Because the Council publication came out in 2005, it put references to this technology in the future tense: "Certainly, dedifferentiation of somatic cells back to their corresponding progenitor cells will likely be welcomed as a powerful new way to produce large quantities of multipotent adult stem cells."[625] Robert P. George, in the same publication, refers to somatic cell dedifferentiation as "likely to be . . . the best long-term solution" to the problem of working with stem cells without harming embryos.[626]

In 1998, Dr. James Thomson of the University of Wisconsin/ Madison first isolated embryonic stem cells. A team led by Thomson and a team led by Dr. Shinya Yamanaka of Kyoto University, Japan, then worked simultaneously to try to induce the dedifferentiation of somatic cells; the teams sought to bring about a sort of regression on the part of the cell back into a pluripotent state by causing different transcription genes (Oct3/4, Sox2, Klf4, and c-Myc) to incorporate themselves into the differentiated somatic cell, thus transforming it over the course of about two weeks into pluripotency. Yamanaka's team

---

[623] Ibid., n.p.

[624] Junying Yu, James A. Thomson, et al. "Induced Pluripotent Stem Cell Lines Derived from Human Somatic Cells." *Science* 318.5858 (20 November 2007): 1917-20; and Kazutoshi Takahashi and Shinya Yamanaka. "Induction of Pluripotent Stem Cells from Mouse Embryonic and Adult Fibroblast Cultures by Defined Factors." *Cell* 126 (20 November 2007): 663-76.

[625] The President's Council on Bioethics. *Alternative Sources of Human Pluripotent Stem Cells*, pp. 50, 51, and 54.

[626] Ibid., p. 79.

used this technique, called "direct reprogramming," on mice cells with success, while Thomson's team worked with human somatic cells. The resulting cells, called "induced pluripotent stem cells" or iPS cells, "displayed several characteristics of embryonic stem cells, including the ability to grow into nerve and heart cells."[627] According to Dr. Markus Grompe, director of the Oregon Stem Cell Center, this discovery "represents a phenomenal breakthrough, more important than cloning"[628]; likewise, Dr. Maureen L. Condic calls direct reprogramming "one of the most exciting scientific discoveries of modern times."[629] If iPS cells function as hoped in humans, "a simple skin biopsy could be used to create embryonic stem cell equivalents" while using neither embryos nor eggs (human or animal), nor even oocyte cytoplasm.[630] In fact, Ian Wilmut, leader of the team which first cloned a mammal from adult cells, after hearing of the breakthrough, publicly renounced his plans to attempt to clone human embryos for research purposes, an attempt for which he had already obtained permission from the British government.[631] It certainly seems ironic that the very scientist (Thomson) who first isolated ES cells led one of the research teams which possibly made ES-cell experimentation obsolete, and the very scientist (Wilmut) who led the research team which first successfully cloned a mammal from adult cells has now apparently rejected further experimentation in human embryonic cloning. Human cloned embryos would no longer be necessary for clinical applications, since iPS cells, derived directly from the patients themselves, would be perfect genetic matches to the patients and thus ideal both for the study of the development of diseases and for the testing of treatments.

Condic lists seven immediate advantages to iPS-cell technology in three categories of benefit. *Scientific* benefits include "the ability to generate patient-specific stem cell lines for research on human genetic diseases," which Condic calls "a tremendous scientific advantage." Moreover, multiple stem cell lines can be generated "from an individual

---

[627] Nidhi Thareja, M.D., "Human Embryonic Stem Cells—Without an Embryo," n.p.

[628] Ibid., n.p.

[629] Maureen L. Condic. "Getting Stem Cells Right." *First Things* 180 (February 2008): 10-12, p. 10.

[630] Joseph Bottum. "Embryonic Stem Cells and Those Pro-Science Pro-Lifers." Firstthings.com, n.p. 20 November 2007. Accessed 20 November 2007.

[631] Ryan T. Anderson. "The End of the Stem-Cell Wars." *The Weekly Standard* 13.12 (3 December 2007), n.p. Weeklystandard.com/Content/Public/Articles. Accessed 26 November 2007.

patient without any extra cost or effort." In the area of *practical* advantages, iPS cells are simpler and less time-consuming to bring about than ES cells; they face none of the ethical obstacles laid out in federal guidelines and are therefore "fully eligible for federal funding"; and since iPS cells do not involve human embryos or eggs, they are subject merely to "simpler regulatory requirements." Of course, the *ethical* benefits include the fact that no human embryos are destroyed, but also that iPS cell research "can be conducted without subjecting women to the medical risks associated with egg donation."[632] In fact, as of early 2009, the iPS technique according to Yuval Levin "has begun to over-take the use of embryos in many stem-cell labs." Approximately 800 laboratories use iPS cells in their research projects, "which has cut sharply into the number of those using human embryos or cells derived from embryos."[633]

For all of these benefits and for the apparent possible resolution of the ES-cell controversies, thanks are due not only to the brilliant scientists involved in these research projects (Hurlbut, Thomson, Yamanaka, and so on), but also to the widely reviled politicians and intellectual leaders (Dr. Leon Kass and U.S. President George W. Bush come immediately to mind) who insisted all along in this process that sources of pluripotent cells besides embryos had to be found. Without their leadership, "Most likely, science and the public would have accom-modated themselves to the mass production and mass killing of human embryos. . . . Having political leaders of principle who insist on ethical standards in scientific research, then, is always of the utmost import-ance."[634] As Richard John Neuhaus puts it, "Those who in recent years insisted that science accommodate itself to moral principle, rather than the other way around, have been vindicated. . . . And one may, without being unpleasant about it, note that the mainstream media and the scientific establishment who beat the drums for the necessity of killing embryos in order, they said, to find cures for all kinds of illnesses, along with politicians who agitated for multibillion-dollar referendums in California, Missouri, and New Jersey, were, not to put too fine a point on it, dead wrong."[635]

## 5. The Question of Utilitarian Benefits Re-Considered

As may be seen, any area of scientific research involving human lives

---

[632] Condic, "Getting Stem Cells Right," p. 11.

[633] Yuval Levin. "Biotech: What to Expect." *First Things* 191 (March 2009): 17-20, pp. 17-18.

[634] Ryan T. Anderson, "The End of the Stem-Cell Wars," n.p.

[635] Neuhaus. "While We're At It." *First Things* 180, p. 67.

must be thought out in terms of its bioethical implications, publicly discussed, specified, and then *limited.* "We deceive ourselves if we come to believe that there are no limits to what we *can* do or what it is *right* for us to do in an effort to improve the world," as Neil Messer writes.[636] Especially with these new advances in cell reprogramming, and given the Thomistic anthropology laid out earlier in this work, along with the definition of "human being" at which we have arrived,[637] neither reproductive enhancement nor therapeutic cloning for the purposes of ES cell research seems otherwise morally right. In the words of Leon Kass, quoted earlier, "We should do all that we can to prevent human cloning from happening, by an international legal ban if possible, by a unilateral national ban, at a minimum."[638] In both reproductive and therapeutic human cloning, one is dealing with a separate human being in the person of the developing embryo, whether to enhance its capabilities (in the case of reproductive enhancement) or to destroy it altogether (usually required in the case of therapeutic cloning, since the embryo is used therapeutically for the sake of another). In both cases, the will of another is imposed upon the embryo, in the one case mortally, and the conditions of the future of another human being are chosen which that human being might not have accepted if given the choice.

The objection might be raised, "But these conditions are imposed in a variety of ways, most considered more 'natural'—for example, a woman addicted to drugs throughout her pregnancy passes on certain conditions for the future of the embryo which would not have been otherwise accepted by the resulting offspring." This is true; however, in the case of cloning, one is dealing with a still-developing technology which society has the power to steer, regulate, or abolish altogether. If this responsibility is abdicated, it could very well be that the future will judge today's society even more harshly than today's society judges the drug-addicted mother. As Maureen Junker-Kenny puts it, "The way in which we define and treat the embryo—as human tissue and raw material for our rational purposes, or at least as human life with a moral claim—says something about how we see ourselves and who we want

[636] Messer, *Christian Ethics*, p. 114. Emphasis in original. See also Messer's "Human Cloning and Genetic Manipulation: Some Theological and Ethical Issues" (*Studies in Christian Ethics* 12.2 [January 1999]: 1-16).
[637] "A human being is a rational, embodied member of the species *Homo sapiens* (the species being determined by the genetic structure of its embodiment), created in God's image but fallen, at any level of development, from conception to death" (Chapter 2).
[638] Kass, "For an International Ban on Human Cloning," n.p.

to be in the future."[639] It seems that much of the justification for the continued development and use of cloning technology relies substantially on a sort of consequentialist utilitarian calculus, aiming for the greatest societal good for the greatest number, in particular the greatest good for the greatest number of people in dire medical need. However, one problem with this sort of justification is the same foundational problem one might find in any discussion of utilitarianism in general: The concept of "greatest good" does not itself define the "good" toward which one should strive. If one substitutes any specific quality, such as the goal of enhanced clinical knowledge or the biotechnological goal of "medical benefits," too much of what makes human life worthwhile may readily be left out of the calculation:

> Many public policy discussions about bioethical issues seem to take place within a purely consequentialist framework—they exclude moral arguments other than those concerned with outcomes (such as attempts to weigh up the likely risks against benefits). If the discussion of human reproductive cloning were limited to such a framework, we should probably conclude that we ought to be very cautious about permitting it, but that it may be justifiable in some circumstances. [However] there is more to be said than this.[640]

Even in utilitarian ethics, the "good" for which one should strive must be seen as a total human flourishing; however, this total human flourishing must be defined as a flourishing according to human *nature*. And, of course, any sort of discussion of a flourishing according to human nature leads one directly back into the discussion of Thomistic anthropology. Only by maintaining sight of first-order anthropological principles may one maintain sight of the natural goods one might legitimately seek to maximize: "The conviction that a little evil may rightly be done for the sake of a greater good, or for the sake of preventing a greater evil, puts human beings on the path to losing their grip on good and evil altogether."[641]

A good example of this sort of discussion is set forward by Anne Maclean in her book *The Elimination of Morality*.[642] Seven sailors are stranded on an island; they have plenty of fresh water but no food, and the likelihood is that all will starve to death. The captain urges his men to resign themselves to their fate courageously; the ship's doctor, however, argues that the lives of six men might be saved if one of them

---

[639] Junker-Kenny, "The Moral Status of the Embryo," p. 52.
[640] Neil Messer, *The Ethics of Human Cloning*, p. 22.
[641] Robert P. George, "Sweet Reason," p. 57.
[642] Maclean, *The Elimination of Morality*, pp. 120-21.

(the heaviest) is killed and eaten by the others. When the shocked captain protests, the doctor replies that the heaviest sailor will die anyway, but there is a chance that the other six will live. Since (he continues) the captain regards the death of the one with horror, he should likewise regard with horror the deaths of all seven men, including the one selected out for death by the doctor.

It would seem, given a utilitarian calculus, that the doctor is correct: One death is better than seven. Maclean points out, however, that despite the lack of sophistication of his presentation, it is actually the captain who is correct, for he perceives the difference in moral quality between the deaths described:

> The fattest sailor will not simply lose his life if the doctor's proposal is carried out; he will not simply die, as he would if he were to starve to death along with his companions. His life will be taken from him; he will be murdered. . . . His fate will not be the same. If the proposal is rejected, the sailor will die; but if it is accepted, he will be murdered.[643]

What this example highlights is that when maximizing the continuance of life itself by any means, or maximizing the quality of life by any means, or maximizing the effectiveness of clinical treatment by any means, or any other utilitarian calculation, becomes the prime motivating factor for actions, considerations of morality itself are eliminated from those actions *in the name of* utilitarian "morality." The deaths of the sailors would not be morally equivalent; the one death would outweigh the others, since it is not the result of an event (something that happens), but the result of an action (something that is chosen and therefore possesses moral properties).

In Aquinas's simple statement, "We should not do evil that there may come good."[644] If, based on consequentialist utilitarian considerations, society attempts to justify therapeutic cloning and ES cell research for the good of some, regardless of the moral status of the embryos thus brought into existence, it has precisely done evil in the attempt to bring forth good. Morally, this should not be done, and legally, it should not be allowed: "No evil that there may come good."

---

[643] Ibid., p. 121.
[644] ST III.68.11, where Aquinas is quoting from Romans 3:8.

# Chapter 9: Euthanasia and Assisted Suicide

Historians will write that by the last decade of the twentieth century, great numbers of men and women in the most pampered society on the earth had come to think it normal and desirable that their sick, their weak, and their helpless should be killed. When they were a poor country, they had not so thought; now in the day of their power and prosperity, they changed their minds.[645]

The bioethics lobby never targets anybody who might be able to hit back.[646]

## 1.    Personhood and the End of Life

The specific issues which have been discussed thus far under the aegis of a Thomistic anthropological framework, as well as euthanasia and assisted suicide, the issues to be discussed in this chapter, today have in common the supposed characteristic of "private judgment." In other words, they are supposedly issues best left to the conclusions of the private conscience of the patient or the doctor, rather than issues with which society as a whole has legitimate law-making interest. For some time society seems to have become increasingly "deferent to individual conceptions of the good," as Russell Hittinger writes: "[Society] may not approve of the consequences of abortion, euthanasia, reprogenics, and homosexual marriage, but it feels helpless to use political authority to prohibit—and often, even to publicly discuss—the justice or injustice of these acts." While one may certainly uphold, defend, and even celebrate the liberty of private judgment in a wide realm of decisions, including "individual conceptions of the good," the consistent stance taken throughout this work is that such liberty of conscience and private judgment must be examined and possibly curtailed if the judgments being made (regarding abortion, for instance) involve actions taken against another individual substance of rational nature, a human

---

[645] J. Budziszewski, *The Revenge of Conscience: Politics and the Fall of Man*, p. 125.
[646] Jenny Teichman, "The False Philosophy of Peter Singer," p. 26.

person: "Men and women . . . cannot exercise a private franchise to use lethal force and still enjoy political order."[647]

(1) *The Beginning and Ending of Personal Life*

Judging the motivations of those defining personhood by functional means may serve little good purpose, although admittedly I have made such judgments rather freely throughout this book. However, one may certainly judge the practical results of these functional definitions. Practically, these functional definitions seem to serve only to exclude some entities on the continuous spectrum of human life and development from the protections afforded to fully fledged humans who are themselves entities located on the same spectrum. However, this sort of exclusion does not seem to be warranted, at least by the medical and biological evidence.

In fact, those who exercise liberty of conscience and private judgment to justify the use of lethal force against those incapable of certain functions such as rationality or self-consciousness must now do so *against* the scientific evidence supporting the protection of their victims. Thus one readily can see that the public vs. private reasoning on display in the political debates surrounding these beginning-of-life issues is highly ironic, to say the least. Although the pro-life forces are supposedly the groups seeking to impose their "private" "religious" beliefs on others, the complete reverse is actually true: The pro-life groups are willing to abide by public reasoning based on genetic and embryological evidence, while the pro-choice groups are forced into ever more tortured philosophical convolutions to justify their private judgments on what constitutes the distinctions between "human," "human being," "human person," "possessor of rights," and so on, and their private judgments on when these human-like entities can rightfully be eliminated. As Wesley J. Smith writes, "Those charged by the main-stream media as being purely ideological argue from valid science, and the supposedly objective scientists are forced into making purely emotional and sophistic appeals."[648]

One may segue from this discussion directly into the analysis of the topics of euthanasia and assisted suicide, since many of these same considerations regarding human life as a "continuous process" also have relevance at the other end of human life, in the cases of those humans who are facing imminent death or seem to be facing imminent death.

---

[647] Hittinger, *The First Grace: Rediscovering the Natural Law in the Post-Christian World.* Wilmington, Delaware: ISI Books, 2003, p. 137.

[648] Smith, "On the Square: Observations and Contentions." Firstthings.com, n.p. 18 August 2006. Accessed 18 August 2006.

As bioethicist Daniel Callahan puts this point:

> It is very rare . . . to find a discussion of when life begins (pertinent to abortion) related to a discussion of when life ends (pertinent to euthanasia and the artificial prolongation of life). Yet both problems turn on what is meant by human life, and the illumination we gain in dealing with one of these problems will be useful when we deal with the other.[649]

The "illumination" to which one might look from reflection on beginning-of-life issues is in particular illumination regarding person-hood and the personal status of human beings. It seems that just as consideration of the beginning of human life is complicated by the question "At what point is a human life infused with personhood of a morally relevant nature?" so also end-of-life issues are further compli-cated by the similar question: "At what point does a human person cease to be, and thus that person's human life may be said to end?"

  (2)  *PVS and "Brain Death"*

For example, many patients in U.S. hospitals[650] are currently diagnosed with Permanent Vegetative Syndrome (PVS), in which the patient seems to possess few or no indications of rationality, self-awareness, and so on. The distinction between "permanent" and "persistent" vegetative state is based on a clinical judgment of the condition's "irreversibility," not the condition's severity. The "irreversible" boundary line is usually set at twelve months in PVS. Both states (permanent and persistent) are characterized by non-comatose wakefulness without apparent awareness.[651] Ronald Dworkin describes the situation of PVS patients in this way:

> Some accidents and diseases leave their victims either in comas or in what doctors call a persistent vegetative state. In either case they are unconscious—though many patients in a persistent vegetative state have open, moving eyes—and the higher centers of their brains have

---

[649] Daniel Callahan. *Abortion: Law, Choice, and Morality*. New York: Macmillan, 1970, p. 334. Germain Grisez' book *Abortion: The Myths, the Realities, and the Arguments* (New York: World Publishing Company, 1970) was written in part as a reaction to Callahan's problematic conclusions; however, Callahan's preliminary comment quoted here certainly seems both accurate and pertinent.

[650] Perhaps between 10,000 to 25,000 adults in the United States are currently diagnosed with PVS, according to Borthwick ("The Permanent Vegetative State," p. 169); the uncertainty of the number seems related to the uncertainty of the diagnosis itself. In the United States, some criteria for more uniform diagnosis both of PVS and of death itself have been proposed.

[651] Multi-Society Task Force, "Medical Aspects of the Persistent Vegetative State, Part 1," p. 1499.

been permanently damaged in a way that rules out any return to consciousness. They are capable of no sensation and no thoughts.[652] Does the patient in this situation cease to be a "person," even if the patient is still thought to be a "human"? If the answer is "Yes," one might raise the question: How important is it in the transition from personhood to lack of personhood that the brain damage suffered is such that it "rules out any return to consciousness," as Dworkin has it?[653]

According to the Pontifical Academy of Sciences, in statements released in 1985, 1989, and 2006, the concept of "brain death" (as described by a 1968 Harvard Medical School report, "A Definition of Irreversible Coma") is now the accepted determining criterion for the death of a human being.[654] "Brain death" is defined as an even more

---

[652] Ronald Dworkin. *Life's Dominion: An Argument About Abortion, Euthanasia, and Individual Freedom.* New York: Knopf, 1993, p. 93.

[653] Of course, even the idea that PVS "rules out any return to consciousness" is itself highly problematic. In *The Guardian*, health editor Sarah Boseley covered the following rather astonishing development ("Sleeping Pill Wakes Men in Vegetative State," 23 May 2006): "A drug commonly used as a sleeping pill appears to have had a miraculous effect on brain-damaged patients who have been in a permanent vegetative state for years, arousing them to the point where some are able to speak to their families, scientists report today. The dramatic improvement occurs within twenty minutes of taking the drug, Zolpidem, and wears off after around four hours—at which point the patients return to their permanent vegetative state, according to a paper published in the medical journal *NeuroRehabilitation*. All three patients were men around thirty who had suffered brain damage in car accidents. Patient L had been in a vegetative state for three years, showing no reaction to touch and no response to his family. After he was given the drug, he was able to talk to them. Patient G was also able to interact with family, answer simple questions and catch a baseball. Patient N 'was constantly uttering random screams.' After he was given the drug, the screaming stopped, and he started watching television and reacting to his family." Boseley's comment "at which point the patients return to their *permanent* vegetative state [emphasis added]" is apparently not meant to be ironic. Likewise, Associated Press medical correspondent Marilynn Marchione writes the following regarding 42-year-old Terry Wallis: "Doctors have their first proof that a man who was barely conscious for nearly twenty years [from age 19 to 38] regained speech and movement because his brain spontaneously rewired itself by growing tiny new nerve connections to replace the ones sheared apart in a car crash" ("Man's Brain Rewired Itself, Doctors Say," 4 July 2006). However, Marchione was also careful to point out "doctors said the same cannot be hoped for people in a persistent vegetative state, such as Terri Schiavo."

[654] The nine-page report released in 2006 is entitled "Why the Concept of Brain

severe condition than PVS, since in "brain death" the "whole brain" suffers the loss of functions, including all unconscious functions associated with the brain stem. These functions include spontaneous respiration, pupillary response, and cranial nerve reflex, all of which are absent in the patient. On the other hand, in the condition of PVS, while cerebral cortex function has been lost, unconscious brain stem functions such as respiration, swallowing, and facial reflexes may be retained. Even this condition is enough for some to think of the PVS patient as "a dead human organism": "A living organism in a PVS is, in relevant respects, just like a dead body: they are both instances of the physical remains a person leaves when he or she ceases to exist."[655] However, even when considering the more severe "brain death" diagnosis, some, such as Bishop Fabian W. Bruskewitz of Lincoln, Nebraska, ask "how the Catholic Church can accept a lack of brain function as a definition of death, yet still oppose the willful destruction of human embryos, which have not yet developed a brain."[656] According to Roberto de Mattei, vice-president of the National Research Council of Italy, commenting on the 2006 statement of the Pontifical Academy:

> When faced with questions about the moment of ensoulment at the beginning of life, the church's position [is] to assume the soul enters at conception in order to ensure the greatest possible defense of human life. Those who question whether brain death is really death are simply asking that the Church extend its defense of human life if there is the minimal possibility that the soul remains in a body that has a heartbeat, respiration, and blood circulation, even if those are supported artificially.

De Mattei is particularly concerned with the removal of vital organs for transplant, which he says "would be synonymous with homicide."[657]

The stance taken by Bruskewitz and de Mattei is Thomistic in nature because it contends that a human person exists "so long as their body is

---

Death Is Valid as a Definition of Death." A collection of papers from those dissenting from the Pontifical Academy's conclusions was published separately, outside of the Vatican's auspices, as Roberto de Mattei, ed., *Finis Vitae: Is Brain Death Still Life?* (Rome: Consiglio Nazionale delle Rescherche, 2006).

[655] J. McMahan. *The Ethics of Killing: Problems at the Margins of Life.* New York: Oxford University Press, 2002, p. 447.

[656] Cindy Wooden, "Minority View: Participants Publish Their Side of Brain Death Debate." Vatican Letter, 20 April 2007, n.p. Catholic News Service. Catholicnews. com. Accessed 23 April 2007.

[657] Ibid., n.p.

informed by their rational soul. . . . Rational *activity* is not required to contend that a rational human being continues to exist."[658] Again, a human person is not defined by function, as some kind of Cartesian "embodied mind." Of course, one may hold to the distinction between "actively" killing patients and "allowing" those patients to die, which would be the likely fate of "brain death" patients. However, what de Mattei is pointing out is that in the classical definition of death a patient actually dies when the patient's heartbeat, respiration, and blood circulation end, when the body is no longer informed by its form, not when the patient loses brain-centered activities.

Resolving these anthropological questions of the form/body relationship carries immediate relevance to the discussion of what may and may not be done with patients diagnosed even with the less severe condition, PVS. According to one study of 434 patients with a firm diagnosis of PVS,[659] slightly over half (226) of the patients recovered consciousness within one year.[660] After the twelve-month demarcation, only 7 out of the 434 patients recovered consciousness; however, since 33 percent of the original patients (143) had died before their first year of PVS had ended, this means that 7 out of the remaining 65 patients recovered consciousness, or 10.6 percent of those still alive and still in PVS after one year of the condition.[661] In total, this means that nearly 54 percent of the patients in this study with a firm diagnosis of PVS recovered consciousness, while another third died within a year of the diagnosis. (It must be admitted, however, that only 7 percent of the

---

[658] Jason Eberl, *Thomistic Principles and Bioethics*, p. 96. Emphasis in original.

[659] As reported by the Multi-Society Task Force on PVS, "Medical Aspects of the Persistent Vegetative State, Part 2." *New England Journal of Medicine* 330.22 (1994): 1572-79, pp. 1572-73.

[660] Note also that this study was reported in 1994; the medical technology available to aid patients diagnosed with PVS is today far more advanced and effective.

[661] Although this study does not take into account continuing quality of care for the PVS patients, a consistently high quality of care may have raised the recovery percentages even further. Is it not plausible to assume, as Borthwick asserts, "At the lowest level, a hospital may be influenced by considerations of cost-benefit analysis to give less intense care to a PVS patient" ("The Permanent Vegetative State," p. 177)? In other words, the assumption of the "irreversibility" of the PVS patient's condition may become a self-fulfilling prophecy. Likewise, the "apnea" test for brain death (removing artificial respiration from a patient for ten minutes to see if natural respiration begins) virtually seems to guarantee the non-recovery of the patient and hence the validation of the initial diagnosis.

patients who recovered consciousness had what was regarded medically as a "good recovery," i.e., were not disabled.) Philosophically, one would be forced to conclude, given the restrictiveness of functional definitions of personhood, that over half of these patients *were* persons, then *were not* persons for a few months, then *were* persons again. Although this seems ridiculous, such is potentially the situation whenever one attempts to define personhood by functional means, whether at the beginning of life or at the end.

Likewise, neurologist Steven Laureys, of the University of Liege and head of the university's Coma Science Group, concludes that coma patients are misdiagnosed "on a disturbingly regular basis." Having examined 44 patients diagnosed as being in vegetative states, Laureys found that 18 of them "responded to communication." He now argues that patients diagnosed as being in "non-reversible" coma states should be "tested ten times" before being labeled as such.[662]

(3)  *Two Thomistic Principles and Some Preliminary Conclusions*

Two Thomistic principles in particular apply to this discussion. The first pertains once again to the question of personhood. The reader will recall that to Thomas any human being is also a human person; that is, any human being is an individual substance of rational nature. Further, Aquinas argues that the "powers" of the soul, as well as the actual exercise of the powers of the soul, cannot be the essence of the human's substantial form, since "a power is nothing but a thing's principle of operation."[663] Although some maintain that the "essence itself of the soul is the immediate principle of all its operations" (such as when a human "understands, senses, and acts, and other things of this sort"), according to Thomas, "To be understanding or sensing actually, is not a substantial mode of existing, but an accidental one to which the intellect and sense are directed. It is similar with respect to being large or small, to which the augmentative power is ordered." Therefore, whether or not a human is actually understanding or thinking at any given time has no more to do with the definition of the human essence than whether or not the human is large or small in size (or is functionally disabled). Even though "Man is said to be an intellect because the intellect is said to be the highest thing in man," still "this does not mean that the essence of the soul is the intellective power

---

[662] Connolly, Kate. "Trapped in his own body for 23 years—the coma victim who screamed unheard." Guardian.co.uk (23 Nov. 2009). N.p. Accessed 30 Nov. 2009.

[663] *Quaestiones Disputatae de Anima*, Article 12, "Whether the Soul Is Its Powers?"

itself."[664] In fact, the moral equality of human beings "may legitimately be predicated of [that human] who exercises the use of reason [as well as] one who has lost its exercise through mental dysfunction."[665]

The second relevant principle involves the Thomistic determination of death, which is not based on any concept such as "brain death." In the Thomistic language of the substantial form, at the point of actual death, the body's form no longer serves as its organizing principle and the body begins to decompose: "Existence belongs to a form, which is an act, by virtue of itself. Wherefore matter acquires actual existence as it acquires the form; while it is corrupted so far as the form is separated from it."[666] If the patient's body is not actually losing its self-organization (i.e., decomposing), the patient is not actually dead by these definitions of death, and anything done to the patient's body is being done to a living person:

> Scrutinizing the existence of the symptoms of death as perceived by common sense, science no longer presupposes the "normal" under-standing of life and death. It in fact invalidates normal human perception by declaring human beings dead who are still perceived as living. . . . It is no longer the interest of the dying to avoid being declared dead prematurely, but other people's interest in declaring a dying person dead as soon as possible.[667]

In "normal human perception," a human being is not perceived as "dead" if the human is still breathing and the human's heart is still beating, even if the respiration and heartbeat are artificially sustained. Would such a human, for example, be buried? (In fact, it might well be pointed out that the "brain-dead" child will grow into the "brain-dead" adult![668])

However, the declaration of death can be seen as furthering the interests of others involved. The two primary reasons given for this "third-party interest" in declaring the patient dead are (1) "guaranteeing

---

[664] Ibid., Article 12.
[665] Donald G. McCarthy and Albert S. Moraczewski, eds., *An Ethical Evaluation of Fetal Experimentation: An Interdisciplinary Study*, p. 73.
[666] ST I.75.6.
[667] Dr. Robert Spaemann, quoted in Paul A. Byrne, Cicero G. Coimbra, Robert Spaemann, and Mercedes Arzú Wilson, "Brain Death Is Not Death." Essay presented to the Pontifical Academy of Sciences, February 2005. Published by Compassionate Healthcare Network, 29 March 2005. Chninternational.com, n.p. Accessed 15 February 2008.
[668] Nicanor Pier Giorgio Austriaco, O.P. "In Defense of the Loss of Bodily Integrity as a Criterion for Death: A Response to the Radical Capacity Argument." *The Thomist* 73 (Oct. 2009): 647-59, pp. 657-58.

legal immunity for discontinuing life-prolonging measures"; and (2) "collecting vital organs for the purpose of saving the lives of other human beings through transplantation."[669] In a similar vein, Dr. David Hill, a British anesthetist and Cambridge lecturer, points out that "brain death" as the criterion of actual death was at least partially adopted because "the earliest attempts at transplanting vital organs often failed because the organs, taken from cadavers, did not recover from the period of ischemia following the donor's death." He further argues that the general public is not generally aware "that life support is not withdrawn before organs are taken; nor that some form of anaesthesia is needed to control the donor whilst the operation is performed."[670] As Roberto de Mattei observes, if a patient must be anesthetized in order to facilitate the removal of the patient's still-functioning organs, the distinction between this operation and the act of homicide is quite slight, if the distinction exists at all. It would seem, then, that the principal value of the "brain death" diagnosis lies in the fact that after the diagnosis one may then legally begin to "harvest" organ "donations" from a still-living body, although the patient is now referred to as a "non-living donor" whose body is on life support. Nor is this merely a theoretical possibility: In the first nine months of 2007, there were 670 organ donations from patients ruled dead by the removal of life support and subsequent cessation of heartbeat. However, in the same time period, there were 12,553 organ donations from patients ruled "brain-dead" but still on life support to maintain heartbeat and circulation.[671]

To some, these assertions of the grounds for "brain death" diagnoses might seem far-fetched. No one, they might reply, would declare a patient "brain dead" simply to procure the patient's organs while the patient is yet alive. However, as bioethicist Gilbert Meilaender points out, the biomedical history subsequent to the release of the 1968 "Harvard criteria" paper has revealed a definite trend:

> More than a quarter century ago, when this move to "update" criteria for determining death began, it was met with suspicion. At that time the technology of transplant surgery was beginning to make progress, and some people suspected that the desire to establish in law a concept of brain death was motivated only by the

---

[669] "Brain Death Is Not Death," n.p.

[670] Ibid., n.p.

[671] The figures on organ donation are from the United Network for Organ Sharing, as quoted in Jesse McKinley, "Surgeon Accused in Death of Patient to Get Organs" (*New York Times*, U.S. Section. 27 February 2008. Nytimes.com, n.p. Accessed 27 February 2008).

wish to obtain organs for transplant before those organs had deteriorated. . . . The suspicions may not have been entirely groundless, however—or, perhaps better, they may have been ahead of their time. For it has become clear in recent years that the thirst for transplantable organs is so strong that we *are*, in fact, tempted to redefine death *in order* to secure the "needed" organs. For example, in 1994 the Council on Ethical and Judicial Affairs of the American Medical Association (AMA) issued an opinion holding that it is "ethically permissible" to use "the anencephalic neonate" [severely disabled newborn infant] as an organ donor, even though, as the Council recognized, under current law anencephalic babies are not dead.[672]

In 1988 this same Council "had concluded that it was not permissible to remove organs for transplantation from anencephalic infants while they were still alive"[673]; however, as Meilaender reports, by 1994 the members of the Council had changed their minds. In December 1995 the Council reversed its recommendation yet again, on the grounds that anencephalic babies might possibly possess consciousness. Anencephalic babies, although usually dying soon after birth, often do not need assistance in respiration or heartbeat; they may even respond to touch. In other words, one could conclude that, given these fluctuations in medical opinion, perhaps at some point in the future even the "brain death" diagnosis of death may not be necessary for the removal of organs from a patient.

This possibility is quite real; already some have discussed suspending even the minimal requirement of "brain death" prior to organ removal. This option has been rather candidly promoted in an article in the *New England Journal of Medicine* (14 August 2008), in which doctors Robert D. Truog of Harvard Medical Center and Franklin G. Miller of the National Institutes of Health point out that current safeguards on donations limit "the number and quality of organs available to those in need." They propose obtaining "valid informed consent" regarding organ removal "from patients or their surrogates ahead of time." Given this consent, organs can be removed not only from people who have suffered "brain death," but also from those who "have devastating, irreversible neurologic injuries that do not meet the technical requirements of brain death."[674] Furthermore, although rare, operations

---

[672] Meilaender, *Bioethics*, pp. 97-98. Emphasis in original.
[673] Ibid., p. 98.
[674] Truog and Miller are quoted in Anita Kuhn's article "Down on the Trans-plantations." *Touchstone* (Oct. 2008): 46-47, p. 47.

involving organ removal after "cardiac death" ("DCD," or "Donation after Cardiac Death"), *prior* to "brain death," already occur in the United States.

One might recapitulate at this point: The two Thomistic principles under consideration are simply that (1) the actual functions of rationality or self-consciousness are not necessary in a biological human being in order to consider that human being also as a human person; and (2) in consequence, the Thomistic determination of death is not based on any concept such as "brain death." After due consideration of these two principles and the manner in which these principles may be applied in specific cases, some conclusions regarding PVS and "brain death" may be made:

First premise: In natural law ethical reflection, the deliberate killing of an innocent human person (an embodied individual substance of a rational nature) is morally wrong and should not be legally allowed. Since natural law ethics is not generally utilitarian in nature, this first premise would hold true regardless of the good or bad consequences of its acceptance.

Second premise: Insufficient evidence exists to say with any certainty that the victim of PVS or "brain death" is actually dead and is therefore no longer a living human person. In fact, since the integrity of the human's embodied state persists, the presumption of personhood should perhaps go the other direction, toward acceptance of the patient as a living human person.

First conclusion: Therefore, insufficient evidence exists to permit either morally or legally the active killing of a victim of PVS or "brain death." Removal of life support systems or extraordinary means of prolonging life may be permitted, but should not be permitted insofar as these systems are actually part of the treatment of a condition.

Second conclusion: It is therefore certainly the case that active organ removal or "harvesting" should not be performed upon the patient who is being kept artificially alive only for that very purpose. Such a practice dehumanizes the patient, the doctors performing such operations, the patients receiving the organs thus "harvested," and society as a whole.

Regarding "extraordinary means of prolonging life," questions may arise as to what exactly constitutes "ordinary" and "extraordinary" care, especially for PVS and "brain death" patients. Ethically, it does not seem that one is required to pursue any more than "strictly necessary steps to preserve life and health" in the effort to reach the spiritual ends of human life.[675] However, are life support systems such as respirators and circulatory pumps to be considered strictly necessary steps to preserve one's life, especially if the patient would die if removed from them? Here again, it seems that the best course of treatment to pursue would be that which grants the presumption of personhood and the acceptance of the patient as a living human person, since the integrity of the human's embodied state persists. "Extraordinary" life-prolonging measures would then be those measures or treatments "which would *prevent* a person from pursuing the spiritual goals of life, *disabling* him or her . . . because of the terrible burden it would impose upon them."[676] On the other hand, those treatments which simply continue a person's life without necessarily enabling him or her to recover and to pursue those spiritual goals should not consequently be considered "extra-ordinary." For the most part, the majority of "brain death" patients (over 90 percent) do die within a few weeks, even when connected to life support systems, according to a study by pediatric neurologist D. Alan Shewmon. However, the fact that some survive for months or even years indicates a "somatic unity" which is not integrated solely by the brain, but which is rather a holistic property "founded on the mutual interaction among all the parts of the body."[677] Simple technology such as ordinary feeding and hydration systems, therefore, should not be considered "extraordinary" life support for these patients, even if these systems do not increase the likelihood of the patient's overall recovery.

This recommendation runs contrary to that of a well-known article written by noted Dominican bioethicists Kevin O'Rourke and Patrick Norris, which surveys Catholic viewpoints on this and other issues. The authors report that in general opinions regarding artificial hydration and nutrition [AHN] fall into three categories: There are those who view AHN as "ordinary care and morally obligatory"; those who view AHN as "a medical treatment that should be offered unless it is physio-logically futile or excessively burdensome"; and those who argue AHN "may be discontinued in the case of the patient in PVS primarily because it offers no benefit to the patient and secondarily because it

[675] William E. May. *Catholic Bioethics and the Gift of Human Life*. Huntingdon, Indiana: Our Sunday Visitor Publishing, 2000, p. 254.
[676] Ibid., pp. 255-56. Emphasis in original. Finnis's *Fundamentals of Ethics* also provides a helpful analysis of this distinction between ordinary and extra-ordinary forms of treatment (pp. 106-ff.).
[677] D. Alan Shewmon. " 'Brainstem Death,' 'Brain Death,' and 'Death': A Critical Re-Evaluation of the Purported Evidence." *Issues in Law & Medicine* 14.2 (1998): 125-45, p. 140.

may at times impose a grave burden."[678] The authors argue for the last viewpoint. However, again, if the somatic unity of the patient's body is a holistic property of that body, this fact in itself would indicate that the morally safest course of treatment would be to continue the simple hydration and nutrition of the patient. Such a course of treatment is a "work of charity," to borrow Aquinas's phrase, and depends nothing on whether society is or is not moved by pity or utilitarian considerations regarding these patients' conditions: "It is more praiseworthy to do a work of charity from the judgment of reason than from the mere passion of pity."[679] Even if this course of treatment does not and seemingly cannot result in the patient's betterment (which is the natural end or goal of treatment), the precept of charity may be "imperfectly fulfilled" when "the order to that end is not departed from."[680] This partial fulfillment of the charitable precept results ethically in a better situation than if the precept of charity is not fulfilled at all, which would be the case were the care of the patient to be abandoned entirely.

This discussion is far from being a mere academic exercise. For instance, a certain conception of "extraordinary" life support was upheld by several state and federal courts (and denied judicial review four times by the United States Supreme Court) in the widely publicized case of Terri Schiavo, who was dehydrated and starved to death over the course of two weeks in a hospice in Pinellas Park, Florida. Schiavo's tombstone reads in part, *Departed this earth February 25, 1990, At peace March 31, 2005.* How one defines the death of a human being will determine which date one accepts as the date of Schiavo's death.

In terms of merely remaining alive, the only thing Schiavo could not do was feed herself. In other words, in her case, the simple feeding and hydration of a patient was determined to be "extraordinary" life support in the U.S. court system, and removed.

## 2.    Euthanasia and Assisted Suicide

So far this discussion has only considered the case of patients who are in PVS or "brain death" conditions, in the effort to determine first of all whether or not these patients are actually dead, and secondly whether or not they are still human persons. The second determination may be said to dovetail with the first: On the one hand, if the patients are actually dead, the patients are no longer human persons. On the other hand, even if the patients are seen as potential sources of viable and valuable

---

[678] O'Rourke and Norris, O.P. "Care of PVS Patients: Catholic Opinion in the United States." *Linacre Quarterly* 68 (August 2001): 201-17, p. 202.
[679] ST I-II.24.3.
[680] ST II-II.44.6.

organs, if they cannot be determined actually to be dead, the possibility of their continued personhood cannot be discounted and thus their organs should not be removed.

However, in all such cases of PVS and "brain death," it is assumed that the patients have no consciousness or voice to speak for themselves. What about the cases in which patients either consciously acquiesce in their own killing (euthanasia) or else are aided by a physician in carrying out their own killing (assisted suicide)? Does the fact of a patient's conscious consent change the moral implications of the action of killing the patient or aiding the patient to kill himself or herself?

These issues would seem to have been already addressed in most respects by the extended argument presented thus far regarding the killing of innocent human persons. However, the problems surrounding the assignment of personhood do not in fact arise as such in the cases of euthanasia or assisted suicide precisely because the request for euthanasia or assisted suicide would under ideal conditions originate with a conscious, rational, self-volitional human agent; no one, presumably, would question this human agent's personhood. However, the ideal conditions of uncoerced consciousness, rationality, and self-volition are usually not present in such cases; often those requesting euthanasia or assisted suicide are dealing with a variety of influences such as physical pain, mental exhaustion, economic duress, family pressures, fear of the unknowns involved in the aging process or the disease process, and so on. For example, a 2008 study revealed that fully one-third of those who chose assisted suicide in that year in the state of Oregon "cited the burden on their families and care-givers as a reason." Even more grievously (and contrary to Dutch law):

> A study in the Netherlands found that one in four doctors said they had killed patients without an explicit request—including one doctor who believed that a dying Dutch nun was prevented from requesting euthanasia because of her religion, so he felt the just and merciful thing to do was to decide for her.[681]

However, even if one assumes the ideal conditions of unquestioned personhood and of uncoerced, rational, and repeated requests for euthanasia or assisted suicide, moral problems still remain with these procedures.

For example, in the previous arguments regarding abortion, infanticide, cloning, ES cell research, PVS, and "brain death," something like the following premise typically has been stated: "In

---

[681] Nancy Gibbs. "Dying Together." *Time* (3 August 2009): 64, p. 64.

natural law ethical reflection, the deliberate killing of an innocent human person (an embodied individual substance of a rational nature) is morally wrong and should not be legally allowed. Since natural law ethics is not generally utilitarian in nature, this first premise would hold true regardless of the good or bad consequences of its acceptance." As noted, the personhood of the patient requesting euthanasia or assisted suicide is unquestioned, and certainly a deliberate killing, whether physician- or self-inflicted, is involved in the process; therefore, one is here dealing precisely with "the deliberate killing of an innocent human person." Of course, the patient's fully rational (as assumed) consent has been given to the process. Even so, however, ". . . with the exception of the common law principle of self-defense, the right of private persons to kill is not to be found in the organic, statutory, or written constitutional laws of our polity," as Russell Hittinger observes. "The common law principle has never been construed to condone either (a) the deliberate use of lethal force by private agents, or (b) suicide."[682] In other words, given the nature of the action, whether performed upon a fully rational and consensual patient or upon one suffering from PVS or "brain death," and even given the intricacies of the doctor/patient relationship, euthanasia still must be seen as "the deliberate use of lethal force by private agents." In general, no matter the variety of difficult cases presented, such lethal force should not be given into the hands of private agents, even doctors—or perhaps *especially* not into the hands of those private agents who, like doctors, have readily available the means of death.

### 3. A Natural Law Response to Euthanasia and Assisted Suicide

#### (1) *Aquinas on Suicide*

Even more explicitly, Aquinas's account of natural law principles seems immediately contrary to any form of suicide, whether it be a patient's assisted suicide or the patient's requesting of another to perform the act of killing (euthanasia): "It is altogether unlawful to kill oneself," as he writes. He quotes Augustine in support of his statement: "For he who kills himself, kills nothing else than a man."[683] Aquinas delineates three primary reasons for his stance, which may be labeled "natural," "social," and "theological" in nature. The "natural" objection to suicide is based on the general principle "every substance seeks the preservation of its own being, according to its nature."[684] All things seek naturally to keep themselves in being and to resist "corruptions" of their being insofar as

---

[682] Hittinger, *The First Grace*, p. 140.
[683] ST II-II.64.5.
[684] ST I-II.94.2.

they are able, death being the prime corruption of a living substance. Aquinas also points out that self-murder not only violates the natural inclination toward self-preservation, but also theologically is a violation of that "charity whereby every man should love himself"; therefore, "Suicide is always a mortal sin, as being contrary to the natural law and to charity." It is in this respect "a sin in relation to oneself."[685] Although he does not here make any exceptions to this rule, Aquinas does elsewhere say of human rationality that "reason dictates that certain things should be shunned and some sought after."[686] It is possible, given this, that even though suicide "should be shunned" by those in possession of their rational faculties, perhaps it is not a "mortal sin" for those who commit suicide while in the grip of mental illness such as severe mania or depression; such theological issues seem beyond human judgment. Of course, the situation of an apparently uncoerced, rational patient who repeatedly requests euthanasia or assisted suicide would not fall in this category, but would rather be strictly forbidden both by the natural law and by the virtue of charity toward oneself.

Aquinas's "social" and "theological" objections to suicide follow from this first, for in addition to being a sin against charity toward oneself, suicide is also sinful "in relation to the community and to God." Just as self-mutilation injures the unitary body, so suicide injures society: "Every part, as such, belongs to the whole. Now every man is part of the community, and so, as such, he belongs to the community. Hence by killing himself he injures the community." Moreover, theologically speaking, the self-murderer implicitly seeks by that very action to raise himself or herself to the level of that One commanding the power of death and life. The oft-heard phrase "Death with Dignity" hence might well be re-labeled "Death with Self-Deification":

> Life is God's gift to man, and is subject to His power, Who kills and makes to live. Hence whoever takes his own life, sins against God . . . as he who usurps to himself judgment of a matter not entrusted to him. For it belongs to God alone to pronounce sentence of death and life.[687]

One should note, however, that Aquinas's prohibition of murder and self-murder does not necessarily prohibit execution by properly ordained public authority, killing in self-defense, or accidental killing, which are allowed for in ST II-II.64.2-3, 7, and 8, respectively. All of these actions Aquinas thinks of as distinct from the action of murder.

---

[685] ST II-II.64.5.
[686] ST II-II.125.1.
[687] ST II-II.64.5.

Other issues might also be raised regarding euthanasia and assisted suicide. By requesting assistance in pursuing death, the patient is thereby making another not only an accessory in the deliberate killing of an innocent person, but the actual perpetrator of the killing. Does the patient indeed possess such power? Does the doctor? "We are no longer debating *whether* there is life and whether it is viable, but rather the meanings and values assigned to the life, as well as who has the power to assign those meanings."[688] It does not seem that morally it is within the power of a rational human person to commit suicide, nor to request death at the hands of another. "The passage from this life to another and happier one is subject not to man's free-will but to the power of God."[689] Nor is it morally within the power of the one who is so requested to actually perform the killing: "It is in no way lawful to slay the innocent," as Thomas concludes.[690]

(2)　*An Objection Based on the Possibility of a Blessed Afterlife*

Thus far any allowance of either euthanasia or assisted suicide has been rejected, whether in the case of the rational, consensual patient or in the cases of PVS or "brain death" patients. However, there exist numerous objections to this negative position. For example, some might reason as follows: "Would not the possibility of a blessed afterlife be sufficient justification for removing oneself from this current life of suffering?" This line of reasoning might also be applied to the PVS patient who receives artificial hydration and nutrition:

> Removal of artificial nutrition is not only tolerated, morally, it is a good moral act. It discontinues a costly procedure that offers no proportionate benefit, and it enables the transition from biological life to eternal life. . . . It would seem that [a patient's] biological confinement by tube-feeding is preventing the completion of her life's journey, and her release into eternal life.[691]

However, Aquinas flatly rejects this thesis as a legitimate possibility for conscious agents: "It is not lawful for man to take his own life that he may pass to a happier life, nor that he may escape any unhappiness whatsoever of the present life, because the ultimate and most fearsome evil of *this* life is death."[692] It would seem the same principle would

---

[688] Hittinger, *The First Grace*, p. 145. Emphasis in original.
[689] ST II-II.64.5.
[690] ST II-II.64.6.
[691] Ruth Caspar, O.P. "Wisdom and Light: Contributions from Aquinas to Contemporary Bioethics." The Aquinas Convention Address: Ohio Dominican University. 28 January 2004: 1-24, pp. 19-20.
[692] ST II-II.64.5. Emphasis added.

apply to those making the decision of death on behalf of patients who are no longer conscious.

Humans are unitary creatures. Even if the life which awaits the patient after death may be a blessed one, free of pain and suffering, that future life would seem necessarily to be non-corporeal in nature. This would be the case even if death is suffered in the hope of a bodily resurrection such as that upheld by historic Christian teaching. This human life itself, as the composite of corporeal and non-corporeal, is a good in itself, and this particular good is lost even if only for a time by death; that is, the good human life of a human being is lost at death precisely in its character as the life of a human being, since the displaced soul in Thomistic thinking is not strictly speaking a human person as such. The goodness of *this* mode of existence will be lost as the totality of the human person is ended. The humane social order will thus seek to affirm the goodness of this life, even as one's religious faith points toward an afterlife free of infirmity: "The response of an individual or a community that values the intrinsic dignity of persons, however, is not to kill the sufferer or eliminate the wounded [or function as an "enabler" for their possible suicidal desires] but to alleviate the suffering and affirm the sufferer's goodness, regardless of the deprivation, the loss, or the presumed shame of human frailty."[693]

(3) *An Objection Based On Ending Suffering*

Another objection might be raised at this point, namely, that the arguments against assisted suicide and euthanasia thus far have mischaracterized the very nature of these actions, by focusing on the action of ending human life rather than the intended action of ending human suffering. Do not all people, when confronted with horrible or even slight suffering, yearn for the alleviation of that suffering? However, this objection uncovers a good example of what Aquinas means when he argues that all desire the good as an intrinsic end, even if some do not apprehend clearly the wrongfulness of their means toward that end. The desire to end human suffering in a pain-wracked patient is a good desire and rightful goal; the means, on the other hand, is wrongful, since in the rightful desire to end suffering the one who administers euthanasia or who aids in assisted suicide both commits some form of homicide and wrongfully brings to an end the goodness of the patient's corporeal existence. As Aquinas writes, "Therefore to bring death upon oneself in order to escape the other afflictions of this life, is to adopt a greater evil in order to avoid a lesser"; in support of

[693] John F. Kavanaugh, *Who Count as Persons? Human Identity and the Ethics of Killing.* Washington, D.C.: Georgetown University Press, 2001, p. 137.

his position, he quotes St. Paul, "Evil must not be done that good may come."[694] How can one benefit one's hylomorphic unity of self by ending the existence of that hylomorphic self, this totality of existence which is in itself a good?

On the other hand, Lisa Sowle Cahill makes a contrary argument which is founded on Aquinas himself. Aquinas writes, "Every part is naturally for the sake of the whole. For this reason we observe that if the health of the whole body demands the excision of a member, through its being decayed or infectious to the other members, it will be both praiseworthy and advantageous to have it cut away."[695] Cahill uses the principle behind this passage to argue that occasionally the body should be "cut away" from the soul, for the good of the human person:

> Since the distinctive and controlling element of human nature is the personal self or spirit, then according to the principle of totality, the body which is a "part" may in some cases be sacrificed for the good of the "whole" body-soul entity.[696]

However, as has been argued in response to the previous objection, this seems a misunderstanding of Aquinas's "totality" stance. Again, humans are unitary creatures, and any life "cut off" from the body would seem necessarily to be non-corporeal in nature. The corporeal/non-corporeal composite that is the human life presently known is a good in itself, and this particular good is lost at corporeal death precisely in its character as the life of a human being, since the displaced soul is not strictly speaking a human person as such. Jason Eberl makes this point well in his comment on the passage quoted from Cahill:

> It is thus a mischaracterization to construe euthanasia as merely the "cutting off" of one's body as one would sever a gangrenous limb to preserve one's overall health and well-being. Without their bodies, though human beings may continue to exist composed of their souls alone, their existence will be quite deficient because many of their capacities—vegetative and sensitive—will not be actualizable and they will not be able to gain knowledge in the natural way through sensation.[697]

Therefore, euthanasia and assisted suicide, even if done for the purpose of ending the physical suffering of the one being killed, intrinsically are not actions that give adequate account of or can be performed for the

---

[694] ST II-II.64.5. The biblical quotation is from Romans 3:8.
[695] ST II-II.64.2.
[696] Lisa Sowle Cahill. *Euthanasia: A Protestant and a Catholic Perspective.* Dissertation. University of Chicago, 1976.
[697] Eberl, *Thomistic Principles and Bioethics*, p. 101.

good of the total human person.

"The champions of suicide allege reasons that drip altruism: remorse, failure, disgracing his family, fear of sin, or violation of body," Walter Farrell writes in his discussion of Aquinas on suicide:

> Of course none of these is valid; it is never permissible to do murder that good might come; that the particular murder is cowardly neither justifies nor ennobles it. Direct suicide must always stand condemned as evil, for human life is a sacred thing. . . . There is a profound significance in the fact that this fundamental truth is so seriously challenged today; challenged, you understand, not in a class-room or a letter to the editor, but in the concrete actions of governments and men. . . . On the personal side there is the mercy killing calculated to relieve a man of his suffering; the painless killing of the hopelessly wounded, of the old, the misfit, the insane, social nuisances. . . . All this is murder. The smooth, somniferous length of the words we use to describe it—liquidation, euthanasia, mercy-killing, solicitude for suffering mothers—does not destroy the ugliness of murder.[698]

The reader should note that this passage was originally published in 1945. One wonders how Farrell, were he alive now, would describe the influence of "the champions of suicide" upon today's society and medical practice.

### (4)   End-of-Life Indeterminacy

Furthermore, as has been seen in the discussion of PVS and "brain death" patients, the very indeterminacy of the occasionally opaque boundary between life and death is a primary reason to resist mortally prejudging a patient's condition. One should resist "any direct action that would be violative" of a patient "who may be this side of the inexact and doubtfully known borderline between life and death."[699] As Hans Jonas has argued, "Giving intrinsic vagueness its due is not being vague."[700] If contemporary bioethicists are not completely sure that "brain death" actually is death, they should stop acting as if they were completely sure—no matter the utilitarian benefits such a surety would provide were it to exist.

Rather than encouraging the choice of death, medicine should rather encourage the best life possible while one is dying: "The conviction that

---

[698] Walter Farrell, O.P. *A Companion to the Summa. Volume III—The Fullness of Life*, pp. 198-200.

[699] Ramsey, *Ethics at the Edges of Life*, p. 223.

[700] Hans Jonas. *Philosophical Essays: From Ancient Creed to Technological Man.* Chicago: University of Chicago Press, 1974, p. 134.

one should always choose life lies at the heart of the practice of medicine and nursing. In that sense, medical ethics must be pro-life."[701] This will not always mean the patient will or should take advantage of every means possible to prolong life; however, it does mean that the physician will take no action to cause the end of that life, nor encourage the patient in any way to choose the end of his or her life. This ethical stance is appreciably weakened when euthanasia or assisted suicide are accepted as more or less normal medical procedures. For example, the rather startling results of surveys conducted anonymously among physicians in the Netherlands (where both euthanasia and assisted suicide are legal) in both 1990 and 1995 indicate that euthanasia *without the patient's consent or request* is being carried out in that country at a rate averaging around 1,000 victims per year.[702] Only about 41 percent of euthanasia cases are officially reported, and over 50 percent of Dutch physicians actively encourage patients to choose euthanasia.[703] In other words, over 400 reported involuntary euthanasia cases per year (at a minimum) are taking place in a relatively small country in which euthanasia has been legalized for many years; this does not even take into account the unreported cases revealed in the surveys. Moreover, these cases are completely dependent upon the private judgment of the physicians performing the killing. The abuse of this power seems not only possible, but frighteningly likely.

Moreover, many potential cases involve patients who are in possession of their rational faculties, who themselves are making the request for euthanasia (for example, voluntary euthanasia requests in the Netherlands run to around 2,500 or more cases per year). How much greater the possibility of abuse of the power of life and death when the patients under consideration are those clinging to life by the thinnest of threads, those who cannot speak for themselves? If diagnostic errors in these cases are to be made, such errors should rather be made on the morally safe ground of granting still-living but otherwise helpless patients the benefit of the doubt.

---

[701] Ramsey, *Ethics at the Edges of Life*, p. 146.

[702] M. Angell. "Euthanasia in the Netherlands—Good News or Bad?" *New England Journal of Medicine* 335.22 (28 November 1996): 1676-78, p. 1676.

[703] Paul J. van der Maas, et al. "Evaluation of the Notification Procedure for Physician-Assisted Death in the Netherlands." *New England Journal of Medicine* 335.22 (28 November 1996): 1706-12, p. 1706.

# Chapter 10: A Culture of Life

By common grace, the gleam never quite dies out.[704]

### 1. A Culture of Life

"The pace of change in biotechnology and medicine shows no immediate signs of slackening, and each new development brings its own ethical questions in its wake," as Neil Messer writes. "It is my conviction that the Christian tradition contains great resources for addressing these questions and that if bioethical discussions become detached from these resources, they cannot but be impoverished."[705] To a great extent, it might be the case that this impoverishment has already occurred. "Modern medicine, it might be said, is *sick*," according to Anne Maclean. "The sickness must be diagnosed, the causes of it established, and the patient restored to health." Her prescription for this modern sickness follows: "It is philosophical reflection that must not only put medicine back on the right path, but keep it there."[706] To this one must only add: It is philosophical reflection of a *certain kind* that might restore health to modern medicine, since it was precisely philosophical reflection of a different kind in the first place, largely a nominally Lockean reflection upon the nature of personhood, which helped usher medicine into its modern sickness. Furthermore, this sickness is not only localized to the field of medicine. Certainly it is in that field that the sickness finds its most virulent outbreaks, since medicine deals with issues of life and death on a daily basis; however, the sickness seems society-wide:

> It is something to recognize that there is something wrong. But obviously it is not enough. A merely negative attitude will get us nowhere. The West is decadent—and the deepest decadence is to be found in those circles that loudly proclaim the youthful vigor and purity

---

J. Budziszewski, *Natural Law for Lawyers.* , p. 35
[705] Messer, *Theological Issues in Bioethics*, p. 6.
[706] Maclean, *The Elimination of Morality*, p. 197. Emphasis in original.

of their way of life; but it will hardly recover its lost vitality unless it can rightly diagnose the causes of its disease.[707]

    (1)   *What Would Thomistic Anthropology Promote?*

Specifically, Thomistic anthropology and the bioethical judgments following from it, I have argued throughout this work, comprise the path back to biomedical and societal health in the area of human-life issues such as abortion, cloning, ES cell research, assisted suicide, and euthanasia. If such a seemingly outdated anthropology has not proven thus far either compelling or effective, perhaps a part of the reason is a lack of promulgation outside of exceedingly narrowly focused academic venues: "The triumph of St. Thomas is yet to come."[708] Like the taste of salt on bland food, the tang of moral truth introduced to the minds of the general populace might prove both invigorating and rehabilitating once adequately explained. In fact, in limited segments of academia itself, in the late twentieth and early twenty-first century, Aquinas's view of human nature has seen a revival even outside of the "neo-Thomist" movement within the Catholic Church. Many non-Catholics and even non-Christians are "peeping Thomists," in Ralph McInerny's wonderful phrase. However, even though one may wish "moral appeals to nature could be demonstrated more easily," as one author has it, one must admit that in an unstable society "such moves are more difficult."[709]

    As has been seen, Thomistic anthropology and its associated natural law theory have much to say regarding many specific contemporary issues. However, what would a society look like constructed around this particular view of human nature? What would such a society promote? From one perspective, this question does not make a great deal of sense. If Thomistic anthropology in fact is an accurate depiction of human nature, one would expect most societies *already* to be constructed around certain remarkably similar moral principles—and this is exactly what is discovered. Most principles of natural law ethics may already be found institutionalized in most human societies: principles regarding murder, self-protection, familial responsibilities toward one's children, truthfulness and contractual relationships, the quest to eliminate ignorance, the avoidance of needless offense to fellow members of society, and so on. Although much of modern philosophy seems to consist of the attempt to cast out the restraints of nature and natural law from human ethical conduct, such an attempt, if ethical conduct is in fact rooted in

---

[707] Gerald Vann, *The Aquinas Prescription*, p. xvi.
[708] Ibid., p. 174.
[709] Anthony Battaglia, *Toward a Reformulation of Natural Law.* New York: The Seabury Press, 1981, p. 137.

human nature, will always be inevitably frustrated: "You may cast Nature out with a pitchfork, but she will always return,"[710] after all. "In the civil kingdom, where God's people intermix with people outside their religious kingdom for common cultural purposes," as David VanDrunen writes, "natural law rather than special divine revelation serves as the basis for their moral reasoning." Such moral reasoning is valid for shared cultural purposes and societal guidelines because of its natural accessibility; in fact, the basic principles of natural law "afford an impressive foundation for a civilized and orderly society."[711]

On the other hand, the social and ethical issues raised by the questions of when the life of a human person begins or ends have not yet gained the societal consensus these other issues have gained. Although some change on this front may be observed over the past few years, society has not yet completely accepted a view such as that of Robert P. George: "Even the life of an early embryo or a severely retarded child or a comatose person has value and dignity. . . . They enjoy a moral inviolability that will be respected and protected in any fully just regime of law."[712] This respect and protection, this "moral inviolability," is certainly not what is seen in contemporary societies; rather, since arguments such as George's are contested by some, the "default position" in the argument seems to be that even in a "just regime of law," little or no protections are offered to those whose personhood is called into question.

Therefore, what sort of specific appeals might one make who wishes to help call society back to a foundational Thomistic anthropological viewpoint, in particular in the realm of biomedical issues? First of all, one might simply argue for the basic natural inclinations recognized as foundational by Aquinas himself. These include those inclinations humans share with all other substances, such as the desire for self-preservation and the preservation of health in a variety of areas (spiritual, mental, social, physical, and emotional), as well as the specialized inclinations which humans share with other animals. These specialized inclinations would include the rearing of children, the preservation of the dual-sexed unions typified by humans' natural bodies, and so on. These basic human goods would also include the good of reason peculiar to humanity; this good of reason teaches humans as social creatures to desire knowledge, to desire a peaceful and productive human society, and so on.[713] Although these basic human

---

[710] *Naturam expelles furca, tamen usque recurret.* Horace, *Epistles* I.X.24-25.

[711] VanDrunen, *A Biblical Case for Natural Law*, pp. 53-54.

[712] George, *The Clash of Orthodoxies*, pp. 8-9.

inclinations and goods may seem too vague to be applicable to specific recommendations and prohibitions, such is not altogether the case, once it is recognized that what they all have in common is "the rule of conduct which is prescribed to us by the Creator in the constitution of the nature with which He has endowed us."[714] Many bioethical debates would be helped toward resolution if the focus of these debates were directed toward the natural constitutions of the patients involved rather than toward the patients' functional abilities. These Thomistic inclinations toward certain goods "are not themselves precepts of natural law," as McInerny points out; however, their importance in bioethical discussion lies in the fact that "their presence within us assures that we have immediate access to certain types of good, of objects of desires and inclinations."[715] The type of society centered around these inclinations, in other words, would be based on humanity's rational analysis of its own nature, rather than on humanity's willful assertion of its ever-shifting popular fashions and desires: "Each of the natural inclinations experienced by man will result in the apprehension of a self-evident moral precept."[716] For instance, the first and most general natural inclination, that of self-preservation, points toward the apprehension of the wrongness of euthanasia and assisted suicide.

This point should perhaps be repeated: The sort of society under discussion here would be a society based on the rational acceptance and analysis of the natural human constitution, rather than on the willful urge toward self-definition manifested primarily as the abandonment of nature. It would be a society based on *reason* rather than on *will*, in which the rule of law is not determined by a judiciary's latest fiat or by the latest media-popularized intellectual craze, but rather by "an objective moral standard inherent in the natural order. . . . a standard that transcend[s] political and religious boundaries of decency, justice, and judicial wisdom."[717] Certainly the protections of law in this type of society would be extended toward all those recognized as human persons, those recognized both biologically and logically as innocent individual substances of rational nature.

---

[713] ST I-II.94.2.

[714] James J. Fox, "Natural Law," n.p.

[715] McInerny, *St. Thomas Aquinas*. Notre Dame and London: Univ. of Notre Dame Press, 1982, p. 67.

[716] Giuseppe Butera, "The Moral Status of the First Principle of Practical Reason in Thomas's Natural-Law Theory." *The Thomist* 71.4 (October 2007): 609-31, p. 615.

[717] VanDrunen, *A Biblical Case for Natural Law*, pp. 44-45.

Secondly and more generally, this type of society would have a certain sort of attitude toward the intrinsic goodness of human life in particular and the intrinsic goodness of nature in general. The Thomistic anthropology and the Aristotelian metaphysical stance underlying it provide a remarkably explicit example of this sort of attitude toward the intrinsic goodness of life and nature; therefore, the last few pages of this book will comprise a discussion of the goodness of existence itself and what specifically this means in Aquinas's philosophical vision.

A good way of taking up this discussion might lie in considering the criticisms made by Friedrich Nietzsche toward Christianity's attitude toward the goodness of life, since Nietzsche according to Alasdair MacIntyre is "*the* moral philosopher of the present age." MacIntyre goes on to argue that, since in his view Enlightenment-era ethical philosophies cannot stand against Nietzsche's critique, if any premodern moral philosophy (such as natural law) is "to be vindicated against modernity, it will be in *something like* Aristotelian terms or not at all"[718]—in fact, our question for our moral and cultural future is simply "Nietzsche or Aristotle?"[719] Although in this particular work quoted (*After Virtue*) MacIntyre himself does not necessarily do so, one may assume that Aquinas's incorporation of Aristotle makes Thomism one of the greatest heirs, and probably the greatest, of the Aristotelian metaphysical terminology. Let us see, therefore, what Aquinas may have to say to Nietzsche regarding the intrinsic goodness and sacrality of human existence.

(2)  *The Goodness of Existence*

Occasionally one encounters thinkers who seem brilliantly wrong, like flawed diamonds. They reason forcefully from their fundamental premises, and these premises are typically stated in a pungent style. However, the premises themselves often seem simply *mistaken*. Hobbes and Machiavelli may be seen as examples of this type of thinker, but clearly the prime specimen is the many-faceted Nietzsche, whose influence on contemporary society it would be difficult to overstate. For relevant examples of these mistaken premises, one might examine a few of Nietzsche's numerous criticisms of Christianity, which often seem based on the notion that Christianity in general and Christian morality in particular are "life-denying," i.e., that Christian faith and practice are based on the denial of the inherent goodness of life. Nietzsche also attacks Christianity as having "spiritualized" itself into denying the validity of the physical senses, the senses necessary for corporeal interaction with life. In short, Nietzsche perceives Christianity as being

---

[718] MacIntyre, *After Virtue*, pp. 114 and 118. Emphasis in original.

[719] Ibid., title of Chapter 9.

anti-physical, even anti-life itself, and many of his attacks upon the Christian faith follow from this perception.

Nietzsche himself is incessantly clear on the point, like the village crank with his *idée fixe*. He writes in *The Antichrist*, "What was formerly just sick is today indecent—it is indecent to be a Christian today. . . . All the concepts of the church have been recognized for what they are, the most malignant counterfeits that exist, the aim of which is to devalue nature and natural values."[720] In *Twilight of the Idols*, Nietzsche describes these "natural values" in terms of the "passions" and "instincts": "All that is good is instinct."[721] One might wish to "spiritualize" or sublimate the passions, but, holds Nietzsche, the aim of Christianity, with its "hatred of the body" or "hostility against sensuality," is to *extirpate* the passions of life. Christians are thus the enemies of life: "The church fights passion with excision in every sense: its practice, its 'cure,' is castratism. . . . But an attack on the roots of passion means an attack on the roots of life: the practice of the church is *hostile to life*."[722] According to Nietzsche, Christianity's hostility toward life is manifested especially in its moral prescriptions:

> Every naturalism in morality—that is, every healthy morality—is dominated by an instinct of life. . . . *Anti-natural* morality—that is, almost every morality which has so far been taught, revered, and preached—turns, conversely, *against* the instincts of life: it is *condemnation* of these instincts, now secret, now outspoken and impudent. . . . It says No to both the lowest and the highest desires of life, and posits God as the *enemy of life*. The saint in whom God delights is the ideal eunuch. Life has come to an end where the "kingdom of God" begins.[723]

To Nietzsche, Christianity's anti-natural bias is also apparent in the prejudice against the "senses." He describes the "other-worldly" Christians as crying out against the deception of this world, a deception that prevents them from coming to know what they see as the only "real" world, the world of the spirit. Christians supposedly find the source of this deception in the senses: "These senses, which are so immoral in other ways, too, deceive us concerning the *true* world. . . . And above all, away with the body. . .!" Nietzsche praises the pre-

---

[720] Nietzsche. *The Antichrist* [1895]. *The Portable Nietzsche*. Walter Kaufmann, ed. and trans. New York: Penguin, 1976: 565-656, p. 611.
[721] Nietzsche. *Twilight of the Idols* [1889]. Kaufmann, ed. and trans.: 463-563, p. 494.
[722] Ibid., p. 487. Emphasis in original.
[723] Ibid., pp. 489-90. Emphasis in original.

socratic Heraclitus for "his assertion that being is an empty fiction. The 'apparent' world [discerned by the senses] is the only one: the 'true' world [of the spirit] is added by a lie."[724] Any philosophical division between a "true" and an "apparent" world is thus "only a suggestion of decadence, a symptom of the *decline of life* [as especially represented by Christianity]."[725] One could go on in this vein indefinitely; as mentioned earlier, Christianity's supposed "life-denying" stance is one of Nietzsche's primary preoccupations, arising often in his work.

One sees, therefore, that Nietzsche's "revaluation of all values" (his phrase), as well as his assertion of the "natural" morality as the only true morality, are fundamentally based on these concepts, that Christianity teaches that *this life is evil, the body is evil, the senses are deceptive,* and so on. Further, Christian morality is thus seen as artificial, as a life-denying restriction on the "natural" forces which, if followed, would lead one to "true" morality. However, this entire edifice of polemic seems constructed on a misunderstanding of the natural law and its principles and applications, whether specifically Christian or not. What happens to the superstructure of Nietzsche's critique of Christianity if the very foundation is shown to be, quite simply, mistaken? What happens if his most fundamental concepts are founded on clear factual errors, both theological and historical in nature?

"What a paradox," comments Mircea Eliade in Volume II of his *Journal.* "The Greeks, who . . . loved life, existence in the flesh, the perfect form, had, as an ideal of survival, the survival of the pure intellect (mind, *nous*). Christians, who are apparently ascetics and scorn the body, insist on the necessity of the resurrection of the body, and cannot conceive of paradisiac blessedness without the union of the soul and the body."[726] As validation of Eliade's point, one might recall Aquinas's hylomorphic union of the human form and body which compose the complete human person and which will be re-united at the resurrection of the body.[727] Yet Nietzsche proclaims that Christians cry out "above all" for the rejection of the body—while in fact what Christians cry out "above all" is that "God became flesh in Christ" and "I believe in the resurrection of the body." This "paradox" did not appear to have entered Nietzsche's understanding, given his extravagant praise of the pre-Christian Greeks and his equally extreme condem-

---

[724] Ibid., pp. 480-81. Emphasis in original.

[725] Ibid., p. 484. Emphasis in original.

[726] Mircea Eliade. *Journal II: 1957-1969*. Fred H. Johnson, Jr., trans. Chicago and London: The University of Chicago Press, 1989, p. 95.

[727] ST I.75.4.

nation of the "anti-natural" Christians. However, as Eliade points out elsewhere, "For religious man, nature is never only 'natural'. . . . Nature always expresses something that transcends it."[728]

What is the actual attitude on the part of orthodox Christianity, specifically from a Thomistic viewpoint, toward the goodness of this world and human existence? One should begin with the opening chapter of the Bible itself: "And God saw every thing that he had made," reads the biblical account, "and, behold, it was very good" (Genesis 1:31). This intuition of the inherent goodness of the natural order (inherently good both because it is created by God and because of its native excellence) lies behind much of the development of Thomistic thought regarding the *identification of goodness with being itself.* In other words, far from seeing life as "evil," Thomas sees *the whole of existence as good, insofar as it possesses being*—for God is seen as the ground of all being.

Both Augustine and Aquinas may be taken as representative of traditional Christian theology in this respect. For example, Aquinas argues that all that has being—all that possesses real existence—to that extent is good: "Goodness and being are really the same, and differ only in idea."[729] The terms "being" and "good" are the same in reference (*secundum rem*) and differ only in "idea" or sense (*secundum rationem*). Stated differently, to say of something that it is "good" expresses the idea of its end or desirability, while to say of it that it has "being" is to say of it that it possesses actual existence. However, both ideas express the same set of natural properties, i.e., the "properties in virtue of which that thing has actualized its specifying potentialities," as medievalist Scott MacDonald puts it.[730] One may see this stated more clearly by Aquinas a bit later, in the third Article of the same section quoted above:

> Every being, as being, is good. For all being, as being, has actuality and is in some way perfect; since every act implies some sort of perfection; and perfection implies desirability and goodness. . . . Hence it follows that every being as such is good.[731]

For example, though Aristotle speaks of humans as "the rational animal," this in itself does not imply that if one does not possess full rationality one is not human. However, it does imply that a healthy adult human will possess functioning rationality, and will thus be in that

---

[728] Eliade, *The Sacred and the Profane*, pp. 116 and 118.
[729] ST I.5.1.
[730] Scott MacDonald. "The Relation Between Being and Goodness." *Being and Goodness: The Concept of the Good in Metaphysics and Philosophical Theology.* Scott MacDonald, ed. Ithaca, New York: Cornell University Press, 1991: 1-28, p. 17.
[731] ST I.5.3.

respect a good example of the human "being," or the being of a human. The relevant moral point follows from this: What is it that makes a human "good," i.e., ethically and morally sound? Is it not, according to Aristotle, habitual reference to the very rationality and soundness of soul that also defines human *qua* human? So it seems that the "being" and the "goodness" of a human should be identified, since the defining characteristic of both "human-ness" and human morality is the same in reference (the rational nature of the intellectual soul) and differs only in idea (rationality as defining characteristic on the one hand, and as moral guide on the other).

This is why Aquinas can say (quoting Augustine's *On Christian Teaching*, I.42) that "inasmuch as we exist we are good."[732] In fact, Augustine also makes this point elsewhere, in his *City of God* (XII.4): "All natures, then [he is here speaking specifically of *bodily* natures], inasmuch as they are, and have therefore a rank and species of their own, and a kind of internal harmony, are certainly good."[733] No fair judge would say these representative Christian thinkers "devalue nature," as Nietzsche would have it. To the contrary, Aquinas goes even further than Augustine, from whom he is drawing: "No being can be spoken of as evil, formally as being, but only so far as it lacks being."[734] A cup with a hole in its base, for example, lacks "being" or complete existence as a cup. But the point is that it also lacks "goodness" as a cup (it is, in fact, a bad cup) exactly to the same extent that it lacks "being." Both the being of the cup and the goodness of the cup are reduced simultaneously by the hole in the cup's base, since they both specify the same property of the cup, but from different perspectives.

This identification of being and goodness is easy enough to see in something like a cup. The nature of a cup is to hold liquid; if it does not hold liquid, it lacks both being as a cup and goodness as a cup. On the other hand, what about this identification in humans? The Thomistic argument is certainly also applicable to humanity, and one could plausibly maintain that human "being" is also equivalent to human "goodness." However, this is only plausible if humans have a functional nature or constitution in themselves as surely as do cups. "If man is an artifact of God's," as Ralph McInerny writes, "man has a nature that provides a measure of his action. Acts that thwart his nature are bad; those that fulfill its potential are good. That is, there are criteria of good

[732] ST I.5.1.
[733] From Vernon J. Bourke, ed., *The Essential Augustine*. Indianapolis: Hackett Publishing, 1978, p. 101.
[734] ST I.5.3.

and bad action antecedent to this person's doing anything at all." In the case of humanity just as in the case of the cup, "Creation is thought of on the model of the human artisan who, when he fashions something, does so with an eye to some purpose."[735] Because he accepts humanity's creation by God, Aquinas believes, as does Nietzsche, that humans should act according to their true "natures." The difference lies in the fact that Aquinas thinks of this rational nature as the fundamental trait of rational beings (i.e., those with an intellectual substantial form), while Nietzsche seems to reject this idea ("All that is good is *instinct*"). Aquinas, to the contrary, would identify moral goodness in humans and their behavior as that which follows their deepest, truest nature, the nature based on reason, not on their "instinct."

Of course, there is more to the complete human nature than one's logical capability, and Aquinas's view of rationality does encompass this wider view of nature, incorporating the affections, emotions, instincts, natural pleasures, and so on, if they "be taken according to reason: for reason itself demands that the use of reason be interrupted at times."[736] In fact, intuitive knowledge, "the knowledge in which the heart is necessarily involved," is for Aquinas "the summit of human knowledge."[737] According to Gerald Vann, an anthropology of any value must "take account of the whole man and of the destiny of the whole man [and of] the value of personality. . . . Man cannot live on reason alone any more than he can live on bread alone":

> We shall not win the world back to reason unless we can first show that by *reason* is not meant the impoverished reason of rationalism, but reason as one of the elements in a whole approach to reality—necessary but not the only thing necessary, important but not the only thing important.[738]

Still, despite this crucial caveat, reason remains the marker of humanity's intellectual nature as opposed to its animal attributes: "*Rational* is included in the meaning of *man* [but] not in the meaning of *animal*," as Aquinas writes.[739]

However, Nietzsche argues that this identification of reason as the primary differentiating characteristic of humans is to be "*absurdly*" rational. He speaks of the position of Socrates among the Greeks in these terms:

---

[735] McInerny, *Ethica Thomistica*, pp. 53-54.

[736] ST I-II.34.1.

[737] Gerald Vann, *The Aquinas Prescription*, p. 153.

[738] Ibid., pp. 160, 162, and 167.

[739] ST I.29.4. Emphasis in original.

The fanaticism with which all Greek reflection throws itself upon rationality betrays a desperate situation; there was danger, there was but one choice: either to perish or—to be *absurdly rational*. The moralism of the Greek philosophers from Plato on is pathologically conditioned. . . . Reason-virtue-happiness, that means merely that one must imitate Socrates and counter the dark appetites with a permanent daylight—the daylight of reason.[740]

It can be seen, therefore, that the real division here is not between the "nature-loving" Nietzsche and the "nature-hating" Christian, for the Christian is also "nature-loving." The real division is over what *constitutes* the primary human nature which is to be loved. On the one hand, a strand of thinking typified by philosophers such as Nietzsche and Schopenhauer argues that humanity's fundamental nature is composed of instinct, passion, the non-rational will. In this view, "What is right is simply what instinct affirms to be conducive to success, success in its turn being measured simply in terms of power and force."[741] On the other hand, Thomistic anthropology, amongst other philosophical strands, argues for rationality as humanity's key trait. Aquinas certainly does not hate human nature, or any kind of nature. He asserts that what is "good" for something is what is "natural" to it, and what is "unnatural" for something is also "bad"; the good is what is "according to nature."[742] When something is "good," just as when something has "being," it has "actualized its specifying potentialities"—its natural potential given its natural form. In fact, *what is evil for something—for anything—cannot be natural to it.*[743]

This conflict plays itself out today in many ways in society, notably in the continuing debate over same-sex "marriage"; it is a struggle for definition. One side has decided that same-sex unions must be as valid as more traditional marriages, for these unions come from within the

---

[740] Nietzsche, *Twilight of the Idols*, p. 478. Emphasis in original.

[741] Vann, *The Aquinas Prescription*, p. 158.

[742] ST I-II.18.5.

[743] This, of course, corresponds with the Thomistic doctrine of original sin, for original sin is seen as a moral fall rather than as an ontic fall. Therefore, the human use of natural reason *in itself* cannot be evil, since the use of reason is natural to humans. Of course, the misuses and misdirected objects of rational activity may render such activity evil, because such misuses are unnatural to human reason considered as such in itself. The natural object of the use of reason is inferential knowledge of truth, and the use of reason to reach such knowledge is good.

participants, "naturally" in the Nietzschean sense (i.e., by *instinct*), and must therefore be "right" and "good." The opposing side, Thomistic in fact if not always in name, stubbornly points out that same-sex "marriages" cannot be equivalent to traditional marriage, despite the participants' proclivities, for these unions do not actualize the specifying potentialities of the male and the female; they do not fulfill the natural constitution of dual-sexed humanity. These unions do not complete the natural potential of the humans involved, despite the impulses of their "instincts" (and despite the emotional sympathy and regret one might feel while making this rational judgment). We do not "decide" or "create" what is right for us in our own chosen "reality"; we *discover* what is right for us in the reality given us, and in our own natural constitution.

As for Nietzsche's charge that Christianity devalues the "senses" as "deceptive," perhaps it would be enough of a response merely to quote a sentence from Aquinas's epistemology, taken more or less wholesale from Aristotle: *Nihil est in intellectu quod non sit prius in sensu.* "Nothing is in the intellect that was not first in the senses."[744] Except for the divinely endowed natural capacity to know truth,[745] humans rely first of all on their bodily senses for their access to knowledge. This understanding of the necessity of the senses also counters Nietzsche's claim that Christianity inherently contains a "hatred of the body" and a "hostility against sensuality," and that it desires to extirpate the passions of life. Since in his view the Christian Church is "hostile to life," its remedy for all passions is "castratism." However, such is not the case. As the Ante-Nicene author who wrote under the name of Ignatius argues (in the Epistle of Ignatius to the Philippians), when discussing human sexuality and nudity, "Anything becomes disgraceful when it is polluted by wickedness. But when sin is not present, none of the things that have been created are shameful, none of them evil, but all very good."[746] Physical passion in itself is "very good"; however, when physical passion is put to anti-natural and anti-rational uses, it can quickly become very wrong indeed.

Perhaps an overall summary of this discussion would be helpful at this point:

---

[744] *De Ver.* 2.3.19.

[745] In ST I.80.1, Aquinas makes the distinction between "intellect" and "sense"; both together make up the soul's knowledge. See also Etienne Gilson, *The Unity of Philosophical Experience* (New York: Scribner, 1965), p. 308.

[746] Ignatius. "The Epistle of Ignatius to the Philippians." From *The Ante-Nicene Fathers, Volume 1.* A. Cleveland Coxe, ed. Pub. 1885. 2nd printing. Peabody, Mass.: Hendrickson Publishers, 1999. 116-19, Chapter VI, p. 117.

A.	Existence itself is good, although what is done with that existence may be evil.
B.	The actualization of something's specific capacities, or its "nature" (such as the use of reason in humans), progressively completes or perfects the "being" of that thing as well. "Gaining being" in this way is equivalent to gaining goodness, as follows:
1.	That thing is good as a type of the thing it is, e.g., "rational animal."
2.	It is good as that which is potential becomes actual.
3.	It is good because its "being" is being fulfilled.
C.	Therefore, an "evil" or wrongful existence is one which is still good insofar as it exists, but bad insofar as it fails to actualize its specifying capacities—insofar, using Nietzschean terminology but with Thomistic meaning, as it fails to live according to its true nature.

What, then, is one to say of Nietzsche's repeated contentions that Christianity manifests a "hatred" of this world, that it thinks of nature and the body as "evil"? To the contrary, it seems that in world history, Christianity is one of the truly great *affirmers* of the goodness of life, nature, and the value of the individual. In fact, Christianity believes in this to the extent that it teaches that God Himself took on a physical body and became part of the natural world. If Christians believe the body is "evil," would not that make Christ a partaker in evil? What can one say but that Nietzsche on this fundamental point is wrong? As Alasdair MacIntyre writes:

> What has to be supplied is a cogent theoretical explanation of ideological blindness. . . . Can a Thomist hope to construct [such an explanation] for Nietzsche's [philosophy]? . . . Where then would such [an explanation] have to begin? The answer is: with what Aquinas says about the roots of intellectual blindness in moral error, with the misdirection of the intellect by the will and with the corruption of the will by the sin of pride, both that pride which is an inordinate desire to be superior and that pride which is an inclination to contempt for God.[747]

"There is an ethical problem at the root of our philosophical difficulties," according to Etienne Gilson, "for men are most anxious to find truth, but very reluctant to accept it."[748]

---

[747] MacIntyre, *Three Rival Versions of Moral Enquiry*, p. 147.
[748] Gilson, *The Unity of Philosophical Experience*, p. 61.

## 2.    Thomistic Thought and Contemporary Issues

However, let us make an immense two-fold assumption: Let us assume that our society as a whole becomes convinced of the truth of these Thomistic principles, and let us further assume that the legislators and culture-makers of society press toward some sort of instantiation of these principles in law. What would such a society look like? There would be many, many specific examples brought up or promoted in councils and legislative bodies at all levels of government, as well as many shifts in cultural mood and opinion, but I would like to highlight some general principles instead. In a society constructed around Thomistic principles of natural law, particularly in the realm of bioethical decision-making, one would find as this society's prime characteristics most or all of the following:

(1) the rejection of this Nietzschean pride and the attempt at self-definition, in favor of the celebration and analysis of the given human constitution;

(2) the overall affirmation of the intrinsic goodness of human life, of its value and sacredness;

(3) the affirmation in general of the intrinsic goodness of nature and natural existence;

(4) the attitude of humble reception of the gift of life, at whatever stage and in whatever manifestation;

(5) the care and protection of all humanity in its embodied state, from its inception as a zygote to its final disembodiment;

(6) the general expression of gratitude for life's gifts rather than the pride, recklessness, and consequent spiritual, mental, and moral blindness so characteristic of human societies today. The common devaluation and degradation of life and its goodness would slowly ebb away from its high-tide domination of contemporary popular culture, as moral sanity and health made its return. The very air we breathe would seem cleaner and more free, the very atmosphere less and less *despairing*.

(7) Finally, these general characteristics would be exemplified more specifically in the criminal law's protections of innocent human beings. This moral principle and legal protection would hold sway even in the face of the possibility both of scientific advances and of utilitarian economic benefits. Neither scientific advances nor economic benefits trump the inherent value and dignity of a single human being.

In short, we would be a society truly protective of innocent human life. We would live in a culture of life, a culture which does not depend upon the death of some for the well-being and convenience of others. We would perceive the humanity and personhood inherent in even the least of us. It is my hope that this state of affairs would be the end result of the application of Thomistic thought to contemporary bioethical issues.

# Works Cited

Adams IV, Nathan A. "An Unnatural Assault on Natural Law: Regulating Bio-technology Using a Just Research Theory." *Human Dignity in the Biotech Century: A Christian Vision for Public Policy.* Charles W. Colson and Nigel M. de S. Cameron, eds. Downers Grove, Illinois: InterVarsity Press, 2004: 160-80.

Adler, Mortimer. "Introduction." Robert E. Brennan, O.P. *Thomistic Psychology: A Philosophic Analysis of the Nature of Man.* New York: Macmillan, 1941: vii-xiv.

Aertsen, Jan. *Nature and Creature: Thomas Aquinas's Way of Thought.* Leiden: Brill, 1988.

"An Approach to a Key Theological Question." American Bioethics Advisory Commission Report, Part 10. all.org/abac/clontx10. Accessed 13 Dec. 2013.

Anderson, Ryan T. "The End of the Stem-Cell Wars." *The Weekly Standard* 13.12 (3 Dec. 2007), n.p. Weeklystandard.com/Content/Public/Articles. Accessed 26 Nov. 2007.

---. "Faithful Reason about Stem Cells." Firstthings.com (7 June 2007), n.p. Accessed 7 June 2007.

Angell, M. "Euthanasia in the Netherlands—Good News or Bad?" *New England Journal of Medicine* 335.22 (28 November 1996): 1676-78.

Anon. "Why Keep Some Old Testament Laws and Discard Others?" Associated Press, 26 December 2003.

Aquinas, Thomas. *See* Thomas Aquinas.

Aristotle. *De Anima.* Hugh Lawson-Tancred, trans. New York: Penguin, 1987.

Arkes, Hadley. "That 'Nature Herself Has Placed in Our Ears a Power of Judging': Some Reflections on the 'Naturalism' of Cicero." *Natural Law Theory: Contemporary Essays.* Robert P. George, ed. Oxford: Clarendon Press, 1992: 245-77.

Armstrong, David. *Family Matters: Catholic Theology of the Family.* Melvindale, Michigan: Lulu Publishing, 2007.

Ashley, Benedict M., O.P. "The Anthropological Foundations of the Natural Law: A Thomistic Engagement with Modern Science." *St. Thomas Aquinas and the Natural Law Tradition: Contemporary Perspectives.* John Goyette, Mark S. Latkovic, and Richard S. Myers, eds. Washington, D.C.: Catholic University of America Press, 2004: 3-16.

Athenagoras. *On the Resurrection of the Dead.* In *The Ante-Nicene Fathers, Volume II.* B.P. Pratten, trans. A. Cleveland Coxe, ed. Pub. 1885. 2nd printing. Peabody, Mass.: Hendrickson Publishers, 1999. 149-62.

---. *A Plea for the Christians*. In *The Ante-Nicene Fathers, Volume II*. B.P. Pratten, trans. A. Cleveland Coxe, ed. Pub. 1885. 2nd printing. Peabody, Mass.: Hendrickson Publishers, 1999. 129-48.

Atkinson, Joseph C. "*Familiaris Consortio*: The Biblical and Theological Foundation of an Adequate Anthropology." *Life and Learning XI: Proceedings of the Eleventh University Faculty for Life Conference*. Joseph W. Koterski, S.J., ed. Washington, D.C.: University Faculty for Life, 2001: 248-66.

Augustine. *The City of God*. Gerald G. Walsh, Demetrius B. Zema, Grace Monahan, and Daniel J. Honan, transs. New York: Image Books/ Doubleday, 1958.

Austriaco, Nicanor Pier Giorgio, O.P. "In Defense of the Loss of Bodily Integrity as a Criterion for Death: A Response to the Radical Capacity Argument." *The Thomist* 73 (Oct. 2009): 647-59, pp. 657-58.

Baldner, Steven. "The Soul in the Explanation of Life: Aristotle Against Reductionism." *Lyceum* 3.2 (Fall 1991): 1-14.

---. "An Argument for Substantial Form." *The Saint Anselm Journal* 5.1 (Fall 2007): 1-12.

Balint, Benjamin. "The Life of the World to Come: Review of *Resurrection and the Restoration of Israel: The Ultimate Victory of the God of Life*, by Jon D. Levenson." *First Things* 170 (February 2007): 31-34.

Battaglia, Anthony. *Toward a Reformulation of Natural Law*. New York: The Seabury Press, 1981.

Beckwith, Francis J. "Defending Abortion Philosophically: A Review of David Boonin's *A Defense of Abortion*." *Journal of Medicine and Philosophy* 31 (2006): 177-203.

---. *Defending Life: A Moral and Legal Case Against Abortion Choice*. New York: Cambridge University Press, 2007.

Bentham, Jeremy. *An Introduction to the Principles of Morals and Legislation* [1780]. J.H. Burns and H.L.A. Hart, eds. London: Athlone Press, 1970.

Bobik, Joseph. *Aquinas on Being and Essence: A Translation and Interpretation*. Notre Dame, Indiana: University of Notre Dame Press, 1965.

Bondeson, William B., et al., eds. *Abortion and the Status of the Fetus*. Dordrecht, Holland: D. Reidel Publishing, 1983.

Boonin, David. *A Defense of Abortion*. Cambridge: Cambridge University Press, 2003.

---. "Death Comes for the Violinist: On Two Objections to Thomson's 'Defense of Abortion.'" *Social Theory and Practice* 23.3 (Fall 1997): 329-64.

Borthwick, Chris. "The Permanent Vegetative State: Ethical Crux, Medical Fiction?" *Issues in Law and Medicine* 12.2 (1996): 167-85.

Boseley, Sarah. "Sleeping Pill Wakes Men in Vegetative State." *The Guardian* 23 May 2006.

Bottum, Joseph. "Embryonic Stem Cells and Those Pro-Science Pro-Lifers." Firstthings.com, n.p. 20 November 2007. Accessed 20 November 2007.

Bourke, Vernon J., ed. *The Essential Augustine*. Indianapolis: Hackett Publishing, 1978.

Boyle, Joseph M. "Reverence for Life and Bioethics." *Linking the Human Life Issues*. Russell Hittinger, ed. Lake Bluff, Illinois: Regnery Gateway, 1986:

101-40.

Bradley, Denis J.M. " 'To Be or Not To Be?': Pasnau on Aquinas's Immortal Human Soul." *The Thomist* 68.1 (2004): 1-39.

---. *"Ephemerides Thomisticae Analyticae*: Metaphysics and Ethics in Stump's *Aquinas." The Thomist* 69.4 (October 2005): 593-620.

Brady-Lunny, Edith. "Psychologist Appointed to Help Massey Defense in Murder Case." Decatur *Herald & Review*. Updated 5 Jan. 2007. Herald-Review.com. Accessed 16 May 2007.

Brennan, Robert Edward, O.P. *Thomistic Psychology: A Philosophic Analysis of the Nature of Man.* New York: Macmillan, 1941.

Brody, Baruch. *Abortion and the Sanctity of Human Life: A Philosophical View.* Cambridge, Massachusetts: MIT Press, 1975.

Brower, Jeffrey E. "Making Sense of Divine Simplicity." *Faith and Philosophy* 25.1 (January 2008): 3-30.

Brownlee, Christen. "Do Not Harm: Stem Cells Created Without Destroying Healthy Embryos." *Science News* 168.17 (22 October 2005): 259.

Budziszewski, J. *The Resurrection of Nature: Political Theory and the Human Character.* Ithaca and London: Cornell University Press, 1986.

---. *Written on the Heart: The Case for Natural Law.* Downers Grove, Illinois: InterVarsity Press, 1997.

---. *The Revenge of Conscience: Politics and the Fall of Man.* Dallas: Spence Publishing, 1999.

---. *What We Can't Not Know: A Guide.* Dallas: Spence Publishing, 2003.

---. "Natural Law." *New Dictionary of Christian Apologetics.* W.C. Campbell-Jack, Gavin McGrath, and C. Stephen Evans, eds. Leicester, England: Inter-Varsity Press, 2006: 473-76.

---. *Natural Law for Lawyers.* Jeffery J. Ventrella, ed. Nashville, Tennessee: ACW Press, 2006.

---. *The Line Through the Heart: Natural Law as Fact, Theory, and Sign of Contradiction.* Wilmington, Delaware: ISI Books, 2009.

Burtchaell, James T. "The Child as Chattel: Reflections on a Vatican Document." *Guaranteeing the Good Life: Medicine and the Return of Eugenics.* Richard John Neuhaus, ed. Grand Rapids, Michigan: Eerdmans, 1990: 89-121.

Butera, Giuseppe. "The Moral Status of the First Principle of Practical Reason in Thomas's Natural-Law Theory." *The Thomist* 71.4 (October 2007): 609-31.

Byrne, Paul A., Cicero G. Coimbra, Robert Spaemann, and Mercedes Arzú Wilson. "Brain Death Is Not Death." Essay presented to the Pontifical Academy of Sciences, February 2005. Published by Compassionate Healthcare Network, 29 March 2005. Chninternational.com, n.p. Accessed 15 February 2008.

Cahill, Lisa Sowle. *Euthanasia: A Protestant and a Catholic Perspective.* Dissertation. University of Chicago, 1976.

"California Institute Funds Stem-Cell Research." Associated Press, 11 April 2006.

Callahan, Daniel. *Abortion: Law, Choice, and Morality.* New York: Macmillan, 1970.

Callahan, Sidney. "Zygotes and Blastocysts." *Human Life Review* 28.3 (Summer 2002): 81-82.

Caspar, Ruth, O.P. "Wisdom and Light: Contributions from Aquinas to Contemporary Bioethics." The Aquinas Convention Address: Ohio Dominican University. 28 January 2004: 1-24.

Callahan, Daniel. *Abortion: Law, Choice, and Morality*. New York: Macmillan, 1970.

Callahan, Sidney. "Zygotes and Blastocysts." *Human Life Review* 28.3 (Summer 2002): 81-82.

Chesterton, G.K. *Varied Types*. New York: Dodd and Mead, 1903.

---. "Where Is the Paradox?" *The Well and the Shallows* [1935]. San Francisco: Ignatius Press, 2006: 198-203.

Childress, James. "Bioethics." *A New Dictionary of Christian Ethics*. John Macquarrie and James Childress, eds. London: SCM Press, 1986.

Cicero. *De Legibus*. Loeb Classical Library No. 213. Clinton W. Keyes, trans. Cambridge: Harvard Univ. Press, Loeb Library, 1928.

Clarke, W. Norris, S.J. *Explorations in Metaphysics*. South Bend, Indiana: University of Notre Dame Press, 1994.

---. *Person and Being: The Aquinas Lecture, 1993*. Milwaukee: Marquette University Press, 1993.

Condic, Maureen L. "Getting Stem Cells Right." *First Things* 180 (February 2008): 10-12.

Connolly, Kate. "Trapped in his own body for 23 years—the coma victim who screamed unheard." Guardian.co.uk (23 Nov. 2009). N.p. Accessed 30 Nov. 2009.

Cooper, Adam G. "Redeeming Flesh." *First Things* 173 (May 2007): 27-31.

Crosby, John F. "The Personhood of the Human Embryo." *Life and Learning III: Proceedings of the Third University Faculty for Life Conference*. Joseph W. Koterski, S.J., ed. Washington, D.C.: University Faculty for Life, 1993: 177-93.

Daly, Cahal B. *Natural Law Morality Today*. Dublin/London: Clonmore and Reynolds/Burns and Oates, 1965.

Dauphinais, Michael, Barry David, and Matthew Levering, eds. *Aquinas the Augustinian*. Washington, D.C.: Catholic Univ. of America Press, 2007.

Davis, John Jefferson. *Evangelical Ethics: Issues Facing the Church Today*. Phillipsburg, New Jersey: Presbyterian and Reformed Publishing Company, 1985.

Davis, John K. "Selecting Potential Children and Unconditional Parental Love." *Bioethics* 22.5 (June 2008): 258-68.

Deane-Drummond, Celia. *The Ethics of Nature*. Oxford: Blackwell, 2004.

Deane-Drummond, Celia, and David Clough, eds. *Creaturely Theology: On God, Humans and Other Animals*. London: SCM Press, 2009.

Deckers, Jan. "Why Eberl Is Wrong: Reflections on the Beginning of Personhood." *Bioethics* 21.5 (June 2007): 270-82.

Dombrowski, Daniel A., and Robert Deltete. *A Brief, Liberal, Catholic Defense of Abortion*. Champaign, Illinois: University of Illinois Press, 2000.

Donne, John. "The Exstasie." *Poems of John Donne, Volume I*. E.K. Chambers, ed.  London: Lawrence & Bullen, 1896: 53-56.

---. *Devotions upon Emergent Occasions and Several Steps in My Sickness* [1624]. Ann Arbor, Michigan: University of Michigan Press, 1959.

Dulles, Avery Cardinal. "God and Evolution." *First Things* 176 (October 2007): 19-24.

Dworkin, Ronald. *Life's Dominion: An Argument About Abortion, Euthanasia, and Individual Freedom*. New York: Knopf, 1993.

Eberl, Jason T. "Aquinas's Account of Human Embryogenesis and Recent Interpretations." *Journal of Medicine and Philosophy* 30.4 (August 2005): 379-94.

---. *Thomistic Principles and Bioethics*. London and New York:  Routledge, 2006.

---. "A Thomistic Perspective on the Beginning of Personhood: Redux." *Bioethics* 21.5 (June 2007): 283-89.

Eliade, Mircea. *The Sacred and the Profane: The Nature of Religion*. Willard R. Trask, trans. New York: Harcourt, Brace & World, 1959.

---. *Journal II: 1957-1969*. Fred H. Johnson, Jr., trans. Chicago and London: The University of Chicago Press, 1989.

Engelhardt, Jr., H. Tristram. "Introduction." *Abortion and the Status of the Fetus*. William B. Bondeson, H. Tristram Engelhardt, Jr., Stuart F. Spicker, and Daniel H. Winship, eds. Dordrecht, Holland: D. Reidel Publishing, 1983: xi-xxxii.

---. *The Foundations of Bioethics*. 2nd edition. New York: Oxford University Press USA, 1996.

---. *The Foundations of Christian Bioethics*. Lisse: Swets & Zeitlinger, 2000.

Epictetus. *The Golden Sayings of Epictetus*. Hastings Crossley, trans.  New York: P.F. Collier & Son, 1937.

Farrell, Walter, O.P. *A Companion to the Summa. Volume I—The Architect of the Universe*. New York: Sheed and Ward, 1945.

---. *A Companion to the Summa. Volume III—The Fullness of Life*. New York: Sheed and Ward, 1945.

Fears, J. Rufus. "Natural Law: The Legacy of Greece and Rome." *Common Truths: New Perspectives on Natural Law*. Edward B. McLean, ed. Wilmington, Delaware: ISI Books, 2000: 19-56.

Finnis, John. *Fundamentals of Ethics*. Oxford: Oxford University Press, 1983.

---. *Moral Absolutes: Tradition, Revision, and Truth*. Washington, D.C.: Catholic University of America Press, 1991.

---. "Abortion and Health Care Ethics II." *Principles of Health Care Ethics*. R. Gillon, ed.  New York: Wiley, 1994: 547-57.

FitzPatrick, William. "Surplus Embryos, Nonreproductive Cloning, and the Intend/Foresee Distinction." *Hastings Center Report* 33.3 (May-June 2003): 29-36.

Fletcher, Joseph. *Situation Ethics: The New Morality*. Philadelphia: The Westminster Press, 1966.

---. *The Ethics of Genetic Control*.  Garden City, New York:  Anchor Press, 1974.

Fox, James J. "Natural Law." *The Catholic Encyclopedia, Volume IX*. Robert Appleton Company: 1910. *Online Edition* K. Knight: 2005. Newadvent.org/cathen. Accessed 2 July 2006.

George, Robert P. "Natural Law and Human Nature." *Natural Law Theory: Contemporary Essays*. Robert P. George, ed. Oxford: Clarendon Press, 1992: 31-41.

---. *The Clash of Orthodoxies: Law, Religion, and Morality in Crisis*. Wilmington, Delaware: ISI Books, 2001.

---. "Sweet Reason." Review of *Human Life, Action, and Ethics: Essays by G.E.M. Anscombe*. Mary Geach and Luke Gormally, eds. *First Things* 159: January 2006: 56-59.

George, Robert P., and Patrick Lee. "Bodies: The Exhibition." "On the Square: Observations and Contentions." Firstthings.com (14 August 2006), n.p. Accessed 14 August 2006.

George, Robert P., and Christopher Tollefsen. *Embryo: A Defense of Human Life*. New York: Doubleday, 2008.

Gibbs, Nancy. "Dying Together." *Time* (3 August 2009): 64.

Gill, Robin. "The Challenge of Euthanasia." *Euthanasia and the Churches*. Robin Gill, ed. London: Cassell, 1998: 15-38.

Gilson, Etienne. *The Unity of Philosophical Experience*. New York: Charles Scribner and Sons, 1965.

Glantz, Leonard. "Is the Fetus a Person? A Lawyer's View." *Abortion and the Status of the Fetus*. William B. Bondeson, H. Tristram Engelhardt, Jr., Stuart F. Spicker, and Daniel H. Winship, eds. Dordrecht, Holland: D. Reidel Publishing, 1983: 107-17.

Glover, Jonathan. *Causing Death and Saving Lives*. New York: Penguin [1977], reprinted 1981.

---. "The Sanctity of Life." *Bioethics: An Anthology*. Helga Kuhse and Peter Singer, eds. Oxford: Blackwell, 2006: 266-75.

Gordon, Doris. "Abortion and Thomson's Violinist: Unplugging a Bad Analogy." Wheaton, Maryland: L4L.org/Articles/ThomViol: 1991. Updated 1999, n.p. Accessed 21 April 2007.

Grabill, Stephen J. "Foreword." David VanDrunen, *A Biblical Case for Natural Law*. Grand Rapids, Michigan: Acton Institute, 2000: i-iii.

Grisez, Germain. *Abortion: The Myths, the Realities, and the Arguments*. New York: World Publishing Company, 1970.

Grompe, Markus, and Robert P. George. "Creative Science Will Resolve Stem-Cell Issues." *The Wall Street Journal* (20 June 2005): A14.

Grotius, Hugo. *Hugonis Grotii, De jure belli et pacis libri tres* [1646 edition]. J.B. Scott, ed. Oxford: Oxford University Press, 1913.

Gudorf, Christine E. "Contraception and Abortion in Roman Catholicism." *Sacred Rights: The Case for Contraception and Abortion in World Religions*. Daniel C. Maguire, ed. New York: Oxford University Press USA, 2003: 55-78.

Gunton, Colin E. *A Brief Theology of Revelation: The 1993 Warfield Lectures*. Edinburgh: T & T Clark, 1995.

Haldane, John, and Patrick Lee. "Rational Souls and the Beginning of Life (A Reply to Robert Pasnau)." *Philosophy* 78.4 (October 2003): 532-40.

Harris, John. *The Value of Life*. London: Routledge & Kegan Paul, 1985.

Harris, Sam. *Letter to a Christian Nation*. New York: Knopf, 2007.

Hauerwas, Stanley. "Must a Person Be a Person to Be a Patient? Or, My Uncle

Charlie Is Not Much of a Person but He Is Still My Uncle Charlie." Stanley M. Hauerwas, David B. Burrell, and Richard Bondi. *Truthfulness and Tragedy: Further Investigations in Christian Ethics.* Notre Dame, Indiana: University of Notre Dame Press, 1977.

Hayden, Mary. "Recovering Eudaimonistic Teleology." *The Monist* 75.1 (January 1992): 71-83.

Healy, Nicholas M. *Thomas Aquinas: Theologian of the Christian Life.* Aldershot, Hants, and Burlington, Vermont: Ashgate Publishing, 2003.

Henry, Carl F.H. "Natural Law and a Nihilistic Culture." *First Things* 49 (January 1995): 55-60.

Hern, Warren M., M.D. "Is Pregnancy Really Normal?" *Family Planning Perspectives* 3.1 (January 1971): 5-10.

Herr, William A. *Catholic Thinkers in the Clear: Giants of Catholic Thought from Augustine to Rahner. Basics of Christian Thought, Vol. 2.* Todd Brennan, ed. Chicago: The Thomas More Press, 1985.

Hittinger, Russell. "Natural Law." *Encyclopedia of Bioethics.* Vol. 4. Warren Thomas Reich, ed. New York: Simon & Schuster Macmillan, 1995: 1805-12.

---. *The First Grace: Rediscovering the Natural Law in the Post-Christian World.* Wilmington, Delaware: ISI Books, 2003.

---. "Two Thomisms, Two Modernities." *First Things* 184 (June/July 2008): 33-38.

---. "Examination of Conscience." *First Things* 189 (January 2009): 59-61.

Hume, David. *A Treatise of Human Nature* [1739-40]. T.H. Green and T.H. Grose, eds. London: Longmans, Green, and Co., 1898.

Iglesias, Teresa. "What Kind of Being Is the Human Embryo?" *Embryos and Ethics: The Warnock Report in Debate.* Nigel M. de S. Cameron, ed. Edinburgh: Rutherford House Books, 1987: 58-73.

---. "Review of *Conceiving the Embryo: Ethics, Law and Practice in Human Embryology,* and *Creating the Child: Ethics, Law and Practice of Assisted Procreation.* Donald Evans, ed." *Studies in Christian Ethics* 11 (1998): 83-90.

Ignatius. "The Epistle of Ignatius to the Philippians." From *The Ante-Nicene Fathers, Volume 1.* A. Cleveland Coxe, ed. Pub. 1885. 2nd printing. Peabody, Mass.: Hendrickson Publishers, 1999. 116-19.

Inwood, M.J. "Philosophical Anthropology." *The Oxford Companion to Philosophy.* Ted Honderich, ed. Oxford and New York: Oxford University Press, 1995. 38-39.

Jacob, Edmond. *Theology of the Old Testament* [1955]. Arthur W. Heathcote and Philip J. Allcock, transs. New York: Harper & Row, 1958.

Janz, Denis R. *Luther and Late Medieval Thomism: A Study in Theological Anthropology.* Waterloo, Ontario: Wilfrid Laurier Univ. Press, 1983.

Jeffreys, Derek S. *Defending Human Dignity: John Paul II and Political Realism.* Grand Rapids, Michigan: Baker Book House, 2004.

---. "The Soul Is Alive and Well: Non-Reductive Physicalism and Emergent Mental Properties." *Theology and Science* 2.2 (Oct. 2004): 205-25.

Jenkins, John, C.S.C. "Aquinas, Natural Law, and the Challenges of Diversity." *Common Truths: New Perspectives on Natural Law.* Edward B. McLean, ed.

Wilmington, Del.: ISI Books, 2000: 57-71.

John Paul II. "The Resurrection and Theological Anthropology." The General Audience of Wednesday, December 2, 1981. *L'Osservatore Romano* (Weekly Edition in English) 7 Dec. 1981: 3.

---. *Evangelium Vitae.* London: Catholic Truth Society, 1995.

Johnson, Thomas L. "Why a Human Embryo or Fetus Is Not a Parasite." Wheaton, Maryland: L4L.org/articles: 1974, n.p. Accessed 24 April 2007.

Jonas, Hans. *Philosophical Essays: From Ancient Creed to Technological Man.* Chicago: University of Chicago Press, 1974.

Jones, David Albert. *The Soul of the Embryo: An Enquiry into the Status of the Human Embryo in the Christian Tradition.* London: Continuum, 2005.

---. *Approaching the End: A Theological Exploration of Death and Dying.* Oxford: Oxford University Press, 2007.

Jones, D. Gareth. *Designers of the Future.* Oxford: Monarch Books, Lion Hudson, 2005.

Jonsen, Albert R. *The Birth of Bioethics.* New York: Oxford University Press, 1998.

Junker-Kenny, Maureen. "The Moral Status of the Embryo." *Concilium: The Ethics of Genetic Engineering* (April 1998): 43-53.

---. "Embryos *in vitro*, Personhood, and Rights." *Designing Life? Genetics, Procreation and Ethics.* Maureen Junker-Kenny, ed. Aldershot: Ashgate, 1999: 130-58.

Kass, Leon R. "For an International Ban on Human Cloning." Testimony presented to the National Bioethics Advisory Commission, Washington, D.C. 14 March, 1997. Mindfully.org/GE/Human-Cloning-Ban-Kass, n.p. Accessed 21 January 2008.

Kass, Leon R., and James Q. Wilson. *The Ethics of Human Cloning.* Washington, D.C.: AEI Press, 1998.

Kavanaugh, John F. *Who Count as Persons? Human Identity and the Ethics of Killing.* Washington, D.C.: Georgetown University Press, 2001.

Keck, John W. "The Natural Motion of Matter in Newtonian and Post-Newtonian Physics." *The Thomist* 71.4 (October 2007): 529-54.

Kelly, Anthony J. *An Expanding Theology: Faith in a World of Connections.* Sydney: E.J. Dwyer, 1993. Revised 2003.

Kenny, Anthony. "The Beginning of Individual Human Life." *Daedalus* 137.1 (Winter 2008): 15-22.

Kerr, Fergus. *After Aquinas: Versions of Thomism.* Oxford: Blackwell Publishing, 2002.

---. "Natural Law: Incommensurable Readings." *Aquinas's* Summa Theologiae: *Critical Essays.* Brian Davies, ed. Lanham, Maryland: Rowman & Littlefield, 2006: 245-63.

Kirk, Russell. "The Case For and Against Natural Law." Lecture 469, Heritage Lecture Series. Washington, D.C.: The Heritage Foundation. 15 July 1993: 1-9.

Klotzko, Arlene Judith. *A Clone of Your Own? The Science and Ethics of Cloning.* New York: Cambridge University Press, 2006.

Koch-Hershenov, R. "Totipotency, Twinning, and Ensoulment at Fertiliza-

254

tion." *Journal of Medical Philosophy* 31.2 (April 2006): 139-64.

Koren, Henry J., S.T.D. *An Introduction to the Philosophy of Animate Nature.* London and St. Louis: Herder, 1955. Revised edition, 1960.

Kreeft, Peter. *The Unaborted Socrates: A Dramatic Debate on the Issues Surrounding Abortion.* Downers Grove, Illinois: InterVarsity Press, 1983.

---. *A Summa of the Summa.* San Francisco: Ignatius Press, 1990.

---. *A Refutation of Moral Relativism.* San Francisco: Ignatius Press, 1999.

---. "The Apple Argument Against Abortion." *Crisis* 18.11 (December 2000): 25-29.

Kreeft, Peter, and Ronald K. Tacelli. *Handbook of Christian Apologetics.* Downers Grove, Illinois: InterVarsity Press, 1994.

Kuhn, Anita. "Down on the Transplantations." *Touchstone* (October 2008): 46-47.

Kuhse, Helga. *The Sanctity-of-Life Doctrine in Medicine: A Critique.* New York: Oxford University Press USA, 1987.

Landini, Gregory. Lecture, "Introduction to Ethics." The University of Iowa, Iowa City, Iowa. Summer 1995.

Lee, Patrick. "Human Beings Are Animals." *Natural Law and Moral Inquiry.* Robert P. George, ed. Washington, D.C.: Georgetown University Press, 1998: 135-51.

Levin, Yuval. "Biotech: What to Expect." *First Things* 191 (March 2009): 17-20.

Levine, Aaron D. *Cloning: A Beginner's Guide.* Oxford: Oneworld Publications, 2007.

Lewis, C.S. *The Abolition of Man.* Oxford: Oxford University Press, 1943.

Lisska, Anthony J. *Aquinas's Theory of Natural Law: An Analytic Reconstruction.* Oxford: Clarendon Press, 1996.

Locke, John. *An Essay Concerning Human Understanding* [1689]. Oxford: Oxford University Press, 1975.

Lukac de Stier, María L. "Aristotle's *De Anima* as Source of Aquinas's Anthropological Doctrine." Jacques Maritain Center: Thomistic Institute, www2.nd. edu. Accessed 12 Sept. 2007.

Maas, Paul J. van der, M.D., Ph.D., Gerrit van der Wal, M.D., Ph.D., Ilinka Haverkate, M.Sc., Carmen L.M. de Graaff, M.A., John G.C. Kester, M.A., Bregje D. Onwuteaka-Philipsen, M.Sc., Agnes van der Heide, M.D., Ph.D., Jacqueline M. Bosma, M.D., LL.M., Dick L. Willems, M.D., Ph.D., Gerrit van der Wal, M.D., Ph.D., Jacqueline M. Bosma, M.D., LL.M., Bregje D. Onwuteaka-Philipsen, M.Sc., Dick L. Willems, M.D., Ph.D., Ilinka Haverkate, M.Sc., and Piet J. Kostense, Ph.D. "Evaluation of the Notification Procedure for Physician-Assisted Death in the Netherlands." *New England Journal of Medicine* 335.22 (28 November 1996): 1706-12.

MacDonald, Scott. "The Relation Between Being and Goodness." *Being and Goodness: The Concept of the Good in Metaphysics and Philosophical Theology.* Scott MacDonald, ed. Ithaca, New York: Cornell University Press, 1991: 1-28.

Machuga, Ric. *In Defense of the Soul: What It Means to Be Human.* Grand Rapids, Michigan: Brazos Press, 2002.

MacIntyre, Alasdair. *After Virtue: A Study in Moral Theory.* 2nd edition. Notre Dame, Indiana: Univ. of Notre Dame Press, 1984.

---. *Whose Justice? Which Rationality?* Notre Dame, Indiana: Univ. of Notre Dame Press, 1988.

---. *Three Rival Versions of Moral Enquiry: Encyclopaedia, Genealogy, and Tradition.* Notre Dame, Indiana: Univ. of Notre Dame Press, 1990.

---. *Dependent Rational Animals: Why Human Beings Need the Virtues.* Chicago and LaSalle, Illinois: Open Court, 1999.

---. "Theories of Natural Law in the Culture of Advanced Modernity." *Common Truths: New Perspectives on Natural Law.* Edward B. McLean, ed. Wilmington, Delaware: ISI Books, 2000: 91-115.

---. *God, Philosophy, Universities: A Selective History of the Catholic Philosophical Tradition.* Lanham, Maryland: Rowman & Littlefield, 2009.

---. "Intractable Moral Disagreements." *Intractable Disputes About the Natural Law: Alasdair MacIntyre and Critics.* Lawrence S. Cunningham, ed. Notre Dame, Indiana: Univ. of Notre Dame Press, 2009: 1-52.

Maclean, Anne. *The Elimination of Morality: Reflections on Utilitarianism and Bioethics.* London and New York: Routledge, 1993.

Macquarrie, John. *Three Issues in Ethics.* London: SCM Press, 1970.

Magee, Joseph M. "Thomistic Psychology." *The Thomistic Philosophy Page.* Aquinas-online.com, n.p. Updated August 27, 1999. Accessed 15 Sept. 2006.

---. *Unmixing the Intellect: Aristotle on Cognitive Powers and Bodily Organs.* Westport, Connecticut: Greenwood Press, 2003.

Manchester, Eric. "Locke on Bodily Rights and the Immorality of Abortion: A Neglected Liberal Perspective." *Life and Learning XVI: Proceedings of the Sixteenth University Faculty for Life Conference.* Joseph W. Koterski, S.J., ed. Washington, D.C.: University Faculty for Life, 2007: 383-409.

Marchione, Marilynn. "Man's Brain Rewired Itself, Doctors Say." Associated Press, 4 July 2006.

Marcus Aurelius. *Meditations.* George Long, trans. New York: P.F. Collier & Son, 1909.

Markowitz, Sally. "Abortion and Feminism." *Social Theory & Practice* 16.1 (Spring 1990): 1-17.

Marshall, Bruce D. "Thomas, Thomisms, and Truth." *The Thomist* 56.3 (1992): 499-524.

Martin J.A., B.E. Hamilton, P.D. Sutton, S.J. Ventura, F. Menacker, and S. Kirmeyer. "Births: Final Data for 2004." *National Vital Statistics Reports* 55.1. Hyattsville, Maryland: National Center for Health Statistics, 2006.

Mattei, Roberto de, ed. *Finis Vitae: Is Brain Death Still Life?* Rome: Consiglio Nazionale delle Rescherche, 2006.

May, William E. *Catholic Bioethics and the Gift of Human Life.* Huntingdon, Indiana: Our Sunday Visitor Publishing, 2000.

McCarthy, Donald G., and Albert S. Moraczewski, eds. *An Ethical Evaluation of Fetal Experimentation: An Interdisciplinary Study.* St. Louis, Missouri: The Pope John XXIII Medical-Moral Research and Education Center, 1976.

McInerny, D.Q. *A Course in Thomistic Ethics.* Elmhurst, Pennsylvania: The Priestly Fraternity of Saint Peter, 1997.

McInerny, Ralph. *Ethica Thomistica: The Moral Philosophy of Thomas Aquinas.*

Washington, D.C.: Catholic University of America Press, 1982. Revised edition, 1997.

---. *St. Thomas Aquinas.* Notre Dame and London: University of Notre Dame Press, 1982.

---. *Being and Predication: Thomistic Interpretations.* Washington, D.C.: Catholic University of America Press, 1986.

---. "Are There Moral Truths that Everyone Knows?" *Common Truths: New Perspectives on Natural Law.* Edward B. McLean, ed. Wilmington, Delaware: ISI Books, 2000: 1-15.

---. Praeambula Fidei: *Thomism and the God of the Philosophers.* Washington, D.C.: Catholic University of America Press, 2007.

McInerny, Ralph, and John O'Callaghan. "Saint Thomas Aquinas." *The Stanford Encyclopedia of Philosophy (Spring 2005 Edition).* Edward N. Zalta, ed. plato. stanford.edu/archives/spr2005/entries/aquinas. Accessed 14 Jan. 2006.

McKinley, Jesse. "Surgeon Accused in Death of Patient to Get Organs." *New York Times*, U.S. Section. 27 February 2008. Nytimes.com, n.p. Accessed 27 Feb. 2008.

McLean, Ian A.T. "Criminal Law and Natural Law." *Common Truths: New Perspectives on Natural Law.* Edward B. McLean, ed. Wilmington, Delaware: ISI Books, 2000: 259-89.

McMahan, J. *The Ethics of Killing: Problems at the Margins of Life.* New York: Oxford University Press, 2002.

Meilaender, Gilbert. *The Taste for the Other: The Social and Ethical Thought of C.S. Lewis.* Grand Rapids, Michigan: Eerdmans, 1978.

---. *Bioethics: A Primer for Christians.* Grand Rapids, Michigan: Eerdmans, 1996.

Messer, Neil. "Human Cloning and Genetic Manipulation: Some Theological and Ethical Issues." Studies in Christian Ethics 12.2 (January 1999): 1-16.

---. *The Ethics of Human Cloning.* Cambridge: Grove Books, 2001.

---. *Theological Issues in Bioethics: An Introduction with Readings.* London: Darton, Longman & Todd, 2002.

---. *Christian Ethics.* London: SCM Press, 2006.

---. *Selfish Genes and Christian Ethics: Theological and Ethical Reflections on Evolutionary Biology.* London: SCM Press, 2007.

---. "Humans, Animals, Evolution and Ends." *Creaturely Theology: God, Humans and Other Animals.* Celia Deane-Drummond and David Clough, eds. London: SCM Press, 2009: 211-27.

Milne, Bruce. *The Message of Heaven and Hell: Grace and Destiny.* Derek Tidball, ed. Leicester and Downers Grove: InterVarsity Press, 2002.

Moore, G.E. *Principia Ethica* [1903]. Amherst, New York: Prometheus Books, 1988.

Multi-Society Task Force on PVS. "Medical Aspects of the Persistent Vegetative State: Part 1." *The New England Journal of Medicine* 330.21 (1994): 1499-1508.

---. "Medical Aspects of the Persistent Vegetative State: Part 2." *The New England Journal of Medicine* 330.22 (1994): 1572-79.

Murphy, Nancey. *Anglo-American Postmodernity: Philosophical Perspectives on Science, Religion, and Ethics.* Boulder, Colorado: Westview Press, 1997.

National Consultative Ethics Committee for Health and Life Sciences. "Reply to the President of the French Republic on the Subject of Reproductive Cloning." Section II.3. 22 April 1997. Ccne.ethique.fr/docs.pdf. Accessed 2 February 2008.

Neuhaus, Richard John. "Human Dignity and Public Discourse." *Human Dignity and Bioethics: Essays Commissioned by the President's Council on Bioethics.* Edmund D. Pellegrino, M.D., chair. Adam Schulman and Thomas W. Merrill, eds. Washington, D.C.: Government Printing Office, March 2008: 215-28.

---. "The Politics of Bioethics." *First Things* 177 (November 2007): 23-28.

---. "While We're At It." *First Things* 159 (January 2006): 66-76.

---. "While We're At It." *First Things* 180 (February 2008): 61-72.

Nietzsche, Friedrich. *The Antichrist* [1895]. *The Portable Nietzsche.* Walter Kaufmann, ed. and trans. New York: Penguin, 1976: 565-656.

---. *Twilight of the Idols* [1889]. *The Portable Nietzsche.* Kaufmann, ed. and trans.: 463-563.

Noonan, Jr., John T. "Aquinas on Abortion." *St. Thomas Aquinas on Politics and Ethics.* Paul E. Sigmund, ed. New York: Norton Critical Edition, 1988: 245-48.

Oakley, Francis. *Natural Law, Laws of Nature, Natural Rights: Continuity and Discontinuity in the History of Ideas.* London: Continuum, 2005.

Ocampo, Liza Ruth A. "The Question of the Definition of Man in Thomas Aquinas's *De Unitate Intellectus Contra Averroistas.*" *Talastasan Series 2005.* Diliman, Quezon City: Univ. of the Philippines, September 2005: 1-7.

O'Donovan, Oliver. *Begotten or Made?* Oxford: Oxford University Press, 1984.

---. "Again, Who Is a Person?" *On Moral Medicine.* Stephen E. Lammers and Allen Verhey, eds. Grand Rapids, Michigan: Eerdmans, 1998: 380-86.

---. "John Finnis on Moral Absolutes." *The Revival of the Natural Law: Philosophical, Theological, and Ethical Responses to the Finnis-Grisez School.* Nigel Biggar and Rufus Black, eds. Aldershot, Hants: Ashgate, 2000: 111-28.

O'Rourke, Kevin D., O.P. "The Embryo as Person." *Life and Learning XVI: Proceedings of the Sixteenth University Faculty for Life Conference.* Joseph W. Koterski, S.J., ed. Washington, D.C.: University Faculty for Life, 2007: 281-96.

O'Rourke, Kevin D., and Patrick Norris, O.P. "Care of PVS Patients: Catholic Opinion in the United States." *Linacre Quarterly* 68 (August 2001): 201-17.

Pasnau, Robert. *Thomas Aquinas on Human Nature: A Philosophical Study of* Summa Theologiae *1a 75-89.* Cambridge: Cambridge University Press, 2002.

Payne, Craig. "Fatalist Attraction: Determinism, Freedom, and Moral Choice." *De Philosophia* 14.2 (Fall/Winter 1998): 253-71.

Peach, Andrew J. "Pro-Choice 'Personhood': An Abortive Concept." *Life and Learning XIII: Proceedings of the Thirteenth University Faculty for Life Conference.* Joseph W. Koterski, S.J., ed. Washington, D.C.: University Faculty for Life, 2003: 187-210.

---. "Late- *vs.* Early-Term Abortion: A Thomistic Analysis." *The Thomist* 75.1 (January 2007): 113-41.

Pegis, Anton C. "The Separated Soul and Its Nature in St. Thomas." *St. Thomas Aquinas 1274-1974: Commemorative Studies.* Toronto: Pontifical Institute of

Mediaeval Studies, 1974: 1:131-58.

Perkoff, Gerald T. "A Normative Definition of Personhood." *Abortion and the Status of the Fetus.* William B. Bondeson, H. Tristram Engelhardt, Jr., Stuart F. Spicker, and Daniel H. Winship, eds. Dordrecht, Holland: D. Reidel Publishing, 1983: 159-66.

Pessala, Anne. "Seminary President Criticizes Abortion Opponents." Washington, D.C.: Religion News Service. 4 April 2006.

Peters, Sheila. "The Human Person, Freedom, and Moral Responsibility." *Sapientia et Doctrina* 1.1 (2004): 55-60.

Peterson, Eugene H. *Christ Plays in Ten Thousand Places.* Grand Rapids, Michigan: Eerdmans, 2005.

Pieper, Josef. *Reality and the Good.* Chicago: Regnery Publishing, 1967.

Pojman, Louis P., and Francis J. Beckwith, eds. *The Abortion Controversy: A Reader.* Boston: Jones and Bartlett, 1994.

Pope, Stephen J. *The Evolution of Altruism and the Ordering of Love.* Washington, D.C.: Georgetown University Press, 1994.

Porter, Jean. *Nature as Reason: A Thomistic Theory of the Natural Law.* Grand Rapids, Michigan: Eerdmans, 2005.

President's Council on Bioethics. *Alternative Sources of Human Pluripotent Stem Cells.* Washington, D.C.: Government Printing Office, May 2005.

---. *Human Cloning and Human Dignity: An Ethical Inquiry.* Washington, D.C.: Government Printing Office, July 2002.

---. *Monitoring Stem Cell Research.* Washington, D.C.: Government Printing Office, January 2004.

"Production of Pluripotent Stem Cells by Oocyte Assisted Reprogramming— Joint Statement." Alterednucleartransfer.com, n.p. 20 June 2005. Accessed 5 Feb. 2008.

Rahner, Karl. *Theological Investigations.* Volume IX. G. Harrison, trans. London: Darton, Longman & Todd, 1972.

Ramelow, Anselm, O.P. "Review of *Persons: The Difference Between 'Someone' and 'Something'* by Robert Spaemann (Oliver O'Donovan, trans. Oxford: Oxford University Press, 2007)." *The Thomist* 72.2 (April 2008): 317-21.

Ramsey, Paul. *Ethics at the Edges of Life: Medical and Legal Intersections.* New Haven and London: Yale University Press, 1978.

Rawls, John. *A Theory of Justice.* Cambridge, Massachusetts: Harvard University Press, 1971.

Reiman, Jeffrey. *Abortion and the Ways We Value Human Life.* Lanham, Maryland: Rowman and Littlefield, 1999.

Rice, Charles E. *Fifty Questions on the Natural Law: What It Is and Why We Need It.* San Francisco: Ignatius Press, 1995.

Robb, James H. *Man as Infinite Spirit: The Aquinas Lecture, 1974.* Milwaukee: Marquette University Press, 1974.

Rommen, Heinrich A. *The Natural Law: A Study in Legal and Social History and Philosophy* [1947]. Thomas R. Hanley, O.S.B., trans. Indianapolis: Liberty Fund, reprinted 1998. Originally published as *Die ewige Wiederkehr des Naturrechts* (Leipzig, 1936).

Ruse, Michael. *Darwin and Design: Does Evolution Have a Purpose?* Cambridge,

Massachusetts: Harvard University Press, 2003.

Scarlett, Brian. "The Moral Uniqueness of the Human Animal." *Human Lives: Critical Essays on Consequentialist Bioethics.* David S. Oderberg and Jacqueline A. Laing, eds. New York and London: Macmillan, 1997: 77-95.

Schoonenberg, Piet. *God's World in the Making.* Pittsburgh: Duquesne University Press, 1964.

Schwarz, Stephen D. *The Moral Question of Abortion.* Chicago: Loyola University Press, 1990.

Simon, Yves. *The Tradition of Natural Law: A Philosopher's Reflections.* Vukan Kuic, ed. New York: Fordham University Press. Second printing, 1967.

Singer, Peter. "A German Attack on Applied Ethics." *Journal of Applied Philosophy* 9.1 (1992): 85-91.

---. "All Animals Are Equal." *Philosophic Exchange.* Brockport, New York: Center for Philosophic Exchange, 1974: 103-16.

---. *Animal Liberation* [1975]. New York: Harper Perennial Reprint, 2001.

---. *The Expanding Circle: Ethics and Sociobiology.* Oxford: Clarendon Press, 1981.

---. "Heavy Petting." *Nerve* (March 2001), n.p. Nerve.com/Opinions/Singer. Accessed 4 January 2008.

---. *In Defense of Animals: The Second Wave.* Oxford: Blackwell, 2005.

---. Interview: "Does the End Justify the Means?" *The Examined Life.* DVD. Pasadena, California: Intelecom, 2002.

---. "Killing Babies Isn't Always Wrong." London *Spectator* (16 September 1995): 20-22.

---. *Practical Ethics.* Cambridge: Cambridge Univ. Press. Second edition, 1993.

---. *Rethinking Life and Death: The Collapse of Our Traditional Ethics.* New York: St. Martin's Griffin, 1996.

---. "Sanctity of Life or Quality of Life?" *Pediatrics* 72.1 (July 1983): 128-29.

---. "Science, Religion and Stem Cells" [response to editorial column "Not on Faith Alone," Mario Cuomo, 20 June 2005]. *The New York Times* 23 June 2005.

---. *Unsanctifying Human Life: Essays on Ethics.* Helga Kuhse, ed. Oxford: Blackwell, 2002.

Singer, Peter, and W. Walters, eds. *Test-Tube Babies.* Oxford: Oxford University Press, 1982.

Sloane, Andrew. "Singer, Preference Utilitarianism and Infanticide." *Studies in Christian Ethics* 12.2 (January 1999): 47-73.

Smith, Janet E. "Natural Law and Sexual Ethics." *Common Truths: New Perspectives on Natural Law.* Edward B. McLean, ed. Wilmington, Delaware: ISI Books, 2000: 193-215.

Smith, Wesley J. "On the Square: Observations and Contentions." Firstthings.com (18 August 2006). Accessed 18 August 2006.

Sokolowski, Robert. "What Is Natural Law? Human Purposes and Natural Ends." *The Thomist* 68 (2004): 507-29.

Somme, Luc-Thomas. "The Infallibility, Impeccability and Indestructibility of Synderesis." *Studies in Christian Ethics* 19.3 (2006): 403-16.

Spaemann, Robert. *Persons: The Difference Between 'Someone' and 'Something.'* Oliver O'Donovan, trans. Oxford: Oxford University Press, 2007.

Steinbock, Bonnie. "The Morality of Killing Human Embryos." *The Journal of Law, Medicine & Ethics* 34.1 (Spring 2006): 26-34.

Still, Carl N. "The Search for the Real Aquinas." *The Canadian Journal of History* (April 2005): Online, n.p. Accessed 15 March 2006.

Stith, Richard. "Abortion Is More Than 'Murder.'" *Life and Learning XV: Proceedings of the Fifteenth University Faculty for Life Conference.* Joseph W. Koterski, S.J., ed. Washington, D.C.: University Faculty for Life, 2006: 105-11.

Stith-Coleman, Irene. "Human Embryo Research." Library of Congress Congressional Research Service. Research Report Number 95-910 STM. Updated 29 January 1998. Accessed 22 November 2005.

Strong, Carson. *Ethics in Reproductive and Perinatal Medicine: A New Framework.* New Haven, Connecticut: Yale University Press, 1997.

Stump, Eleonore. *Aquinas.* London and New York: Routledge, 2003.

Sumner, L.W. *Abortion and Moral Theory.* Princeton: Princeton University Press, 1981.

Takahashi, Kazutoshi, and Shinya Yamanaka. "Induction of Pluripotent Stem Cells from Mouse Embryonic and Adult Fibroblast Cultures by Defined Factors." *Cell* 126 (20 November 2007): 663-76.

Talaro, Kathleen Park. *Foundations in Microbiology.* 6th edition. New York: McGraw-Hill, 2008.

Taylor, Kenneth. *The Living Bible.* Carol Stream, Illinois: Tyndale House Publishers, 1974.

Teichman, Jenny. "Dr. Jekyll and Mr. Hyde." *The New Criterion* 19.2 (October 2000): 64-67.

---. "The False Philosophy of Peter Singer." *The New Criterion* 11.8 (April 1993): 25-30.

---. *Social Ethics.* Oxford: Blackwell, 1997.

Thareja, Nidhi, M.D. "Human Embryonic Stem Cells—Without an Embryo." Abcnews.com, n.p. 20 November 2007. Accessed 20 November 2007.

Thomas Aquinas. *Compendium Theologica.* Cyril Vollert, S.J., trans. [1947]. New York: Sophia Institute Press, 1998.

---. *De Veritate.* Robert W. Mulligan, S.J.; James V. McGlynn, S.J.; and Robert W. Schmidt, S.J., transs. Chicago: Henry Regnery Co., 1952-54.

---. *On Being and Essence.* Joseph Bobik, trans. Notre Dame, Indiana: University of Notre Dame Press, 1965.

---. *Quaestiones Disputatae de Anima.* John Patrick Rowan, trans. *The Soul.* St. Louis & London: B. Herder Book Co., 1949.

---. *Quaestiones Disputatae de Potentia Dei.* English Dominican Fathers, transs. [1932]. Westminster, Maryland: Newman Press, reprinted 1952.

---. *Quaestiones Disputatae de Spiritualibus Creaturis.* Mary C. Fitzpatrick and John J. Wellmuth, transs. Milwaukee: Marquette University Press, 1949.

---. *Summa Contra Gentiles.* Anton C. Pegis, James F. Anderson, Vernon J. Bourke, and Charles J. O'Neil, transs. Notre Dame: University of Notre Dame Press. Reprinted edition, 1975.

---. *Summa Theologica.* Fathers of the English Dominican Province, transs. [1920]. New York: Benziger Brothers, 1947.

Thomson, Judith Jarvis. "A Defense of Abortion." *Philosophy and Public Affairs* 1.1 (Fall 1971): 47-66.

Tittle, Peg. *What If: Collected Thought Experiments in Philosophy.* New York: Pearson/Longman, 2005.

Tooley, Michael. *Abortion and Infanticide.* Oxford: Clarendon Press, 1983.

---. "Abortion and Infanticide." *Philosophy and Public Affairs* 2.1 (1972): 37-65.

---. "Personhood." *A Companion to Bioethics.* Helga Kuhse and Peter Singer, eds. Oxford: Blackwell, 1998: 117-26.

Torrell, Jean-Pierre, O.P. *Saint Thomas Aquinas Volume 2: Spiritual Master.* Robert Royal, trans. Washington, D.C.: Catholic Univ. of America Press, 2003.

---. *Aquinas's* Summa: *Background, Structure, and Reception.* Benedict M. Guevin, O.S.B., trans. Washington, D.C.: Catholic Univ. of America Press, 2005.

Trefil, James. "What Is a Human Being?" World Economic Forum Annual Meeting, 29 January 1999. Weforum.org, n.p. Accessed 19 February 2006.

Twain, Mark. *Adventures of Huckleberry Finn* [1876]. Norton Critical Edition, 2nd ed. Sculley Bradley, Richmond Croom Beatty, E. Hudson Long, and Thomas Cooley, eds. New York: Norton, 1977.

VanDrunen, David. *A Biblical Case for Natural Law.* Grand Rapids, Michigan: Acton Institute, 2000.

Vann, Gerald, O.P. *The Aquinas Prescription: St. Thomas's Path to a Discerning Heart, a Sane Society, and a Holy Church.* Published London: Hague and Gill, 1940. Reprinted Manchester, New Hamphire: Sophia Institute Press, 1999.

Verbrugge, Verlyn D., ed. *"Psuche." New International Dictionary of New Testament Theology.* Grand Rapids, Michigan: Zondervan, 2000: 620-23.

Villee, Claude, and Vincent Dethier. *Biological Principles and Processes.* Philadelphia: Saunders, 1976.

Warren, Mary Anne. "On the Moral and Legal Status of Abortion." *The Monist* 57.1 (1973): 43-61. Reprinted in *The Right Thing to Do: Basic Readings in Moral Philosophy.* 3rd edition. James Rachels, ed. New York: McGraw-Hill, 2003: 97-106.

Welsh, Thomas J. "Catholic Faith and Reverence for Human Life." *Linking the Human Life Issues.* Russell Hittinger, ed. Chicago: Regnery Books, 1986: 9-19.

Westerman, Pauline C. *The Disintegration of Natural Law Theory: Aquinas to Finnis.* Leiden: Brill, 1997.

Wilcox, John T. "Nature as Demonic in Thomson's Defense of Abortion" [1989]. *The Ethics of Abortion: Pro-Life vs. Pro-Choice.* Revised edition. Robert M. Baird and Stuart E. Rosenbaum, eds. Buffalo, New York: Pranetheus Books, 1993: 212-25.

Wilmut, Ian, and Roger Highfield. *After Dolly: The Uses and Misuses of Human Cloning.* New York and London: Norton, 2006.

Wilson, James Q. *The Moral Sense.* New York: Free Press, 1993.

Wippel, John F. *The Metaphysical Thought of Thomas Aquinas: From Finite Being to Uncreated Being.* Washington, D.C.: CUA Press, 2000.

Wooden, Cindy. "Minority View: Participants Publish Their Side of Brain Death Debate." Vatican Letter, 20 April 2007, n.p. Catholic News Service. Catholicnews.com. Accessed 23 April 2007.

Yu, Junying, James A. Thomson, et al. "Induced Pluripotent Stem Cell Lines Derived from Human Somatic Cells." *Science* 318.5858 (20 November 2007): 1917-20.

Zuckert, Michael. *Natural Rights and the New Republicanism*. Princeton, New Jersey: Princeton University Press, 1998.

# ABOUT THE AUTHOR

Craig Payne is a professor of humanities at Indian Hills College in Ottumwa, Iowa. He holds a doctorate in theology from the University of Wales/Lampeter. His previous books include *What Believers Don't Have to Believe: The Non-Essentials of the Christian Faith* (2006) and *Why a Fetus Is a Human Person from the Moment of Conception: A Revisionist Interpretation of Thomas Aquinas's* Treatise on Human Nature (2010).

www.ingramcontent.com/pod-product-compliance
Lightning Source LLC
Chambersburg PA
CBHW070344090426
42733CB00009B/1279